Antonio Vieyra

A Grammar of the Portuguese Language

To Which is Added a Copious Vocabulary and Dialogues

Antonio Vieyra

A Grammar of the Portuguese Language
To Which is Added a Copious Vocabulary and Dialogues

ISBN/EAN: 9783337085636

Printed in Europe, USA, Canada, Australia, Japan

Cover: Foto ©Paul-Georg Meister /pixelio.de

More available books at **www.hansebooks.com**

A GRAMMAR

OF THE

PORTUGUESE LANGUAGE;

TO WHICH IS ADDED

A Copious Vocabulary and Dialogues,

WITH

EXTRACTS FROM THE BEST PORTUGUESE AUTHORS.

BY A. VIEYRA.

NEW EDITION, REVISED

BY

A. PEIXOTO, K.C.C.,

PROFESSOR OF PORTUGUESE, KING'S COLLEGE, LONDON;
EXAMINER TO THE CIVIL SERVICE COMMISSIONERS, AND TO THE
SOCIETY OF ARTS AND SCIENCES.

LONDON: DULAU AND CO., 37 SOHO SQUARE.
SIMPKIN, MARSHALL, & CO., STATIONERS' HALL COURT.
1890

LONDON:
Printed by STRANGEWAYS & SONS, Tower Street,
Cambridge Circus, W.C.

AUTHOR'S PREFACE.

As the usefulness of the Portuguese Language is so well known to all English merchants who carry on a general trade with the different parts of the known world, it will be needless to use any arguments here to prove it; and I shall refer what I have to say on the copiousness and energy of this language, to the Preface to my English and Portuguese Dictionary.

The reader will find, in the First Part of this Grammar, what is material as a foundation of the whole.

At the end of the Second Part is a full explanation of the Particles, on which I have bestowed more time and labour, because this subject has been hitherto much neglected, although the principal ornament and elegance, not only of the Portuguese, but of every other language, chiefly consist in the proper arrangement and judicious interspersion of the words.

In the Third Part is a larger collection than hitherto published of the terms of trade, war, navigation, &c., which the present intercourse between the nations renders particularly useful.

I have in the Fourth Part given some passages selected from the best Portuguese Authors, which will facilitate the reading of their most eminent writers.

CONTENTS.

PART I.

CHAPTER I.

	PAGE
Of the Portugese alphabet	1
Of the vowels	2
Of the consonants	3
Of the double consonants	6
Of the five nasal vowels	7
Of diphthongs	8

CHAPTER II.

Of the articles 9

CHAPTER III.

Of the nouns	11
Of the adjectives	19
Of numeral nouns; and first, of cardinal	22
Ordinal nouns	24
A method to learn a great many Portuguese words in a short time	26

CHAPTER IV.

Of pronouns	28
Of personal pronouns	28
Of conjunctive pronouns	32
Of mixed pronouns	33
Of possessive pronouns	34

Remarks upon the possessives	36
Of the pronouns demonstrative	38
Of the pronouns interrogative	42
Of the pronouns relative	44
Of the improper pronouns	46

CHAPTER V.

Of verbs	48
Conjugation of the auxiliary verb *têr*, or *haver*, to have	49
Of the auxiliary verb *haver*	55
Conjugation of the auxiliary verb *ser*, or *estar*, to be	56
An easy method of learning to conjugate the Portuguese verbs	62
First conjugation of the verbs in *ar*	65
Second conjugation of the verbs in *er*	72
Third conjugation of the verbs in *ir*	77
Of the irregular verbs	81
Of neuter verbs	116
Of reciprocal verbs	117
Impersonal verbs	123

CHAPTER VI.

Of the participles	134

CHAPTER VII.

Of the adverbs	134

CHAPTER VIII.

Of the prepositions	138

CHAPTER IX.

Of the conjunctions	139
Interjective particles	141
Abbreviations	143

PART II.

CHAPTER I.

Of the division of syntax 145

CHAPTER II.

Of the syntax of articles 149

CHAPTER III.

Of the syntax of nouns; and first of the substantives . . 154
Of the syntax of adjectives 155
Adjectives which come after the substantives . . . 156
Of the syntax of comparatives and superlatives . . . 158

CHAPTER IV.

Of the syntax of pronouns 159

CHAPTER V.

Of the syntax of verbs 163

CHAPTER VI.

Of the syntax of participles and gerunds 177

CHAPTER VII.

Of prepositions 179
Of further particles 207

CHAPTER VIII.

Of the Portuguese orthography; and of capitals and stops . 219
Of the accents 220
Some observations upon the Portugese orthography . . 222
Of double letters 231
Of the quantity of syllables and their sound . . . 242

CHAPTER IX.

Etymology of the Portuguese tongue from the Latin . . 248

PART III.

	PAGE
Phraseology .	251
Vocabulary of words most used in conversation	255
Of the Portuguese coin .	256
A collection of Portugese proverbs	257
Familiar dialogues	368
Letters on business	387

PART IV.

Several useful and entertaining passages	395
Poetical extracts .	419

A NEW PORTUGUESE GRAMMAR.

PART I.

CHAPTER I.

OF THE PORTUGUESE ALPHABET, AND THE MANNER OF PRONOUNCING EACH SEPARATE LETTER.

THE Portuguese alphabet contains twenty-five single letters and five double consonants, viz.:—

A, B, C, D, E, F, G, H, I, J, K*, L, M, N, O, P, Q, R, S, T, U, V, X, Y, Z.

Of these the following five letters are vowels:—

a, e, i, o, u.

These five letters are pronounced with a nasal sound, when there is a cedilla (˜) over them, viz.:—

ã, ẽ, ĩ, õ, ũ.

The following are the five double consonants:—

ch, lh, nh, ph, rr.

* *K* has been adopted in the Portuguese alphabet [ever since the first (Barros's) Portuguese Grammar was printed, in 1539] for words of foreign derivation originally written with it; it is expressed by a sound like that of the *ca* in the English word *car*, if the *r* is dropped in the pronunciation; its power is the same as in English.

OF THE MANNER OF PRONOUNCING THE PORTUGUESE LETTERS.

OF THE VOWELS.

A

in Portuguese is commonly pronounced like *a* in the following English words:—*adapted, castle, bath,* &c. It is sometimes pronounced with less strength, and closely, as in *ambos,* both, where the *a* is pronounced like *a* in the English word *ambition.*

E.

The letter *e* has two* different sounds: the one open, like *ai* in *daily;* the other close, like that in the English word *mellow.* Examples of the former, *fé,* faith, *pe,* foot, &c. Examples of the latter, *rêde,* a net, *parêde,* a wall, &c. In this consists a great part of the beauty of the Portuguese pronunciation, which, however, cannot be learned but by long use, notwithstanding all the rules that can be given.

I

is pronounced like *ee* in the English word *steel,* aço; or like *i* in the English word *still,* ainda, *visible,* visivel.

---

* *E* has three different sounds (the same as the French ê, é, e, respectively corresponding with the Portuguese é, ê, e) : no notice has been taken of the *e* mute, as in the words *appetite,* appetite; *retrato,* portrait. The accent (ˆ) in the words *rêde, parêde,* is used here only to show which *e* bears the second or close sound (the other *e* being mute), not that the words are generally written with that accent. Indeed, whenever a vowel is found accentuated in Portuguese, the proper sound of the accent must, of course, be given to it; but the student must not expect always to find the respective accents on the vowels whenever any such sound belongs to them.

O.

This vowel has two* sounds: one open, as in the word *dó*, pity, where the *o* is pronounced like our *o* in the word *store;* the other close, as in the Portuguese article *do*, of, and the word *redondo*, round, where the *o* is pronounced like our *u* in *turret* or *stumble*. It is likewise in the different pronunciation of the vowel that the greatest part of the beauty of the Portuguese pronunciation consists; but it can be learnt only by long use.

U.

The vowel *u* is pronounced like *oo* in English.

OF THE CONSONANTS.

B

is pronounced as the *b* in the English word *better*.

C

is pronounced as in the English word *celebrated*.

Before *a, o, u,* and the consonants, *l, r,* it has the sound of a *k;* but before *e* and *i* it takes the hissing

---

* The Portuguese O has three different sounds, as the E, and equally accentuated *ó, ô, o:* the first is open, as in the words *dó*, pity, *tópo*, I hit upon, where the *o* is pronounced much like the English in *top;* the other close, as in *tôpo*, top, *pôr*, to place, for the sound of which I find no sound equivalent in English; the third mute, as in the Portuguese article *do*, of, and the final unaccentuated *o* ending all Portuguese words, where its sound is just the same as in the English verb *do*, or the preposition *to*, when lightly pronounced without stress or emphasis. In the word *redondo*, the *on* somewhat resembles that of the English in *controversy*, and therefore bears no analogy to the *u* in *turret* or *stumble*.

sound of *s*, and also before *a, o, u*, when there is a cedilla under it, thus *ç*.

Double *c* is sounded only before *e* and *c*, the first with the sound of *k*, and the other with the hissing sound of *s* ; as in the word *accidente*, accident, pronounced *aksidente*.

D

is pronounced like the *d* in the first syllable of the English word *declared*.

F

is always pronounced as in English.

G

Before the vowels *a, o, u*, and before consonants, it is pronounced as in English: examples, *ganancia*, gain; *repugnancia*, repugnancy.

G before *e* and *i* denotes the sound of *j* consonant, as in the English word *generation*.

G before *l* and *r* is pronounced as in English: examples, *gladiador*, gladiator ; *gruta*, grotto.

Güa is pronounced as if the English word *guard*, in Portuguese *güarda*, were written *gward*.

Gue, gui are pronounced as *gue, gi* in the words *guest* and *gift* ; but when there are two dots on the *u*, the *u* is then pronounced as in *argüir*, to argue.

H.

This letter is mute in Portuguese, the same as in the English words *honour, heir*, and is preserved in those words that are derived from the Latin.

J

is pronounced like the *j* in English.

K

is only used in the words of foreign derivation originally written with it.

L.

L and *ll* are pronounced as in English.

M

is also pronounced as in English.

N.

Also as in English.

P

has a sound as that of *pe* in the English word *penny*.

Q

is pronounced like *k*: example, *quero*, I am willing, pronounced *kero*.

The vowel *u* in the words *qual*, which; *qualidade*, quality, &c., is pronounced as in the latter word.

R

at the beginning of a word is pronounced as in English in the words *rage, rose, rice*, &c., and between two vowels, as in the name of *Sarah;* but after a consonant and before a vowel it has a strong sound, as in the word *enrich*.

S

and *ss* are pronounced as in English.

S between two vowels is pronounced like a *z;* particularly in the words ending in *oso* and *esa*, as *amoroso cuidadoso, mesa, defensa,* &c.

T

has a sound like that of *ta* in the English word *tame*.

V

is pronounced as in English.

X

is pronounced like our personal pronoun *she*, with *es* added to it, as *shees*, in the words *baixo*, low; *paixão*, passion; *axioma*, axiom.

X after the vowel *e*, and before a consonant, is pronounced like *is* in the words *extensão*, *extenuado*, *expulso*, *excellente*, and some other words.

X between two vowels is pronounced like *iz*, as in the words *exactamente*, *exornar*, *exordio*, &c.

X at the end of a word is pronounced like *s*, as in *Felix*, *simplex*, *duplex*, &c.

Y

has the same sound as an *i* in the English word *visible*, and is called *ypsilon*.

Z

is pronounced as in English; but at the end of words it is sounded like *s*, as *rapaz*, boy; *Francez*, French; *perdiz*, partridge; *voz*, voice; *luz*, light, &c.

OF THE FIVE DOUBLE CONSONANTS, CALLED PROLAÇÕES IN PORTUGUESE.

CH

is pronounced like *sh* in the English word *shoe*, in *chegar*, to arrive; *achar*, to find, with the exception of *architecto*, *monarcha*, &c., when the *ch* has the sound of a *k*.

PH

is pronounced as in English.

LH

is pronounced still softer than the *l* in the word *punctilio*.

NH

has a peculiar sound, of which there is no equivalent in English; it is pronounced as the *n* in the word *cognac* in French.

RR

is only made use of between two vowels, and it is strongly sounded.*

OF THE FIVE NASAL VOWELS.

Words with a nasal sound can be written only with the cedilla over the vowel, thus: ã, ẽ, ĩ, õ, ũ, or with *m* and *n* before it; with this difference, that if they are at the end of a word, or before *b, p, m,* they must be written with *m*, and in all other cases with *n;* as in the words *sãto, santo; sõda, sonda;* and *sĩ, sim; irmã, irmam; tẽpo, tempo.*

* It would be preferable if the learned in Portugal were to follow the resolution of the Royal Academy of Madrid, by expunging the *ph* and placing the *f* in its stead, as in the words *metaphysica, philosophia,* &c., and by writing *c* instead of *ch* in the words *charidade,* charity, *chôro,* choir, when it is pronounced like a *k;* also by replacing the *ç* with an *s*, since they have in both languages the same hissing sound, and by omitting altogether the *h* in the words *throno, theatro,* and many other modifications, already adopted by some, which we shall have occasion to point out in the course of this work.

OF DIPHTHONGS.

There are sixteen diphthongs in Portuguese, ten of which are vocal and six nasal; namely,

VOCAL DIPHTHONGS.

ái, áe, as in *pai*, or *páe*, father.
áo, as in *páo*, a stick.
éi, as in *réi*, king.
êi, as in *lêi*, law.
éo, as in *céo*, heaven.
êo, as in *mêo*, or *meu*, mine.
ió, as in *vio*, he saw.
ói, óe, as in *herói*, or *heróe*, a hero.
ôi, as in *rôido*, gnawed.
uí, as in *fuí*, I went.

NASAL DIPHTHONGS.

ãi, ãe, as in *mãi*, or *mãe*, mother.
ãɔ, as in *mão*, hand.
ẽe, as in *bẽe*, or *bem*, well.
õe, as in *põe*, or *poem*, poem.
õo, as in *bõo*, or *bom*, good.
ũi, as in *rũi*, or *ruim*, mean.

CHAPTER II.

OF THE ARTICLES.

THOSE particles called Articles are properly prepositions, commonly put before nouns, to show their gender, number, and case.

These articles are definite or indefinite.

OF THE DEFINITE ARTICLE.

The definite article marks the gender, number, and case of the nouns which it precedes.

The English tongue has but one definite article, namely, *the*, which serves for both numbers and genders.

The Portuguese has two, viz., *o* for the masculine, and *a* for the feminine.

The definite article has five cases, the nominative, genitive, dative, accusative, and ablative; because the vocative in the nouns is designed and preceded merely by the interjection *oh*.

THE DECLENSION OF THE MASCULINE ARTICLE *O*.

SINGULAR.	PLURAL.
Nom. *o*, the	N. *os*, the
Gen. *do*, of the	G. *dos*, of the
Dat. *ao*, to the	D. *aos*, to the
Acc. *o*, the	A. *os*, the
Abl. *do*, from	A. *dos*, from the
,, *pelo*, by the	,, *pelos*, by the.

Pelo, pela, &c., is the contraction of *por o* or *por a*, &c.

THE DECLENSION OF THE FEMININE ARTICLE *A*.

SINGULAR.	PLURAL.
Nom. *a*, the	N. *as*, the
Gen. *da*, of the	G. *das*, of the
Dat. *á*, to the	D. *ás*, to the
Acc. *a*, the	A. *as*, the
Abl. *da*, from the.	A. *das*, from the.

Observe, that the Portuguese have an article for each gender, both in the singular and the plural.

OF THE INDEFINITE ARTICLE.

A $\begin{cases} \text{m., } um \\ \text{f., } uma \end{cases}$

The indefinite article is declinable in the same way as the definite article: examples, a house, *uma casa;* of a horse, *de um cavallo;* by a road, *por uma estrada*, &c.

As shown above, the different cases are governed by the respective prepositions—viz., of, *de;* to, *a;* from, *de;* and by, *por*.

There are many other prepositions of which we shall speak in the course of this book.

The preposition *de* may also be put before infinitives, and then it signifies *to;* as *é tempo de fallar, de dormir, de lêr*, &c., it is time to speak, to sleep, to read, &c.

When the verb is in the infinitive mood, and serves as nominative to the following verb, put the definite article *o* before it; as *o comer e o dormir são as coisas mais necessarias n'esta vida*, eating and sleeping are the greatest necessaries of life.

When the proposition *in* (*em*) is followed by the article *the* (*o*) or another word beginning by a vowel, we must render it in Portuguese by *no*, or *nos*, for the masculine; and by *na*, or *nas*, for the feminine: examples, in the garden, *no jardim;* in the street, *na rua;*

in thy book, *no teu livro;* in his bed, *na sua cama,* &c. Note that *no* stands for *em o;* *nas* for *em as,* &c.

When after the preposition *with,* which in Portuguese is expressed by *com,* we find the article *the,* or a pronoun possessive, as *with the, with my,* &c., we must say, *com o, com a, com os, com as:* examples, with the prince, *com o principe;* with the sword, *com a espada;* with the eyes, *com os olhos;* with my books, *com os meus livros,* &c.

When the preposition *with* is followed by a pronoun possessive, and this by a noun of quality or kindred, as *with your majesty, with your highness, with your excellency, with his brother,* &c., *with* must then be rendered by the Portuguese *com,* as *com vossa majestade, com vossa alteza, com seu irmão,* without using the article.

Observe, that sometimes the dative and accusative of the indefinite article are not expressed in English, particularly before pronouns personal and proper names: examples, *convêm-nos,* it behoves us; *Antonio matou a Pedro,* Anthony killed Peter.

CHAPTER III.

OF THE NOUNS.

THE Portuguese nouns have various terminations, as will appear hereafter.

They have but two genders, the masculine and feminine.

The Portuguese nouns have no variation of cases, like the Latin; the article only distinguishes the case.

OF NOUNS ENDING IN A; AND OF THEIR DECLENSION.

SINGULAR.	PLURAL.
N. *a rainha*, the queen	N. *as rainhas*, the queens
G. *da rainha*, of the queen	G. *das rainhas*, of the queens
D. *á rainha*, to the queen	D. *ás rainhas*, to the queens
A. *a rainha*, the queen	A. *as rainhas*, the queens
V. *oh rainha*, O queen	V. *oh rainhas*, O queens
A. *da* ou *pela rainha*, from or by the queen.	A. *das* ou *pelas rainhas*, from or by the queens.

We have already observed that the Portuguese nouns have no variation of cases: therefore, there is no occasion to display more examples of their declensions, as it is only necessary to change the article according to their gender.

OF THE GENDER OF NOUNS ENDING IN A.

Nouns ending in *a* are generally of the feminine gender; as *rosa*, rose; *janella*, window, &c. Except *dia*, day; *planeta*, planet; and other nouns ending in *a*, belonging to a man; as *mariola*, rascal; *jesuita*, Jesuit: those derived from the Greek are likewise masculine; as *dogma, epigramma, clima;* except scientific names, as *mathematica, theologia*, &c.

Except also from this general rule some nouns that have the accent upon the last syllable; as *alvará*, a charter, or a prince's letters patent; *Pará*, one of the captainships of the Brazilian empire.

Observe, that the plural of nouns ending in *a* is formed by adding the letter *s* to the singular; as likewise the plural of all nouns that terminate in vowels.

Observe also, that nouns ending in *ãa* are of the feminine gender, and form their plural like those ending in *a*.*

* *ãa* is now scarcely used; *ã* is substituted instead.

OF THE GENDER OF NOUNS ENDING IN *E*.

Nouns ending in *e* are generally of the masculine gender; as *dente*, tooth; *valle*, valley, &c.

The exceptions are *fé*, faith; *fonte*, fountain; *chave*, key; *torre*, tower; *ave*, bird; *carne*, flesh or meat; *gente*, people; *morte*, death; *neve*, snow; *noite*, night; *ponte*, bridge; *peste*, plague; *parte*, part; *serpente*, serpent; *lebre*, hare.

Except also all names of virtues, vices, faculties, and those expressive of the passions of the mind; as *virtude*, virtue; *santidade*, holiness; *bondade*, goodness; *vaidade*, vanity; *ociosidade*, idleness, &c.

Thirdly, *idade*, age; *velhice*, old age; *rusticidade*, rusticity; *capacidade*, capacity; *felicidade*, happiness; *sorte*, lot; *arte*, art; *arvore*, tree; *fertilidade*,* fertility; *sêde*, thirst; *sebe*, a hedge; *couve*, cabbage; *herdade*, farm; *chaminé*, chimney; *parede*, wall; *saude*, health; *rede*, net; *maré*, tide; *febre*, fever; *galé*, galley, &c.

OF THE GENDER OF NOUNS ENDING IN *I*.

Nouns ending in *i* are masculine; as *extasi*, a rapture; *nebri*, a hawk, &c., and also those ending in *ei*, as *réi*, king; and in *ai*, as *pai*, father; and in *oi*, as in *boi*, ox, &c. Except *lei*, law; *mãi*, mother, which are feminine.

OF NOUNS ENDING IN *O*.

Nouns ending in *o* are of the masculine gender; as *livro*, book; *filho*, son; *braço*, arm; *vestido*, garment; *espelho*, looking-glass, &c. Except *náo*, a ship; *filhó*, a fritter or pancake; *eiró*, an eel.

---

* All words ending in *dade*, without exception, or all ending in *ade*, with the exceptions of *alvaiade*, whitelead, *frade*, friar, and *confrade*, fellow-friar, are feminine in Portuguese.

OF NOUNS ENDING IN *U*.

All nouns ending in *u* are masculine; as *peru*, a turkey; *grou*, a crane.

OF THE OTHER TERMINATIONS OF NOUNS, OR OF THOSE TERMINATING IN CONSONANTS.

1. All nouns ending in *al* are masculine; as *sinal*, a sign or token; *sal*, salt. Except *cal*, lime, which is feminine, and has no plural.

The plural of these nouns is formed by changing the letter *l* of the singular into *es*; as *sinaes* from *sinal*; *animaes* from *animal*.

2. Nouns ending in *ar* are of the masculine gender; as *ar*, air.

The plural of these nouns is formed by adding *es* to the singular; as *ares* from *ar*.

Some nouns ending in *as* in the plural are feminine, and have no singular; as *migas*, *exequias*, &c.

3. Nouns ending in *az* are of the masculine gender; as *rapaz*, a boy; except *paz*, peace. The plural is formed by the addition of *es* to the singular.

4. Nouns ending in *el* are masculine; as *annel*, a ring; *papel*, paper, &c.

The plural of these nouns is formed by changing the *l* of the singular into *is*; *anneis*, from *annel*; *papeis*, from *papel*.

5. Nouns ending in *em* are of the masculine gender; as *homem*, a man; *bem*, benefit, &c. Except *ordem*, order; *viagem*, a voyage; *virgem*, a virgin, &c.; but *selvagem*, a savage, is common.

The plural of these nouns is formed by changing the *m* of the singular into *ns*; as *homens* from *homem*, &c.

6. Nouns ending in *er* are of the masculine gender;

as *poder*, power; *prazer*, pleasure, &c. Except *colhér*, a spoon; *mulher*, a woman.

The plural of these nouns is formed by adding *es* to the singular; as *colhéres*, from *colhér*.

7. Nouns ending in *ez* are of the masculine gender; as *freguez*, a customer; *mez*, month; *arnez, levez, revéz*, &c. Except *surdez*, deafness; *torquez, vez*, &c.

The plural of these nouns is formed by adding *es* to the singular, as *freguezes*, from *freguez;* but *tez* has no plural.

8. Nouns ending in *il* are of the masculine gender; as *funil*, a funnel; *barril*, a barrel.

The plural of these nouns is formed by changing the *l* of the singular into *s;* as *funis*, from *funil*, &c. Except *aquatil facil*, &c., which change the *il* into *eis* in the plural; as *faceis*, from *facil;* *aquateis*, from *aquatil;* and *pensil*, which has its plural *pensiles*.

9. Nouns ending in *im* are of the masculine gender; as *espadim*, a little sword.

The plural of these nouns is formed by changing the *m* of the singular into *ns;* as *espadins*, from *espadidim*.

10. Nouns ending in *ir* or *yr* are of the masculine gender; but *martir* or *martyr*, a martyr, is common.

The plural of these nouns is formed by adding *es* to the singular.

11. All nouns ending in *iz* are of the masculine gender; as *apprendiz*, an apprentice; *nariz*, nose; *verniz*, varnish; *matiz*, a shadowing in painting; *chafariz, chamariz*, &c. Except *aboiz, perdiz, raiz, codorniz, matriz*, &c.

The plural of these nouns is formed by adding *es* to the singular; as *perdizes*, from *perdiz*.

12. Nouns ending in *ol* are of the masculine gender; as *anzol*, a hook; *sol*, the sun, &c.

The plural of these nouns is formed by changing the *l* of the singular into *es ;* as *anzoes* from *anzol*, &c.

13. Nouns ending in *om* are of the masculine gender; as *som*, sound; *dom*, gift, &c.

The plural of these nouns is formed by changing the *m* of the singular into *ns ;* as *sons* from *som*, &c.

14. Nouns ending in *or* are of the masculine gender; as *amor*, love; *temor*, fear, &c. Except *dôr*, pain; *côr*, colour, &c.

The plural of these nouns is formed by adding *es* to the singular; as *amôres* from *amôr*.

Nouns ending in *os* are of the masculine gender; as *Deos*, God.

The plural of these nouns is formed by adding *es ;* as *Deoses* from *Deos*.

15. Nouns ending in *oz* are of the masculine gender; as *albernoz*, a Moorish coat; *arrôz*, rice; *algôz*, hangman, &c. Except *noz*, a walnut; *voz*, voice; *foz*, the mouth of a river.

The plural of these nouns is formed by adding *es* to the singular.

16. Nouns ending in *ul* or *um* are of the masculine gender; as *sul*, the south; *atum*, tunny-fish.

The plural of those ending in *ul*, according to the learned Bluteau, is formed by changing the *l* of the singular into *es ;* as *sues* for *sul ;* *azues* from *azul*, blue, &c. Except *consules* from *consul*, a consul.

The plural of those ending in *um* is formed by changing the *m* of the singular into *ns ;* as *atuns* from *atum*.

17. Nouns ending in *uz* are of the masculine gender; as *arcabuz*, an arquebus.

The plural of these nouns is formed by adding *es* to the singular.

18. Nouns ending in *ão* are of the feminine gender;

as *mão*, hand; *composição*, composition; *oração*, oration, &c. Except *pão*, bread; *anão*, dwarf; *oução*, handworm; *trovão*, thunder; *esquadrão*, squadron; *pião*, top; *borrão*, blot; *papelão*, cardboard; *chão*, ground; *quinhão*, share.*

There is no certain rule for the formation of the plural of the nouns ending in *ão;* because some change the *ão* of the singular into *ães*, as *Alemães*, from *Alemão*, German; *capitães*, from *capitão*, captain; *cães*, from *cão*, dog; *pães*, from *pão*, loaf, &c. Some change the *ão* of the singular into *ãos;* as *cidadãos*, from *cidadão*, citizen; *christãos*, from *christão*, Christian; *cortezãos*, from *cortezão*, courtier; *villãos*, from *villão*, villain, &c. Some change the *ão* of the singular into *ões;* as *esquadrões*, from *esquadrão*, squadron; *trovões*, from *trovão*, thunder; *conclusões*, from *conclusão*, conclusion; *orações*, from *oração*, oration; and generally all the Portuguese nouns that may be easily made English by changing their termination *ção* into the English termination *tion*—as *declinação*, declension or declination; *consideração*, consideration, &c.—are of the feminine gender.

19. All nouns signifying a male must be of the masculine gender; as *duque*, duke; *marquez*, marquis; *conde*, count; and those denoting a female are always feminine.

Two general rules may be formed from what has

* The quantity of Portuguese nouns ending in *ão* being very great, and the exceptions to the rule, that they are feminine, numbering a good half of those that conform to it, we will remark in regard to nouns of such termination, that:

1st. All augmentatives are masculine, without exception.

2nd. Verbal nouns are feminine, excepting the following (nearly all of which are real augmentatives): *apertão, arremessão, cevão, empurrão, empuxão, enchemão, encontrão, espião, tendão.*

3rd. Nouns not verbal are masculine, except *amarellidão, constellação, escravidão, lunação, mão, mansidão, multidão, sedição, solidão, tribulação, vereação, vermelhidão.*

been said concerning the formation of the plural of nouns, viz.:

I. That all nouns ending in any of the vowels have their plural formed by adding the letter *s* to the singular.

II. That the plural of nouns ending in *az, ez, iz, oz, uz*, is formed by adding *es* to the singular.

OF AUGMENTATIVES.

The Portuguese have their augmentatives formed by the increase of one or two syllables, which they add to the end of their nouns, and which serve either to augment the signification of nouns, or to declare a thing contemptible: thus, from *homem*, a man, they form *homemzarrão*, a great strong man; from *tolo*, a fool, *toleirão*, a great fool, &c., and some others that may be learned by use. They have also their augmentatives for the feminine; as *mulherona*, a great stout woman; *toleirona*, &c.*

There are a great many nouns that appear, by their termination, to be augmentatives, though they are not: as, *forão*, a ferret; *atafona*, an ass or a horse-mill, &c.

OF DIMINUTIVES.

The diminutives lessen the signification of their primitives.

The diminutives in the Portuguese language are always formed by changing the last vowel of the primitives into *inho*; but they denote either smallness of things, or kindness and flattery: as *bichinho*, a little worm, from *bicho*, a worm; *coitadinho*, from *coitado*, a poor little man; *bonitinho*, a little pretty person or thing, from *bonito*, pretty.

---

* It is a peculiarity of the Portuguese language that augmentatives in *ão* are also formed in it sometimes, as well as in *ona*, from feminine primitives, and that the first then assume the masculine gender; so from *espada*, a sword, is made *espadão*, a great sword; from *mulher, mulherão;* from *canastra, canastrão*, &c.

ADJECTIVES.

Sometimes they are formed by adding *zinho* to the primitives; as *cãozinho*, a little dog, from *cão*, a dog; *irmãozinho*, dear little brother, from *irmão*, &c.*

The diminutives that serve for the feminine have their termination in *inha*, or *zinha*; as *mãozinha*, a little hand, from *mão*, a hand; *cabecinha*, a little head, from *cabeça*, a head. It may be seen, from the last example, that the diminutives serving for the feminine and ending in *inha*, are formed by changing the last syllable *a* of the primitive into *inha*.

Observe that many nouns appear to be diminutives without being so; as *moinho*, a mill; *espinha*, a fish-bone.

Note: the diminutives in Portuguese convey sometimes a bad meaning, and denote contempt.

OF ADJECTIVES.

All adjectives ending in *o* make their feminine by changing the *o* into *a*; as *douta*, from *douto*, learned; but *mao*, bad, make *má* in the feminine.

Those which end in *ão* have their feminine in *ã*; as, *sã*, from *são*, healthy; *louçã*, from *loução*, brisk, gay, beautiful; *meã*, from *meão*, middling, ordinary.

Those ending in *e* are common to both genders; as *forte*, strong, &c.

* No language has so many diminutives of different degrees, especially in its familiar style, as the Portuguese: thus, for instance, the adjective *pequeno*, small, is gradually diminished by being turned into *pequenote, pequenete, pequenito, pequenino, pequenicho*, &c., and *cordeiro*, a lamb, into *cordeirote, cordeirete, cordeirito, cordeirinho*; the same is done with other substantives and adjectives: this for the masculine. For the feminine the nal *o* is changed into *a*.

Those which end in *m* make their feminine by adding an *a* to the masculine; as *uma*, from *um*, one; *alguma*, from *algum*, some, &c.: and sometimes by changing the *m* into *a*; as *boa* from *bom*, good.

Those ending in *u* make their feminine by adding an *a* to the masculine; as *nua*, from *nu*, naked; *crua*, from *cru*, raw.

Those ending in *ez* are common to both genders; as *cortez*, civil, kind; *capaz*, capable, &c.: except some which make the feminine by adding *a* to the masculine; as *Franceza*, from *Francez*, French; *Portugueza*, from *Portuguez*, Portuguese.

Espanhol, Spanish, makes *Espanhola* in the feminine; but generally those which end in *l* are common to both genders; as *affavel*, affable; *cruel*, cruel, &c.

OF THE COMPARISON OF ADJECTIVES.

The comparison of adjectives is the way of increasing their signification by certain degrees, which are three, viz., the positive, comparative, and superlative.

The positive lays down the natural signification of the adjective; as *nobre*, noble; *grande*, great.

The comparative raises it to a higher degree, by comparing it with the positive, which in Portuguese is performed by the adverbs *mais*, more; *menos*, less: as, *mais nobre*, more noble; *menos bella*, less handsome.

The following four comparatives constitute exceptions:—

Maior, greater.
Menor, less.
Peior, worse.
Melhor, better.

Observe, that there can be no comparison made without the word *than;* and that this word is expressed in Portuguese by *que,* or *do que.* Ex. *Mais claro que o sol,* clearer than the sun ; *mais branco que a neve,* more white than the snow. The particle *que* is sometimes preceded by the word *do.* Ex. *Isto é mais do que eu lhe disse,* this is more than I told him ; *é mais prudente do que parece,* he is more wise than it appears.

N.B. The comparatives *superior, inferior,* and some others, do not require *que* before the second term, but the dative of the articles,* viz., *a, á, ás, ao, aos.* Ex. *O outro é superior a este,* the other is superior to this.

When the Portuguese have a mind to heighten their comparisons they make use of *muito mais,* or *muito menos,* a great deal or much less. Ex. *Cæsar é muito mais estimado que Pompeio,* Cæsar is much more esteemed than Pompey ; *Pompeio foi muito menos feliz que Cæsar,* Pompey was much less happy than Cæsar.

OF THE SUPERLATIVE ABLOLUTE.

The Portuguese superlative absolute is formed from the positive by changing the last letter into *issimo* for the masculine, and into *issima,* for the feminine ; thus, from *bello* is formed *bellissimo* and *bellissima,* most handsome.

Observe that some superlatives absolute are differently formed : as, *frigidissimo,* from *frio,* cold ; *amicissimo,* from *amigo,* friend ; *antiquissimo,* from *antigo,* ancient ; *capacissimo,* from *capaz*†, capable ; *nobilissimo,* from *nobre,* noble ; *acerbissimo,* from *acerbo,* sharp, or acerb ; *riquissimo,* from *rico,* rich ; *fertilissimo,* from *fertil,* fertile ;

* It would be more intelligible to say, that these require a dative with its preposition *a*.

† Adjectives in *az* generally change the *z* into *cissimo* in their superlative.

bonissimo, from *bom*, good; *fidelissimo*, from *fiel*, faithful; *sacratissimo*, from *sagrado*, sacred, &c.

The most is expressed also in Portuguese by *o mais* and *a mais*; as, the most fair, or fairest, *o mais bello*, *a mais bella*. But there are some adjectives which do not admit of *muito*, very, *o mais*, or *a mais*; as *morto*, *desterrado*, &c.

Observe, that by changing the last letter of the superlatives into *amente*, superlative adverbs are composed; as from *doutissimo*, learned; *doutissimamente*, most learnedly, &c. But the positive adverbs are formed by adding *mente* to the feminine of the positive; as *doutamente*, learnedly, from *douta*, the feminine of *douto*; *prudentemente*, prudently, from *prudente*, prudent.

OF NUMERAL NOUNS.
AND FIRST OF CARDINAL.

The cardinal nouns are such as express the number of things; as,

Um, Uma, one.
Dous, Duas, two.
Tres, three.
Quatro, four.
Cinco, five.
Seis, six.
Sete, seven.
Oito, eight.
Nove, nine.
Dez, ten.
Onze, eleven.
Doze, twelve.
Treze, thirteen.
Quatorze, fourteen.
Quinze, fifteen.

NOUNS.

Dezaseiz, sixteen.
Dezasete, seventeen.
Dezoito, eighteen.
Dezanove, nineteen.
Vinte, twenty.
Vinte e um, twenty-one.
Vinte e dois, twenty-two.
Vinte e tres, &c., twenty-three, &c.
Trinta, thirty.
Quarenta, forty.
Cincoenta, fifty,
Sessenta, sixty.
Setenta, seventy.
Oitenta, eighty.
Noventa, ninety.
Cento, Cem, a hundred.
Duzentos, duzentas, two hundred.
Trezentos, trezentas, three hundred.
Quatrocentos, four hundred.
Quinhentos five hundred.
Seiscentos, six hundred.
Mil, a thousand.
Dous mil, two thousand.
Milhão, or *conto,* a million.
Uma dezena, half a score.
Uma duzia, a dozen.
Uma vintena, a score.
Duas vintenas, two score.
Tres vintenas, three score.

Observe, that all the cardinals that are adjective nouns are not declined, being of the common gender, except *um, uma,* one ; *dois, duas,* two ; and those composed of *cento,* a hundred ; as *duzentos,* two hundred ; *quatro centos, quatro centas,* four hundred, &c.; and when the feminine *uma* is preceded by *a,* and followed by *a outra,* then *a uma* signifies *first,* and *a outra, secondly.*

The plural *uns, umas,* is taken sometimes instead of *alguns, algumas,* signifying some; as, *uns réis,** some *réis; umas maçãs,* some apples.

N.B. *Cento* loses *to* before a noun, either masculine or feminine, and the *n* is changed into *m;* therefore you must say, *cem soldados,* not *cento soldados.* It only retains *to* and *n* when it is followed by another number, as *cento e um,* &c., a hundred and one, &c., and when it is a substantive.

N.B. Sometimes *cento* is made a substantive; as *um cento de castanhas,* one hundred of chestnuts : likewise all the cardinal numbers, when preceded by an article, or by another noun of number, as *o cinco de páos,* the five of clubs; *um sete,* a seven.

The cardinal number is used in Portuguese instead of the ordinal when it expresses the day of the month, or the date of any act; as, *elle chegou a quatro de Maio,* he arrived the fourth day of May. The first day of the month is, however, an exception to this rule; as, *o primeiro de Maio,* the first of May.

OF ORDINAL NOUNS.

Ordinal nouns are such as express the order of things; as,

Primeiro, primeira, first.
Segundo, segunda, second.
Terceiro, terceira, third.
Quarto, fourth.
Quinto, fifth.
Sexto, sixth.

* Derived from *real,* a Portuguese coin.

Setimo, seventh.
Oitavo, eighth.
Nono, ninth.
Decimo, tenth.
Undecimo, eleventh.
Duodecimo, twelfth.
Decimo-tercio, thirteenth.
Decimo-quarto, fourteenth.
Decimo-quinto, fifteenth.
Decimo-sexto, sixteenth.
Decimo-setimo, seventeenth.
Decimo-oitavo, eighteenth.
Decimo-nono, nineteenth.
Vigesimo, twentieth.
Vigesimo-primeiro, one-and-twentieth.
Trigesimo, thirtieth.
Quadragesimo, fortieth.
Quinquagesimo, fiftieth.
Sexagesimo, sixtieth.
Septuagesimo, seventieth.
Octagesimo, eightieth.
Nonagesimo, ninetieth.
Centesimo, the hundredth.
Millesimo, the thousandth.
Ultimo, the last.

The proportionable numbers are, *simples, duplo* or *duplicado, triplo* or *triplicado, quadruplo, quintuplo, centuplo*; a single, double, threefold, fourfold, fivefold, a hundredfold.

The distributive nouns are *um a um,* one by one; *dois a dois,* two by two.

In English all ordinal numbers may be formed into adverbs; but in Portuguese they have only *primeiramente,* and *secundariamente*, first, secondly; and to express thirdly, fourthly, &c., they say, *em terceiro lugar*, *em quarto lugar*, in the third place, in the fourth place.

A METHOD (FOR THOSE WHO UNDERSTAND FRENCH) TO LEARN A GREAT MANY PORTUGUESE WORDS IN A SHORT TIME.

We must observe, that the French syllable *cha* is generally expressed in Portuguese by *ca*, rejecting the *h*. Ex. *Charbon, charité, chasteté, chapelle, chapitre*, &c., the Portuguese say, *carvão, caridade, castidade, capella, capitulo*, &c. Observe also the following rules:—

French words ending in *ance*, or *ence*, as *constance, vigilance, clémence, prudence*, &c., in Portuguese end in *ancia*, or *encia*; as *constancia, vigilancia, clemencia, prudencia*, &c.

Agne makes *anha*; montagne, *montanha*; campagne, *campanha*.

Ie makes *ia*; comédie, *comedia*. Here the accent is upon the *e*, and not upon the *i*, as in French; poésie, *poesia*.

Oire makes *oria*; gloire, *gloria*; victoire, *victoria*.

Ure makes *ura*; imposture, *impostura*; figure, *figura*.

Ison makes *são*; prison, *prisão*; raison, *ração*.

On makes *ão*; charbon, *carvão*; baron, *barão*.

Ulier makes *ular*; régulier, *regular*; particulier, *particular*.

FRENCH TERMINATIONS ENDING IN PORTUGUESE IN *E*.

Ant, ante; vigilant, *vigilante*; amant, *amante*.

Ent, adjective, *ente*; prudent, *prudente*; diligent, *diligente*.

Té makes *dade*; liberalité, *liberalidade*.

FRENCH TERMINATIONS ENDING IN PORTUGUESE IN *VEL.*

Able, vel ; louable, *louvavel* ; aimable, *amavel.*

FRENCH TERMINATIONS ENDING IN PORTUGUESE IN *EZ.*

Ais, names of nations, *ez* ; Français, *Francez;* Anglais, *Inglez.*

FRENCH TERMINATIONS ENDING IN PORTUGUESE IN *O.*

Ain and *ien,* names of nations, *ano ;* Romain, *Romano ;* Italien, *Italiano ;* Napolitain, *Napolitano.*
Aire, ario ; salaire, *salario ;* téméraire, *temerario.*
Eau, eo ; chapeau, *chapeo.*
Ent, substantive, *ento ;* sacrement, *sacramento.*
Eux, oso ; généreux, *generoso ;* gracieux, *gracioso.*
If, ivo ; actif, *activo ;* passif, *passivo.*
C, co ; Turc, *Turco.*

FRENCH TERMINATIONS ENDING IN PORTUGUESE IN *OR.*

Eur, or ; terreur, *terror ;* humeur, *humor ;* chaleur, *calor.*

CHANGE OF TERMINATIONS OF THE VERBS AND PARTICIPLES.

Er, in the infinitive mood of the first conjugation, makes *ar ;* aimer, *amar ;* chanter, *cantar.*

Ir makes *ir,* in the infinitive mood ; as, partir, *partir ;* sentir, *sentir.*

Oir makes *er,* in the infinitive mood ; as concevoir, *conceber.*

The participles in *é* make *ado ;* aimé, *amado ;* parlé, *fallado.*

The participles in *i* make *ido ;* dormi, *dormido ;* menti, *mentido.*

The participles in *u* make *do;* as, conçu, *concebido;* entendu, *entendido.*

There are a great many Portuguese words that have no manner of analogy with the French, which prevent these rules from being general.

CHAPTER IV.

OF PRONOUNS.

THE pronouns are personal, conjunctive, mixed, positive, demonstrative, interrogative, relative, or improper.

OF PERSONAL PRONOUNS.

The personal pronouns are *eu* and *nós* for the first person; they serve for the masculine and the feminine.

Tu and *vós* for the second; these serve also for the masculine and feminine.

Elle for the third person of the masculine gender, and *elles* in the plural.

Ella for the third person of the feminine gender, makes in the plural *ellas.*

The pronouns personal are declined with the prepositions *de, a,* and *por.*

THE DECLENSION OF PERSONAL PRONOUNS.

First Person.

SINGULAR.	PLURAL.
Nom. *Eu,* I	N. *nós,* we
Gen. *de mim,* of me	G. *de nós,* of us
Dat. *a mim,* or *me,* to me	D. *a nós,* or *nós,* us
Acc. *me,* me	A. *nos,* us
Abl. *de mim,* or *por mim,* from *or* by me.	A. *de nós,* or *por nós,* from *or* by us.

With me is rendered by *commigo*, and sometimes they add the pronoun *mesmo* to it: *me* is expressed by *me* in the Portuguese; as, speak to me, *fallai-me*; tell me, *dizei-me;* send me, *mandai-me;* write to me, *escrevei-me;* he told me, *elle disse-me*, &c.

With us is rendered in Portuguese by *comnosco*.

Us is rendered by *nos*.* Example: tell us, *dizei-nos*; give us, *dai-nos;* show us, *mostrai-nos;* he told us, *elle disse-nos*, &c. In these examples *us* is not a personal pronoun, but conjunctive, as you will see hereafter.

Second Person.

	SINGULAR.		PLURAL.
Nom.	*tu*, thou	N.	*vós*, ye *or* you
Gen.	*de ti*, of thee	G.	*de vós*, or *vos*, you
Dat.	*a ti*, or *te*, to thee	D.	*a vós*, or *vos*, to you
Acc.	*te*, thee	A.	*vos*, you
Abl.	*de ti*, or *por ti*, from *or* by thee.	A.	*de vós*, or *por vós*, from *or* by you.

With thee is rendered by *comtigo;* and sometimes they add to it the pronoun *mesmo*. *You*, or *yourself*, after imperatives, is rendered by *vos*, and not *vós;* as, be you contented, *contentai-vos;* show yourself, *mostrai-vos;* hide yourselves, *escondei-vos*.

Thee, or *thyself*, is expressed after imperatives by *te;* as, *mostra te*, show thyself.

With you is rendered in Portuguese by *comvosco*.

---

* The pronouns *nós* and *nos* are pronounced, the first with the open *ó*, as its accent indicates; the second with the *o* mute. The *o*, therefore, is mute in the conjunctive pronouns. The *c* is equally mute in the same conjunctive pronouns: this it is necessary to remember.

Third Person (*for the Masculine*).

SINGULAR.	PLURAL.
Nom. *elle*, he *or* it	N. *elles*, they
Gen. *d'elle*, of him *or* of it	G. *d'elles*, of them
Dat. *a elle*, or *lhe*, to him, *or* to it	D. *a elles*, or *lhes*, to them
Acc. *o*, him *or* it	A. *os*, them
Abl. *d'elle*, or *por elle*, from *or* by him *or* it.	A. *d'elles*, or *por elles*, from *or* by them.

The Portuguese have no particular pronoun, as the English *it*, for things that are inanimate.

The pronoun *him*, or *to him*, when joined to a verb, is always rendered in Portuguese by *lhe;* and *them*, or *to them*, by *lhes*.

With him is rendered in Portuguese sometimes by *com elle*, and sometimes by *comsigo*, to which they add the pronoun *mesmo*.

Third Person (*Feminine*).

SINGULAR.	PLURAL.
Nom. *ella*, she *or* it	N. *ellas*, they
Gen. *d'ella*, of her *or* of it	G. *d'ellas*, of them
Dat. *a ella*, or *lhe* to her *or* to it	D. *a ellas*, or *lhes* to them
Acc. *a*, her *or* it	A. *as*, them
Abl. *d'ella*, or *por ella*, from *or* by her *or* it.	A. *d'ellas*, or *por ellas*, from *or* by them.

The pronoun *her*, or *to her*, when joined to a verb, is always rendered in Portuguese by *lhe;* and *them*, or *to them*, by *lhes:* as will be seen in the conjunctive pronouns.

With her is rendered in Portuguese by *com ella*, or *comsigo*.

OF THE PRONOUN *SI*, HIMSELF OR ONESELF.

There is another personal pronoun that serves indifferently for the masculine and feminine: this is *si*, oneself. It has no nominative.

Gen. *de si*, of oneself, himself, *or* herself
Dat. *a si*, to oneself, &c.
Acc. *se*, oneself, &c.
Abl. *de si, por si*, from *or* by oneself.

It is joined with the pronoun *mesmo* or *mesma;* as *de* or *por si mesmo*, by himself; *por si mesma*, or *de si mesma*, by herself; *o homem não ama senão a si mesmo*, man loves himself only; *quem não é bom senão para si, não é bem que viva*, who cares for nobody but himself, does not deserve to live; *o vicio é abominavel por si mesmo*, vice is in itself hateful; *a terra de si*, or *de si mesma é fertil*, the earth is fruitful in itself.

Observe, that they join also the pronoun *mesmo* to personal pronouns, as the French do with their pronoun *même*, viz.:—

Eu mesmo, myself	*nós mesmos*, ourselves
Tu mesmo, thyself	*vós mesmos*, yourselves.
Elle mesmo, himself	*elles mesmos*, } themselves
Ella mesma, herself	*ellas mesmas*, }
o homem mesmo, man himself.	*a mesma virtude*, virtue itself.

1st. Observe, that *mesmo* with the article is also an adjective, signifying *the same;* thus, *o mesmo, a mesma, os mesmos, as mesmas*, the same, relating to some nouns expressed or understood.

2ndly. *Note*, also, that the adjective *outro*, other, is joined to the plural of the personal pronouns, *I* and *thou*: thus, *nós outros*, we; *vos outros*, you.

3rdly. *Comsigo* may be rendered in English (as we have said above) by *with him* and *with her;* and it may be rendered also by *with them* in the plural; and sometimes by *about him*, *about her*, or *about them*. Ex. *Elle* or *ella nunca traz dinheiro comsigo*, he *or* she never has money about him, *or* about her.

OF CONJUNCTIVE PRONOUNS.

The pronouns conjunctive are so called, because they always come immediately before or after the verb that governs them.

The conjunctive pronouns bear a great resemblance to the personal pronouns. The personal pronouns are:

Eu, I; *tu*, thou; *elle*, he; *nós*, we; *vós*, ye; *elles*, they.

There are seven pronouns conjunctive, viz, *me*, to me, *or* me; *te*, to thee, *or* thee; *se*, to himself, *or* himself, to herself, *or* herself; *lhe*, to him, *or* him, to her, *or* her; *nos*, to us, *or* us; *vos*, to you, *or* you; *lhes*, to them, *or* them.

EXAMPLES.

Isto me agrada, this pleases me; *é-me necessario*, I want.

Deus te vê, God sees thee.

Ella se louva, she praises herself.

Eu lhe direi, I will tell him, *or* I will tell her.

Eu lhes prometti, I promised them: as well for the masculine as the feminine.

The pronoun conjunctive, *lhe*, is always put after the verb, when it is in the imperative mood; as *dizei-lhe*, tell him; *cortai-lhe as azas*, cut his wings: but when the verb is in some other mood, it may be put either before or after it: as, *elle lhe cortou*, or *elle cortou-lhe a cabeça*, he has cut off his head. The same observation applies to the other conjunctive pronouns.

The conjunctive pronoun, *se*, is sometimes followed by *me, lhe*, &c.; as *offerece-se-me*, it is offered to me; *representou-se-lhe*, it was represented to him, &c.

1st. *Note*, that the pronouns conjunctive are very often joined to a verb, preceded or followed by the verb *haver*. Ex. *Dar-lhe-hei tanta pancada*, or *eu lhe hei de dar tanta pancada, que*, &c., I will cudgel him so much that, &c.

2ndly. *Lhe* is sometimes rendered in English by *you*. Ex. *Que lhe parece aquillo?* What do you think of that? *Assente no que lhe digo*, be persuaded, *or* believe what I tell you.

OF MIXED PRONOUNS.

There are some pronouns in Portuguese which are composed of the pronouns personal and conjunctive, and which therefore are called mixed.

These pronouns are formed by changing the letter *e* of the pronoun conjunctive into *o* for the masculine, and *a* for the feminine; thus, *it* to *me*, instead of *me o*, or *me a*, you must say, *m'o* or *m'a*. In like manner, instead of *lhe o*, or *lhe a*, you must say, *lh'o* or *lh'a*, &c., as you may observe in the following pronouns mixed, or rather contracted.

m'o, m., it *or* him to me
m'a, f., it *or* her to me
m'os, m. ⎫ them to me
m'as, f. ⎭

t'o, it *or* him to thee
t'a, it *or* her to thee
t'os, m. ⎫ them to thee
t'as, f. ⎭

lh'o, m., it to him, *or* to her
lh'a, f., it to him, *or* to her
lh'os, m., them to him *or* to them
lh'as, f., them to her *or* to them

D

nol-o, m.
nol-a, f. } it to us

nol-os, m. pl.
nol-as, f. pl. } them to us

vol-o, m.
vol-a, f. } it to you

vol-os, m. pl.
vol-as, f. pl. } them to you

EXAMPLES.

Para dar-lh'o, to give it to him, *or* to her.
Dai-m'o, give it to me.
Eu t'o darei, I will give it you.
Entrego-t'o, I deliver it to you.
Dize-lh'o, you tell it him, *or* her.
Entrega-lh'os, deliver them to him, *or* to her.
Elle nol-o disse, he told us of it.
Eu vol-os mandarei, I will send them to you.

If the verbs are in the infinitive, the pronouns mixed may be put either before or after the verbs; as, *para dtzerm'o,* or *para m'o dizer,* to tell me it: but if the verbs are in the gerund, the pronouns mixed must be transposed; as, *dizendom'o,* and not *m'o dizendo,* in telling me it.

You must make use of these pronouns, both masculine and feminine, according to the gender of the thing named, sent or delivered, and not of the person to whom the thing is said, sent, given, &c.

OF POSSESSIVE PRONOUNS.

Pronouns possessive, so called because they denote that the thing spoken of belongs to the person or thing they are connected with, are of two sorts, absolute and relative. See the remarks hereafter.

The English have no article in the nominative before

the pronouns possessive; but the Portuguese have: as, *my*, *o meu*, masc., *a minha*, fem. Plural, *os meus*, masc.; *as minhas*, fem.

The pronouns possessive in Portuguese are the following:—

Sing. *meu*, m.; *minha*, f. } my
Plur. *meus*, m.; *minhas*, f.

Sing. *teu*, m.; *tua*, f. } thy
Plur. *teus*, m.; *tuas*, f.

Sing. *seu*, m. } his, her, *or* its
Plur. *seus*, m.

Sing. *sua*, f. } his, her, *or* its
Plur. *suas*, f.

Sing. *nosso*, m.; *nossa*, f. } our
Plur. *nossas*, m.; *nossas*, f.

Sing. *vosso*, m.; *vossa*, f. } your
Plur. *vossos*, m.; *vossas*, f.

The pronouns possessive are declined with the definite article *o* for the masculine, and *a* for the feminine.

EXAMPLE.

SINGULAR.

Nom. *o meu livro*, my book
Gen. *do meu livro*, of my book
Dat. *ao meu livro*, to my book
Acc. *o meu livro*, my book
Abl. *do* or *pelo meu livro*, from *or* by my book

PLURAL.

Nom. *os meus livros*, my books
Gen. *dos meus livros*, of my books
Dat. *aos meus livros*, to my books
Abl. *dos* or *pelos meus livros*, from *or* by my books

Decline all the other masculines after the same manner, and their feminines by the article *a;* as, my house, *a minha casa;* of my house, *da minha casa,* &c.

Note, you must not use the definite article when the pronouns possessive precede nouns of quality, as well as those of kindred, but the indefinite article, *de, a,* &c.

EXAMPLES.

Vossa magestade, your majesty.
De vossa magestade, of your majesty, &c.
Meu pai, my father.
De meu pai, of my father, &c.

From the above examples it appears that nouns declined with the definite article have no article in the nominative, in the singular number.

Seu is sometimes used instead of *vosso* and *vossa,* in the polite way of speaking: thus, *tenho o seu livro,* I have your book; *fallei ao seu criado,* I spoke to your servant; *os seus olhos são formosos,* your eyes are handsome.

REMARKS UPON THE POSSESSIVE.

The pronouns possessive absolute always come before the noun they belong to. We have expressed them above.

To express in Portuguese *it is mine, it is thine,* &c., we must say *é meu, é teu,* &c.

The pronouns possessive absolute do not agree in gender with the noun of the possessor, as in English, but with that of the thing possessed: as, *a mãi ama a seu filho,* the mother loves her son; *o pai ama a sua filha,* the father loves his daughter. Thus the pronoun masculine *seu,* in Portugue e, is in this case rendered by *her* in English, and the feminine *sua* by *his.*

The same observation is to be made upon the possessives relative, according to the gender of the noun that is understood: we say of a hat (for instance) belonging to a lady, *é o seu*, it is hers; because the noun understood, viz., *chapéo*, hat is of the masculine gender.

We have already said that *seu* and *sua* are sometimes rendered into English by *your* when they are absolute: they are also sometimes rendered into English by *yours*, when they are pronouns relative, speaking politely of anything belonging to a gentleman or lady, *é o seu*, or *é a sua*, it is yours; but if the gentleman or lady is not present, or if they are not directly spoken to, though present, then the pronouns, *seu* and *sua* must be rendered into English by *his* or *hers*.

Note, that the pronouns possessive absolute, in Portuguese, agree also in number with the noun of the thing possessed; hence we say, *a sua historia*, its history, speaking of a kingdom, province, &c.; or, his history, speaking of any history composed by a man; or, her history, speaking of that written by a woman; or, their history, speaking of that written by several hands or by several people. From this example, it will be seen that the Portuguese have no particular pronoun possessive for things that are inanimate, corresponding with the English pronoun *its*. Hence, finally, it follows that, when the Portuguese possessives *seu* and *sua* are relative, they are rendered into English by *his* or *hers*, or *theirs*, according to the gender and number of the noun of the possessor that is understood.

The possessives absolute are left out when they are preceded by a verb, or by a pronoun conjunctive, which sufficiently denote whose thing it is they speak of; the article alone being sufficient; as, *devo-lhe a vida*, I owe my life to him, *or* to her, *or* to it.

When the pronouns possessive absolute are before nouns of different genders in the same sentence, and with which they are grammatically construed, they ought to be repeated, as, *seu pai e sua mãi*, his father and mother; not *seu pai e mãi*.

The pronoun possessive absolute is also used as in the following case, when we use the possessive relative; a friend of mine, *um dos meus amigos*.

The possessives *minha, tua, sua, nossa, vossa*, may be also relative, but with a different meaning. Examples: *Levarei a minha avante*, I will insist upon it, I will obtain it; *elle levará a sua avante*, he will insist upon it, he will do it; *levai a vossa avante*, go on with your resolution; *fazer das suas* to play tricks, to dodge.

Os meus, os seus, &c., signifying my relations or my friends, thy relations, or thy friends: as, *os seus não o querem*, his parents or relations do not like him; *deixa-o ir com os seus*, let him go with his people, his countrymen, &c.

When the pronoun possessive is accompanied by a pronoun demonstrative, we do not put the article in the nominative; we do not say, *o este meu livro*, but *este meu livro*, this book of mine. But in all other cases the indefinite article is used; as, *d'este*, or *d'este vosso livro*, &c.

OF THE PRONOUNS DEMONSTRATIVE.

They are called pronouns demonstrative, because they serve to point out or demonstrate any thing or person; as, this book, *este livro;* that man, *aquelle homem*.

There are three principal demonstratives, viz., *este*, this; *esse*, that; *aquelle*, that: *este* shows the thing or person that is just near or by us; *esse* shows the thing that is a little further, or near the person; and *aquelle* shows what is very distant from the person who speaks, or is spoken of, and is expressed in English by *that there* or *yonder*. *Esse, essa*, are used in writing to any person to express the place or town wherein he dwells; as, *tenho fallado n'essa cidade com muitos amigos*, I have spoken in your city with many friends.

These pronouns are declined thus:—

		MASC.	FEM.	NEUT.	
Sing.	Nom.	*este*	*esta*	*isto*	this
	Gen.	*d'este*	*d'esta*	*d'isto*	of this
	Dat.	*a este*	*a esta*	*a isto*	to this
	Acc.	*este*	*esta*	*isto*	this
	Abl.	*d'este*	*d'esta*	*d'isto*	from this
Plur.	Nom.	*estes*	*estas*	No Neuter	these
	Gen.	*d'estes*	*d'estas*		of these
	Dat.	*a estes*	*a estas*		to these
	Acc.	*estes*	*estas*		these
	Abl.	*d'estes*	*d'estas*		from these

		MASC.	FEM.	NEUT.	
Sing.	Nom.	*esse*	*essa*	*isso*	that or it
	Gen.	*d'esse*	*d'essa*	*d'isso*	of that, &c.
	Dat.	*a esse*	*a essa*	*a isso*	to that
	Acc.	*esse*	*essa*	*isso*	that
	Abl.	*d'esse*	*d'essa*	*d'isso*	from that
Plur.	Nom.	*esses*	*essas*	No Neuter	those
	Gen.	*d'esses*	*d'essas*		of those
	Dat.	*a esses*	*a essas*		to those
	Acc.	*esses*	*essas*		those
	Abl.	*d'esses*	*d'essas*		from those

		MASC.	FEM.	NEUT.	
Sing.	Nom.	*aquelle*	*aquella*	*aquillo*	that
	Gen.	*d'aquelle*	*d'aquella*	*d'aquillo*	of that
	Dat.	*á quelle*	*á quella*	*á quillo*	to that
	Acc.	*aquelle*	*aquella*	*aquillo*	that
	Abl.	*d'aquelle*	*d'aquella*	*d'aquillo*	from that
Plur.	Nom.	*aquelles*	*aquellas*	No Neuter	those
	Gen.	*d'aquelles*	*d'aquellas*		of those
	Dat.	*á quelles*	*á quellas*		to those
	Acc.	*aquelles*	*aquellas*		those
	Abl.	*d'aquelles*	*d'aquellas*		from those

There is an elision of the vowel of the preposition *de* in the genitive and ablative of the pronouns *este* and *esse*, both in the singular and plural; as *d'este, d'estas*, &c., instead of *de este, de estas;* so also in the neuter, as *d'isso, d'isto*, instead of *de isso, de isto*. The same observation applies to the pronoun *aquelle*, wherein you will see another elision besides in the dative case.

Both Portuguese and Spaniards have demonstratives of the neuter gender, though they do not agree with the substantives, as in Latin; they do not say *isto homem*, but *este homem*, this man. But the word *cousa*, or *coisa*, thing, is always understood, though the neuter demonstrative does not agree with it; so that it is indifferently said, *isto* or *esta coisa*, this thing; *isso* or *essa coisa*, that thing, &c. Examples: *isso é* or *essa é a coisa de que nós estamos fallando*, that is the thing we are speaking of; *aquillo é* or *aquella é a coisa que vós deveis fazer*, that is the thing you must do, &c.

When the preposition *em*, in, comes before the pronouns demonstrative, the vowel is cut off, and the consonant *m* is changed into *n;* thus, instead of *em este, em esta, em isto, em isso, em aquillo*, they write and pronounce, *n'este, n'esta, n'isto, n'isso*, &c., in this, in that, &c.

The words *outro, outra*, are often joined to the pronouns demonstrative, cutting off the final *e;* as *est'outro, ess'outro, aquell'outro*. Examples: *est'outro homem*, this other man; *est'outra molher*, this other woman; *ess'outro homem*, that other man.

The pronoun *mesmo*, the same, is also frequently joined to the demonstrative; as, *este mesmo homem*, this very same man; *aquillo mesmo*, that very same thing. *Aqui, ali*, and *lá* are sometimes added to the demonstrative, or to the noun that comes after it, in order to specify and particularise it still more; as, *este homem aqui*, this man here; *aquella mulher lá*, that woman there; *aqui*, denoting a near or present object; and *lá*, a distant and absent one.

The pronouns *aquelle, aquella, aquelles, aquellas*, when they relate to persons, and are followed by the relative *que*, are rendered into English by *he who* or *he that, she who* or *that, they who* or *that*: as, *aquelle que ama a virtude é feliz*, he who loves virtue is happy; *aquelles que desprezão a sciencia não conhecem o valor d'ella*, they who despise learning know not the value of it. Observe, that when *aquelle, aquella*, &c., are preceded by *este, esta*, &c., then *este* signifies the last thing or person spoken of, and *aquelle*, &c., the first; as, *Carlos foi grande, Frederico ambicioso, este valente, aquelle poderoso:* Charles was great, Frederic ambitious, the first powerful, the last courageous.

The pronoun possessive absolute *his, her, their*, construed in English with a noun followed by the pronoun relative *who* or *that* before a verb, is rendered in Portuguese by the genitive of the pronouns *aquelle, aquella, aquelles*, followed by *que*, and the possessive is left out; as, all men blame his manners who often says that which himself does not think, *todo o mundo censura o procedimento d'aquelle que tem por costume dizer o que não tem no pensamento;* Providence does not prosper the labours of those that slight their best friends, *a Providencia não abençôa o trabalho d'aquelles que desprezão os seus melhores amigos.*

The English pronoun *such*, followed by *as* or *that* (but not governed by the verb substantive *to be*), is also rendered into Portuguese by *aquelle que,* or *aquelles que;* as, such as do not love virtue do not know it, *aquelle* or *aquelles que não amão a virtude não a conhecem.*

The pronouns *isso, isto, aquillo,* before *que,* are rendered into English by *what;* as, *elle diz aquillo que sabe,* he says what he knows.

Aquelle is also used to show contempt; as, *que quer aquelle homem?* What does that man desire?

OF THE PRONOUNS INTERROGATIVE.

The pronouns interrogative serve to ask questions, and are as follows : who, what, which, *quem, que, qual.*

EXAMPLES.

Quem é?	Who is it?
Quem vos disse isso?	Who told you so?
Que quereis?	What will you have?
Com que se sustenta?	What do you maintain yourself with?
Que estais fazendo?	What are you doing?
De que se faz isto?	From what is this done?
Que livro é este?	What book is this?
Que negocios tendes?	What affairs have you?
Que casa é?	What house is it?
De qual fallais vós?	Which do you speak of?
Qual d'elles?	Which of them?
Quem or *qual dos dois?*	Which of the two?

PRONOUNS.

These pronouns are thus declined:—

Masculine and Feminine.

SINGULAR AND PLURAL.

Nom.	*quem*	who	N.	*que*	what
Gen.	*de quem*	of whom	G.	*de que*	of what
Dat.	*a quem*	to whom	D.	*a que*	to what
Acc.	*quem*	whom	A.	*que*	what
Abl.	*de quem*	from whom	A.	*de que*	from what
,,	*por quem*	by whom	,,	*pelo que*	by what.

Qual is used in speaking both of persons and things, and is declined thus:—

Masculine and Feminine.

SINGULAR.

Nom.	*qual*	which *or* what
Gen.	*de qual*	of which *or* what
Dat.	*a qual*	to which *or* what
Acc.	*qual*	which *or* what
Abl.	*de qual*	from which *or* what
,,	*por qual*	by which *or* what.

Masculine and Feminine.

PLURAL.

Nom.	*quaes*	which *or* what
Gen.	*de quaes*	of which *or* what
Dat.	*a quaes*	to which *or* what
Acc.	*quaes*	which *or* what
Abl.	*de quaes*	from which *or* what

Observe, that when the word *quer* is added to *quem*, or *qual*, it quite alters the meaning; *quemquer* signifying whoever, or any person, and *qualquer*, any one, whether man, woman, or thing; and sometimes they add the particle *que* to them, as *quemquer que*, &c.

OF THE PRONOUNS RELATIVE.

Pronouns relative are those which show the relation or reference which a noun has to what follows it. They are the following: *qual*, which; *que*, that *or* which; *cujo*, whose; *quem*, who.

Qual, in a sense of comparison, is followed by *tal*, and then *qual* is rendered in English by *as*, and *tal* by *of*.

N.B. When *qual* is only a relative, it is declined with the definite articles *o* or *a*.

The pronoun *que* may be relative both to persons and things, and is common to all numbers, genders, and cases; as, *o livro que*, the book which; *os livros que*, the books which; *a carta que*, the letter which; *as cartas que*, the letters which; *o mestre que ensina*, the master who teaches; *a mulher que tenho*, the wife that I have; *o homem que eu amo*, the man whom I love. It is thus declined:—

SINGULAR AND PLURAL.

Nom.	*que*	which *or* who
Gen.	*de que*	of which *or* of whom
Dat.	*a que*	to which or to whom
Acc.	*que*	which or whom
Abl.	*de que*	from which *or* from whom.

Que is sometimes a conjunction; as, *creio que irei*, I believe that I shall go. See the *Syntax*.

The relative *quem*, who, is only relative to persons; but in the nominative case of the singular is rendered into English by *he who* or *who;* as *quem falla deve considerar*, &c., he who speaks ought to consider, &c.; *eu não sei quem*, I know not who.

Observe, that *quem* is common to all numbers, genders, and cases; but it has no nominative in the plural.

SINGULAR AND PLURAL.

Quem is declined thus :—

Nom.	*quem*	he who, *or* she who, *or* whoever
Gen.	*de quem*	of whom
Dat.	*a quem*	to whom
Acc.	*quem*	whom
Abl.	*de quem*	from whom
,,	*por quem*	by whom.

Quem sometimes serves for exclamation; as, *quem me déra estar em casa!* how fain would I be at home!

Cujo, cuja, are declined thus :—

		MASC.	FEM.	
	Nom.	*cujo*	*cuja*	whose
	Gen.	*de cujo*	*de cuja*	of whose
Sing.	Dat.	*a cujo*	*a cuja*	to whose
	Acc.	*cujo*	*cuja*	whose
	Abl.	*de cujo*	*de cuja*	from whose.

The plural is formed by adding *s* to the singular; as, *cujos, cujas,* whose, &c.

Observe that *cujo* must be followed by the noun or term to which it refers, and with which it agrees in gender, number, and case: as, *a pessôa cuja reputação é grande,* the person whose reputation is great; *o céo cujo soccorro nunca falta,* heaven, whose assistance never fails; *cuja bella cara,* whose fair visage; *cujas bellezas,* whose beauties; *a cujo pai,* to whose father; *de cujos irmãos tenho recebido,* from whose brothers I have received. Observe also that *cujo* is not to be repeated, though the terms to which it refers be of different number; as, *cuja valia e obras,* whose valour and deeds.

Observe, that *o, a, os, as, ló, lá,* &c., are also relative pronouns when joined to verbs. See the *Syntax,* chap. iv.

OF THE IMPROPER PRONOUNS.

These pronouns are called *improper*, because indeed they are not properly pronouns, although they bear a great resemblance to pronouns as well as to adjectives. They are the following:—

Um	one
Alguem	somebody
Algum	some
Ninguem	nobody
Nenhum	none
Cadaum	every one, each
Cada	every
Outro, outra	other
Outrem	another person.

Qualquer, any one; whether man, or woman, or thing.

Qualquer dos dois, either of the two, or whichsoever of the two.

Quemquer, whoever, or any person.

Todo, all, or every. *Tal*, such, &c.

Um has two terminations for the two genders, viz., *um, uma*; and in the plural it makes *uns, umas*. It is declinable.

Alguem has only one termination, and is declinable.

Algum has two terminations, viz., *algum, alguma;* and in the plural, *alguns, algumas*. It is declinable.

Ninguem has only one termination and is declinable; *ninguem o crê*, nobody believes it.

Nenhum has two terminations, viz., *nenhum, nenhuma*, and in the plural, *nenhuns, nenhumas;* and is declinable: *nenhum homem*, no man; *de nenhum effeito*, of no effect.

Cada um has two terminations, viz., *cada um, cada uma;* but it has no plural and is declinable.

Cada has but one termination. It has no plural, and is declinable: *cada dia*, every day; *cada mez*, every month.

Outro has two terminations, viz., *outro, outra*, and in the plural, *outros, outras*. It is declinable.

Outrem has only one termination. It has no plural, and is declinable.

Qualquer has but one termination. It makes *quaesquer* in the plural, and is declined. *Qualquer* is said both of persons and things.

Quemquer has but one termination. It has no plural, and is declined. It is rendered in English by *anybody: quemquer vos dirá*, anybody will tell you. *Quemquer* is used in speaking of a person.

Todo has two terminations, viz., *todo, toda*, and in the plural *todos, todas*. It is declinable, and sometimes taken substantively, and then it signifies *the whole;* as, *o todo é maior que a sua parte*, the whole is bigger than its part.

Tal has only one termination. It makes *taes* in the plural, and it is declined with the indefinite article. It is common to the masculine and to the feminine genders; and sometimes it is joined to *qual;* as, *tal qual elle é*, such as it is.

Tal supplies sometimes the place of the person whose name is not specified; as, *um tal velhaco deve ser castigado*, such a rogue ought to be punished.

CHAPTER V.

OF VERBS.

THE verb is a part of speech which serves to express that which is attributed to the subject in denoting the *being* or *condition* of the things and persons spoken of, the *actions* which they do, or the *impressions* they receive.

The first and the most general division of Verbs is into personal and impersonal.

A verb personal is conjugated by three persons.

EXAMPLE.

Sing.
- *eu amo* — I love
- *tu amas* — thou lovest
- *elle ama* — he loves

Plur.
- *nós amamos* — we love
- *vós amais* — you love
- *elles amão** — they love

A verb impersonal is conjugated by the third person of the singular number only; as, *chove*, it rains; *convem*, it behoves.

A verb, considered in regard to syntax, is of four sorts, viz., active, passive, neuter, and reciprocal.

Some of the verbs are regular and others irregular.

---

* The termination in *ão* (often found written *aõ*), in the third person plural in Portuguese verbs, is at present most generally printed *am*; whilst the form *ão* is kept for words that are not verbs, the three modes of writing this termination having the same value.

Some are also called auxiliary verbs. We shall give their definitions in their proper places.

Before you begin to learn the conjugations, it will be proper to observe, that all the verbs may be conjugated with the personal pronouns, *eu, tu, elle,* &c., or without them.

OF THE AUXILIARY VERBS.

The auxiliary verbs are so called because they aid the conjugation of other verbs. They are four in Portuguese: viz., *haver, ter,* to have; *ser, estar,* to be. The auxiliary verb *ser,* to be, is also called the verb substantive, because it affirms what the subject is, and is always followed by a noun that particularises what that subject is; as, *ser rico, prudente, douto,* to be rich, wise, learned, &c.

CONJUGATION OF THE AUXILIARY VERB *TER* OR *HAVER*,
TO HAVE.

The Indicative Mood.

PRESENT.

Sing.
- *eu tenho,* or *hei* — I have
- *tu tens,* or *has* — thou hast
- *elle tem,* or *ha* — he has *or* hath.

Plur.
- *nós temos,* or *havemos,* or *hemos* — we have
- *vós tendes,* or *haveis,* or *heis* — you have
- *elles teem,* or *hão* — they have

PRETERIMPERFECT.

Sing.
- *eu tinha,* or *havia* — I had
- *tu tinhas,* or *havias* — thou hadst
- *elle tinha,* or *havia* — he had

Plur.
- *nós tinhamos,* or *haviamos* — we had
- *vós tinheis,* or *havieis* — you had
- *elles tinhão,* or *havião* — they had

E

PRETERPERFECT DEFINITE.

Sing.
- eu *tive*, or *houve* — I had
- tu *tiveste*, or *houveste* — thou hadst
- elle *teve*, or *houve* — he had

Plur.
- nós *tivémos*, or *houvemos* — we had
- vós *tivestes*, or *houvestes* — you had
- elles *tiverão*, or *houverão* — they had

PRETERPERFECT.

Sing.
- eu *tenho tido* — I have had
- tu *tens tido* — thou hast had
- elle *tem tido* — he has had

Plur.
- nós *temos tido* — we have had
- vós *tendes tido* — you have had
- elles *teem tido* — they have had

PRETERPLUPERFECT.

Sing.
- eu *tinha tido* — I had had
- tu *tinhas tido* — thou hadst had
- elle *tinha tido* — he had had

Plur.
- nós *tinhamos tido* — we had had
- vós *tinheis tido* — you had had
- elles *tinhão tido* — they had had.

This tense may also be conjugated thus : *tivéra, tivéras, tivéra, tivéramos, tivéreis, tivérão.*

FIRST FUTURE.

Sing.
- eu *terei*, or *haverei* — I shall *or* will have
- tu *terás*, or *haverás* — thou shalt *or* wilt have
- elle *terá*, or *haverá* — he shall *or* will have

Plur.
- nós *teremos*, or *haveremos* — we shall *or* will have
- vós *tereis*, or *havereis* — ye shall *or* will have
- elles *terão*, or *haverão* — they shall or will have

SECOND FUTURE.

Sing. *eu hei de ter,* or *haver,* &c.   I must have, &c.

THIRD FUTURE.

Sing. *eu haverei de ter,* or *haver,* &c.   I shall be obliged to have, &c.

FOURTH FUTURE.

Sing. *eu havia de ter;* or *haver,* &c.   I was to have, &c.

Imperative Mood.

Sing.
{ *tem tu,* or *hajas tu* — have thou
{ *tenha elle,* or *haja elle* — let him have

Plur.
{ *tenhâmos,* or *hajâmos nós* — let us have
{ *tende,* or *havei vós* — have ye
{ *tenhão,* or *hajão elles* — let them have

The imperative has no first person, because it is impossible to command oneself.

Optative and Subjunctive Moods.

I join them together because their tenses are similar.

PRESENT.

Sing.
{ *que eu tenha,* or *haja* — that I may have
{ *que tu tenhas,* or *hajas* — that thou mayest have
{ *que elle tenha,* or *haja* — that he may have

Plur.
{ *que nós tenhâmos,* or *hajâmos* — that we may have
{ *que vós tenhais,* or *hajais* — that ye may have
{ *que elles tenhão,* or *hajão* — that they may have

FIRST PRETERIMPERFECT.

Sing. { *que eu tivéra* or *tivésse, houvéra* or *houvésse*
que tu tivéras or *tivésses, houvéras* or *houvésses*
que elle tivéra or *tivésse, houvéra* or *houvésse* . } that I had, should, would, could, *or* might have, &c.

Plur. { *que nós tivéramos* or *tivéssemos, houvéramos* or *houvéssemos*
que vós tivéreis or *tivésseis, houvéreis* or *houvésseis*
que elles tivérão or *tivéssem, houvérão* or *houvéssem* } that we had, should, would, could, *or* might have, &c.

SECOND PRETERIMPERFECT.

Sing. { *eu teria*, or *haveria*
tu terias, or *haverias*
elle teria, or *haveria* } I should, would, *or* could have, &c.

Plur. { *nós teriamos*, or *haveriamos*
vós terieis, or *haverieis*
elles terião, or *haverião* } we should, would, *or* could have, &c.

PRETERPERFECT.

Sing. { *que eu tenha tido*, or *havido*   that I have had
que tu tenhas tido, or *havido*   that thou hast had
que elle tenha tido, or *havido*   that he has had

Plur. { *que nós tenhâmos tido* or *havido*   that we have had
que vós tenhais tido, or *havido*   that you have had
que elles tenhão tido, or *havido*   that they have had

PRETERPLUPERFECT.

It is compounded of the first preterimperfect subjunctive and the participle.

Sing. { se eu tivéra or tivésse
       se tu tivéras or tivésses
       se elle tivéra or tivésse
Plur. { se nós tivéramos or tivessemos
       se vós tivéreis or tivésseis
       se elles tivérão or tivéssem } tido, { if I had had, &c.

SECOND PRETERPLUPERFECT.

It is compounded of the second preterimperfect subjunctive and the participle.

Sing. { eu teria
       tu terias
       elle teria
Plur. { nós teriamos
       vos terieis
       elle terião } tido, I should have had, &c.

FIRST FUTURE.

Sing. { se eu tivér   if I shall have
       tu tivéres   thou shalt have
       elle tivér   he shall have
Plur. { se nós tivérmos   if we shall have
       vós tivérdes   you shall have
       elles tivérem   they shall have

The verb *Haver* is conjugated also thus: *houver, houveres, houver; houvermos, houverdes, houverem.* See Syntax of the Auxiliary Verbs.

SECOND FUTURE.

It is composed of the first future and the participle.

Sing. { *se eu tiver*
tu tiveres
elle tiver* } *tido*, if I shall have had, &c.

Plur. { *se nós tivermos
vós tiverdes
elles tiverem* }

Infinitive Mood.

PRESENT.

ter   to have

PRETERPERFECT.

ter tido   to have had.

PARTICIPLES.

Preterit. Sing. *tido, tida*   Plur. *tidos, tidas*, had.

FUTURE.

que ha de ter   that is to have.

GERUNDS.

tendo, having, *or* in having   *tendo tido*, having had.

SUPINE.

The supine is supplied by the prepositions *a* or *para* and the verb in the infinitive; as,

para ter   to have.

In like manner are conjugated its compounds *contenho, detenho, mantenho*, &c.

REMARKS UPON THE AUXILIARY VERB *ter*, TO HAVE.

The verb *ter*, to have, is an auxiliary or helping verb, which serves to conjugate other verbs: examples, *ter lido*, to have read; *nós temos feito,* we have done; *elles teem visto,* they have seen, &c.

When the verb *ter* is followed by the participle *que,* before an infinitive mood, it denotes the duty, inclination, &c., of doing anything: as, *que tendes que fazer?* what have you to do? *tenho que fazer uma visita,* I must pay a visit; *elle tem muito que dizer-vos,* he has a great many things to tell you.

OF THE AUXILIARY VERB *haver.*

The verb *haver* is seldom used now as an auxiliary in Portuguese, since *ter* is an auxiliary to itself, as well as to all other verbs.

The verb *haver,* with the particle *de* after it, denotes a firm resolution, possibility, or necessity of doing anything, as, *eu hei de ter,* I must have; *eu hei de cantar,* I will sing; *eu havia de fallar,* I was to speak; also before the passive voice, as, *o principe ha de ser respeitado,* the prince ought to be, *or* must be respected.

The same verb *haver* implies also duty without the particle *de;* but then it is put after the verb to which it is auxiliary: thus, *dar-vos-hei,* I will give you; *dar-lhe-hei,* I will give to him, &c. In which examples you may observe, that the verb *haver* is put after the verb and the pronouns conjunctive, *te, lhe,* &c., and sometimes it is put after the verbs and the pronoun mixed; as, *mandar-vol-o-hei,* I will send it to you. In the foregoing examples the verb *haver* may be put before the other verb; but then it requires the particle *de,* and has a different meaning: as, in the first example, you may say, *hei de dar-vos,* I must give to you. Observe, also, that when the indicative present of the verb *haver* is auxiliary to other verbs, as in the foregoing examples, you must cut off the last letters *ei* from the future of the verbs, and say *dar-lhe-hei*, or *hei de dar-lhe;* but not *darei-lhe-hei*, nor *hei de darei-lhe.* When the preterimperfect *havia* is to be auxiliary to any verb, and it is to be placed after it, you must make use of *hia, hias, hia, hiamos, hieis, hião;* and say, *dar-lhe-hia, hias*, &c., but not *dar-lhe-havia, havias*, &c., I should give to him, thou shouldst, &c.

To express interrogation, put the personal pronoun after the verb, as in English, thus, *terei eu?* shall I have? *temos nós?* have we? *tens tu?* hast thou? *tem elle?* has he? Sometimes the pronouns are omitted; as, *que faremos?* what shall we do? *cantaremos?* shall we sing?

Haver is sometimes rendered in English by *to become;* as, *que ha de ser de mim?* what will become of me?

When we speak by negation, we must use the word *não* before the verb; as, *não tenho*, I have not; *vós não conheceis*, you do not know, &c.

CONJUGATION OF THE AUXILIARY VERB *SER*, OR *ESTAR*, TO BE.

Indicative Mood.

PRESENT.

Sing.
- *eu sou*, or *estou* — I am
- *tu és*, or *estás* — thou art
- *elle é*, or *está* — he is

Plur.
- *nós somos*, or *estamos* — we are
- *vós sois*, or *estais* — you are
- *elles são*, or *estão* — they are

PRETERIMPERFECT.

Sing.
- *eu era*, or *estava* — I was
- *eras*, or *estavas* — thou wast
- *era*, or *estava* — he was

VERBS. 57

Plur.	nós eramos, or estavamos	we were
	ereis, or estaveis	you were
	erão, or estavão	they were

PRETERPERFECT DEFINITE.

Sing.	eu fui, or estive	I was
	foste, or estiveste	thou wast
	foi, or esteve	he was
Plur.	nós fomos, or estivémos	we were
	fostes, or estivéstes	you were
	forão, or estivérão	they were

PRETERPERFECT.

The preterperfect is composed of the present indicative of the auxiliary verb *ter*, to have, and its own participle, *sido* or *estado*.

PRETERPLUPERFECT.

The tense is compounded of the preterimperfect indicative, and the participle *sido* or *estado*.

Sing.	eu tinha sido, or estado	I had been
	tinhas sido, or estado	thou hadst been
	tinha sido, or estado	he had been
Plur.	nós tinhamos sido, or estado	we had been
	tinheis sido, or estado	you had been
	tinhão sido, or estado	they had been

It may also be conjugated thus: *fora*, or *estivera; foras*, or *estiveras; fora*, or *estivera; foramos*, or *estiveramos; foreis*, or *estivereis; forão*, or *estiverão*.

FUTURE.

Sing.	eu serei, or estarei	I shall *or* will be
	serás, or estarás	thou shalt be
	será, or estará	he shall be

Plur.	nós seremos, or estaremos	we shall be
	sereis, or estareis	you shall be
	serão, or estarão	they shall be

Imperative Mood.

Sing.	sê tu, or esta	be thou
	seja, or esteja elle	let him be
Plur.	sejamos, or estejamos nós	let us be
	sede, or estai vós	be ye
	sejão, or estejão elles	let them be

Optative and Subjunctive Moods.

PRESENT.

Sing.	que eu seja, or esteja	that I may be, or that I be
	sejas, or estejas	thou mayest be
	seja, or esteja	he may be, &c.
Plur.	que nós sejâmos, or estejâmos	that we may be
	sejais, or estejais	you may be
	sejão, or estejão	they may be

FIRST PRETERIMPERFECT.

Sing.	que eu fôra or fosse, estivera or estivesse	that I were, or might be
	fôras or fosses, estiveras or estivesses	thou wert
	fôra or fosse, estivera or estivesse	he were
Plur.	que nós fôramos or fossemos, estiveramos or estivessemos	that we were
	fôreis or fosseis, estivereis or estivesseis	you were
	fôrão or fossem, estiverão or estivessem	they were

SECOND PRETERIMPERFECT.

Sing.
- eu *seria,* or *estaria* — I should or would be
- *serias,* or *estarias* — thou shouldst be
- *seria,* or *estaria* — he should be

Plur.
- *seriamos,* or *estariamos* — we should be
- *serieis,* or *estarieis* — you should be
- *serião,* or *estarião* — they should be

PRETERPERFECT.

It is compounded of the present conjunctive of the auxiliary verb *ter,* and its own participle *sido,* or *estado.*

Sing.
- *que eu tenha sido,* or *estado* — that I have been
- *tenhas sido,* or *estado* — thou hast been
- *tenha sido,* &c. — he has been

Plur.
- *nós tenhâmos sido,* &c. — we have been
- *tenhais sido,* &c. — you have been
- *tenhão sido,* &c. — they have been

PRETERPLUPERFECT.

It is compounded of the first preterimperfect subjunctive of the verb *ter,* and its own participle.

Sing.
- *se eu tivera,* or *tivesse sido,* or *estado* — if I had been
- *tiveras,* &c. — thou hadst been
- *tivera,* &c. — he had been

Plur.
- *nós tiveramos,* &c. — we had been
- *tivereis,* &c. — you had been
- *tiverão,* &c. — they had been

SECOND PRETERPLUPERFECT.

Compounded of the second preterimperfect subjunctive of the verb *ter,* and its own participle *sido,* or *estado.*

Sing.	*eu teria sido,* or *estado*	I should *or* would have been
	terias, &c.	thou shouldst have been
	teria, &c.	he should have been
Plur.	*teriamos,* &c.	we should have been
	terieis, &c.	you should have been
	terião, &c.	they should have been

FIRST FUTURE.

Sing.	*quando eu fôr,* or *estiver*	when I shall be
	fôres, or *estiveres*	thou shalt be
	fôr, or *estiver*	he shall be
Plur.	*nós fôrmos,* or *estivermos*	we shall be
	fôrdes, or *estiverdes*	you shall be
	fôrem, or *estiverem*	they shall be

SECOND FUTURE.

Compounded of the future subjunctive of the verb *ter* and its own participle.

Sing.	*quando eu tiver sido,* or *estado*	when I shall have been
	tiveres sido, &c.	thou shalt have been
	tiver sido, &c.	he shall have been
Plur.	*nós tivermos sido,* &c.	we shall have been
	tiverdes sido, &c.	you shall have been
	tiverem sido, &c.	they shall have been

VERBS.

Infinitive Mood.

PRESENT.

ser, or *estar*   to be

PRETERPERFECT.

ter sido, or *estado*   to have been

Participles.

PRETERIT.

sido, or *estado*   been

FUTURE.

que ha de ser, or *estar*   that is to be

GERUNDS.

sendo, or *estando*   being
tendo sido, or *estado*   having been

SUPINE.

para ser, or *estar*   to be

REMARKS UPON THE VERBS *ser* AND *estar*.

There is a considerable difference between these verbs, *ser* and *estar*, both in Portuguese and Spanish. In English there is no word to distinguish them, being both rendered into English by *to be*. *Ser* signifies the proper and inseparable essence of a thing, its quality or quantity; *ser homem*, to be a man; *ser bom*, to be good; *ser alto*, to be tall; *ser largo*, to be wide; *ser branco*, to be white, &c. But *estar* denotes a place, or any adventitious quality: as, *estar em Londres*, to be in London; *estar de saude*, to be in health; *esta frio*, to be cold;

estar quente, to be warm; *estar doente*, to be sick; *estar enfadado*, to be angry; *estar alegre*, to be merry, &c.

Estar may be used before the gerund, but not *ser;* therefore you may say, *estou fallando, lendo*, &c., I am speaking, reading, &c., but not *sou fallando*, &c.

THE THREE CONJUGATIONS OF REGULAR ACTIVE VERBS.

A regular verb is such as is confined to general rules in its conjugation.

A verb active denotes the action or impression of the subject, and governs a noun which is the object of that action or impression; as, *amar a virtude*, to love virtue; *receber cartas*, to receive letters.

The regular Portuguese verbs have three different terminations in the infinitive; viz., in *ar, er, ir:* as, *amar*, to love; *temer*, to fear; *admittir*, to admit.

AN EASY METHOD OF LEARNING TO CONJUGATE THE PORTUGUESE VERBS.

I have reduced all the tenses of the Portuguese verbs to eight; four of which are general, and have the same terminations in all the verbs; and the other four may be likewise made general by changing some letters, and all the conjugations reduced to one.

The general tenses are the future indicative, the first and second preterimperfect subjunctive, and the first future subjunctive.

The future indicative is terminated in all the verbs in *rei, rás, rá; remos, reis, rão*.

The imperfect subjunctive, in *ra* or *sse, ras* or *sses, ra* or *sse; ramos* or *ssemos, reis* or *sseis, rão* or *ssem*.

The second imperfect, in *ria, rias, ria; riamos, rieis, rião*.

The first subjunctive, in *es, mos, des, em*.

I have only given the termination of the second person singular of the future subjunctive, because the first and third of the same number are like their respective infinitives of the three conjugations, which, however, keep both their last consonant and vowel before the terminations I have marked for the second person singular, and for the whole plural. As to the future indicative, you have only to add *ei* to the respective present infinitive of the three conjugations, in order to form the first person singular; and if you add to the same infinitive present *as*, you will form the second person singular of it, and so of all the rest, by adding to the infinitive present *a, emos, eis, ão*.

The imperfect subjunctive has two terminations for every person, both in the singular and plural; but if you cut off the last consonant, *r*, of the infinitive, and then add to it the terminations above mentioned, you form the imperfect subjunctive, according to its two different terminations. Lastly, if you cut off the last consonant of the infinitive, and add to it the terminations above mentioned, you will form the second imperfect subjunctive.

The present indicative of the three conjugations is formed by changing the last letters of the infinitive, viz., *ar, er, ir*, into *o ;* as *amo, entendo, admitto*, from *amar, entender, admittir*.

The preterimperfect indicative is formed in the first conjugation by changing the last consonant of the infinitive, viz. *r*, into *va, vas, va, vamos, veis, vão ;* but in the second conjugation it is formed by changing the termination *er* of the infinitive into *ia, ias, ia, iamos, ieis, ião;* and in the third by changing the last consonant, *r*, of the infinitive into *a, as, a, amos, eis, ão*.

The perfect definite in the first conjugation is formed

by changing the termination *ar* of the infinitive into *ei, aste, ou, ámos, ástes, árão;* and in the second conjugation it is formed by changing the termination *er* of the infinitive into *i, este, eo, emos, estes, erão.* In the third conjugation, the same tense is formed by changing the termination *ir* of the infinitive into *i, iste, io, imos, istes, irão.*

The present subjunctive in the first conjugation is formed by changing the termination *ar* of the infinitive into *e, es, e, emos, eis, em;* and in the second conjugation it is formed by changing the termination *er* of the infinitive into *a, as, a amos, ais, ão.* In the third conjugation, the same tense is formed by changing the termination *ir* of the infinitive into the same terminations, *a, as, a,* &c.

As to the imperative mood, you have only to observe that the second person singular is always the same as the third person singular of the present indicative, in all the conjugations.

The participles of the preterperfect tense in the first conjugation are formed by changing the last consonant, *r*, of the infinitive into *do* of the masculine, and *da* for the feminine; and into *dos, das,* for the plural; but when you come to verbs of the second conjugation, you change the termination *r* of the infinitive into *ido, ida,* &c.

In the third conjugation, the last consonant, *r*, of the infinitive must be changed into *do* for the masculine, *da* for the feminine, &c.

FIRST CONJUGATION OF THE VERBS IN *AR*.

Indicative Mood.

PRESENT.

Sing.
- *eu amo* — I love
- *amas* — thou lovest
- *ama* — he loves

Plur.
- *nós amamos* — we love
- *amais* — you love
- *amão* — they love

PRETERIMPERFECT.

Sing.
- *eu amava* — I did love
- *amavas* — thou didst love
- *amava* — he did love

Plur.
- *nós amavamos* — we did love
- *amaveis* — you did love
- *amavão* — they did love

PRETERPERFECT DEFINITE.

Sing.
- *eu amei* — I loved
- *amaste* — thou lovedst
- *amou* — he loved

Plur.
- *nós amámos* — we loved
- *amástes* — you loved
- *amárão* — they loved

PRETERPERFECT.

This tense is composed of the participle *amado* and the present indicative of the auxiliary verb *ter*.

Sing.
- *eu tenho amado* — I have loved
- *tens amado* — thou hast loved
- *tem amado* — he has loved

Plur.	nós temos amado	we have loved
	tendes amado	you have loved
	teem amado	they have loved

PRETERPLUPERFECT.

This tense is composed of the participle *amado* and the imperfect of the auxiliary verb *ter*.

N.B. It may be conjugated thus: *amára, amáras, amára, amáramos, amáreis, amárão,* or

Sing.	eu tinha amado	I had loved
	tinhas amado	thou hadst loved
	tinha amado	he had loved
Plur.	nós tinhamos amado	we had loved
	tinheis amado	you had loved
	tinhão amado	they had loved

FUTURE.

Sing.	eu amarei	I shall *or* will love
	amarás	thou shalt love
	amará	he shall love
Plur.	nós amaremos	we shall love
	amareis	you shall love
	amarão	they shall love

Imperative Mood.

Sing.	ama tu	love thou
	ame elle	let him love
Plur.	amemos nós	let us love
	amai vós	love you
	amem elles	let them love

Optative and Subjunctive Moods.

PRESENT.

Sing. { *que eu ame* — that I may love
ames — thou mayst love
ame — he may love

Plur. { *que nós amemos* — we may love
ameis — you may love
amem — they may love

FIRST PRETERIMPERFECT.

Sing. { *que eu amára,* or *amasse* that I might or could love
amáras, or *amasses* — thou mightest love
amára, or *amasse* — he might love

Plur. { *que nós amáramos,* or *amassemos* — we might love
amáreis, or *amasseis* — you might love
amárão, or *amassem* — they might love

When we find the conjunction *if* before the indicative imperfect, we must use the imperfect of the subjunctive or optative, when we speak by way of wish or desire: as, if I did love, *se eu amasse,* or *amára,* and not the preterimperfect indicative, *se eu amava;* if I had, *se eu tivera, tivesse,* and not *se eu tinha;* and so in all the verbs.

SECOND PRETERIMPERFECT.

Sing. { *eu amaria* — I should love
amarias — thou shouldst love
amaria — he should love

Plur. { *nós amariamos* — we should love
amarieis — you should love
amarião — they should love

PRETERPERFECT.

It is composed of the participle *amado* and the present subjunctive of the auxiliary verb *ter.*

Sing. { que eu *tenha amado*   that I have loved
          tenhas amado   thou hast loved
          tenha amado   he has loved

Plur. { que *nós tenhâmos amado*   we have loved
          tenhais amado   you have loved
          tenhão amado   they have loved

PRETERPLUPERFECT.

It is composed of the participle *amado* and the first preterimperfect subjunctive of the auxiliary verb *ter*.

Sing. { se eu *tivera*, or *tivesse amado*   if I had loved
          tiveras, or *tivesses amado*   thou hadst loved
          tivera, or *tivesse amado*   he had loved

Plur. { se *nós tiveramos*, or *tivessemos amado*   we had loved
          tivereis, or *tivesseis amado*   you had loved
          tiverão, or *tivessem amado*   they had loved

SECOND PRETERPLUPERFECT.

It is composed of the participle *amado* and the second preterimperfect subjunctive of the auxiliary verb *ter*.

Sing. { eu *teria amado*   I should have loved
          terias amado   thou shouldst have loved
          teria amado   he should have loved

Plur. { *nós teriamos amado*   we should have loved
          terieis amado   you should have loved
          terião amado   they should have loved.

FUTURE.

Sing. { *quando eu amar*   when I shall love
          amares   thou shalt love
          amar   he shall love

Plur. { *quando nós amarmos*   we shall love
          amardes   you shall love
          amarem   they shall love

SECOND FUTURE.

It is composed of the participle *amado* and the future subjunctive of the auxiliary verb *ter*.

Sing.
- *quando eu tiver amado* — when I shall have loved
- *tiveres amado* — thou shalt have loved
- *tiver amado* — he shall have loved

Plur.
- *quando nós tivermos amado* — we shall have loved
- *tiverdes amado* — you shall have loved
- *tiverem amado* — they shall have loved

Infinitive Mood.

PRESENT.

amar — to love

PRETERPERFECT.

ter amado — to have loved

Participles.

PRESENT.

que ama, or *amante* — that loves

PRETERIT.

masc. *amado*, fem. *amada*   Plur. *amados, amadas,* loved

FUTURE.

que ha de amar — that is to love

GERUNDS.

amando — loving
tendo amado — having loved

SUPINE.

para amar — to love

Note, the verbs terminating in the infinitive in *car* take *qu* in those tenses where the *c* would otherwise meet with the vowel *e ;* and those terminating in the infinitive in *gar* take an *u* in those tenses where the *g* would otherwise meet with the same vowel *e ;* that is to say, in the first person singular of the preterperfect definite, in the third person singular, in the first and third plural of the imperative, and in the whole present subjunctive, which are the tenses I shall give by way of example in the verbs *peccar* and *pagar.*

Peccar, TO SIN.

PRETERPERFECT DEFINITE.

eu pequei, I sinned, &c., instead of *peccei.*

Imperative Mood.

péque elle, let him sin ; *pequemos nós,* let us sin ; *péquem elles,* let them sin ; and not *pecce elle,* &c.

PRESENT SUBJUNCTIVE.

que eu péque, tu péques, that I may sin ; and not *que eu pecce, pecces,* &c.

Pagar, TO PAY.

PRETERPERFECT DEFINITE.

eu paguei   I paid, &c.

Imperative Mood.

pague elle, paguemos nós, paguem elles, let him pay, &c.

PRESENT SUBJUNCTIVE.

que eu pague, pagues, pague, paguemos, pagueis, paguem, that I may pay, &c.; and not *page, pages,* &c.

The other tenses are conjugated like *amar.*

REGULAR VERBS IN *ar*.

Abafar, to choke, or to smother
Abalar, to shake
Abanar, to fan
Abastar, to satiate
Abaixar, to let down
Abençoar, to bless
Abocanhar, to carp
Abominar, to abominate
Abotoar, to button
Acabar, to finish
Admoestar, to admonish
Affrontar, to abuse
Agarrar, to lay hold of
Alagar, to overflow
Amaldiçoar, to curse
Annular, to annul
Apressar, to hasten
Aquentar, to warm
Argumentar, to argue
Assoprar, to blow
Atar, to tie
Avassalar, to subdue
Azedar, to sour

OF THE VERBS PASSIVE.

Before we proceed to the second conjugation, it is necessary to know that the passive verbs, which express the suffering of an action, are nothing more than the participles of active verbs, conjugated with the verb *ser*, to be.

EXAMPLE.

PRESENT TENSE.

Sing.
eu sou amado — I am loved
tu es amado — thou art loved
elle é amado — he is loved

Plur.
nós somos amados — we are loved
vós sois amados — you are loved
elles são amados — they are loved

and so throughout the other moods and tenses.

SECOND CONJUGATION OF THE VERBS IN *ER*.

Indicative Mood.

PRESENT.

Sing. { eu vendo — I sell
vendes — thou sellest
vende — he sells

Plur. { nós vendemos — we sell
vendeis — you sell
vendem — they sell

PRETERIMPERFECT.

Sing. { eu vendia — I did sell
vendias — thou didst sell
vendia — he did sell

Plur. { nós vendiamos — we did sell
vendieis — you did sell
vendião — they did sell

PRETERPERFECT DEFINITE.

Sing. { eu vendi — I sold
vendeste — thou soldest
vendeo — he sold

Plur. { nós vendemos — we sold
vendestes — you sold
venderão — they sold

PRETERPERFECT.

Sing. { eu tenho vendido — I have sold, &c.
tens vendido — „
tem vendido — „

Plur. { nós temos vendido — „
tendes vendido — „
teem vendido — „

VERBS.

PRETERPLUPERFECT.

Sing. { eu tinha vendido — I had sold, &c.
tinhas vendido — ,,
tinha vendido — ,,

Plur. { nós tinhamos vendido — ,,
tinheis vendido — ,,
tinham vendido — ,,

This tense may also be conjugated thus: *vendêra, vendêras, vendêra, vendêramos, vendêreis, vendêrão.*

FUTURE.

Sing. { eu venderei — I shall *or* will sell, &c.
venderás — ,,
venderá — ,,

Plur. { nós venderemos — ,,
vendereis — ,,
venderão — ,,

Imperative Mood.

Sing. { vende tu — sell thou
venda elle — let him sell

Plur. { vendamos nós — let us sell
vendei vós — sell ye
vendão elles — let them sell

Optative and Subjunctive Moods.

PRESENT.

Sing. { que eu venda — that I may sell, &c.
vendas — ,,
venda — ,,

Plur. { que nós vendamos — ,,
vendais — ,,
vendão — ,,

VERBS.

PRETERIMPERFECT.

Sing.
- *que eu vendêra,* or *vendesse* — that I might or could sell, &c.
- *vendêras,* or *vendesses* — ,,
- *vendêra,* or *vendesse* — ,,

Plur.
- *que nós venderamos,* or *vendessemos* — ,,
- *vendêreis,* or *vendesseis* — ,,
- *vendêrão,* or *vendessem* — ,,

SECOND PRETERIMPERFECT.

Sing.
- *eu venderia* — I should or would sell, &c.
- *venderias* — ,,
- *venderia* — ,,

Plur.
- *nós venderiamos* — ,,
- *venderieis* — ,,
- *venderião* — ,,

PRETERPERFECT.

Sing.
- *que eu tenha vendido* — that I have sold, &c.
- *tenhas vendido* — ,,
- *tenha vendido* — ,,

Plur.
- *que nós tenhamos vendido* — ,,
- *tenhais vendido* — ,,
- *tenhão vendido* — ,,

PRETERPLUPERFECT.

Sing.
- *se eu tivéra,* or *tivésse vendido* — if I had sold, &c.
- *tivéras,* or *tivésses vendido* — ,,
- *tivéra,* or *tivésse vendido* — ,,

Plur.
- *se nós tivéramos,* or *tivéssemos vendido* — ,,
- *tivéreis,* or *tivésseis vendido* — ,,
- *tiverão,* or *tivessem vendido* — ,,

SECOND PRETERPLUPERFECT.

Sing. { eu teria vendido — I should *or* would have sold, &c.
terias vendido — ,,
teria vendido — ,,

Plur. { nós teriamos vendido — ,,
terieis vendido — ,,
terião vendido — ,,

FUTURE.

Sing. { quando eu vender — when I shall sell, &c.
venderes — ,,
vender — ,,

Plur. { quandó nos vendermos — ,,
venderdes — ,,
venderem — ,,

SECOND FUTURE.

Sing. { quando eu tivér vendido — when I shall have sold, &c.
tivéres vendido — ,,
tivér vendido — ,,

Plur. { quando nós tivérmos vendido — ,,
tivérdes vendido — ,,
tivérem vendido — ,,

Infinitive Mood.

PRESENT.

vender — to sell

PRETERPERFECT.

ter vendido — to have sold

Participles.

PRESENT.

que vende   that sells

PRETERIT.

masc. *vendido,* fem. *vendida*   Plur. *vendidos, vendidas,* sold

FUTURE.

que ha de vender   that is to sell

GERUNDS.

vendendo   selling
tendo vendido   having sold

SUPINE.

para vender   to sell

After the same manner as the verb *vender,* are conjugated all the other regular verbs of the second conjugation ending in *er;* as the following:—

Acometer, to attack
Beber, to drink
Comer, to eat
Comprehender, to perceive, or apprehend
Cometer, to commit
Conceder, to grant
Correr, to run
Dever, to owe
Esconder, to hide
Emprender, to undertake
Meter, to put in
Offender, to offend
Prometer, to promise
Responder, to answer
Reprehender, to reprove
Temer, to fear
Varrer, to sweep, &c.

THIRD CONJUGATION OF THE VERBS ENDING IN *IR*.

Indicative Mood.

PRESENT.

Sing. { *eu admitto* I admit, &c.
admittes ,,
admitte ,,

Plur. { *nós admittimos*
admittis
admittem

PRETERIMPERFECT.

Sing. { *eu admittia* I did admit, &c.
admittias ,,
admittia ,,

Plur. { *nós admittiamos*
admittieis
admittião

PRETERPERFECT DEFINITE.

Sing. { *eu admitti* I admitted, &c.
admittiste ,,
admittio ,,

Plur. { *nós admittimos*
admittistes
admittirão

PRETERPERFECT.

This tense is composed of the participle *admittido* and the present indicative of the auxiliary verb *ter*.

Sing. { *tenho admittido*
tens admittido, &c.

I have admitted
thou hast, &c.

PRETERPLUPERFECT.

Composed of the participle *admittido* and the imperfect of the auxiliary verb *ter*.

Sing. { *tinha admittido*
tinhas admittido, &c.

I had admitted
thou hadst, &c.

It may also be conjugated thus: *admittira, admittiras, admittira, admittiramos, admittireis, admittirão*.

VERBS.

FUTURE.

Sing.
- *eu admittirei* — I shall or will admit, &c.
- *admittirás* — ,,
- *admittirá* — ,,

Plur.
- *nós admittiremos* — ,,
- *admittireis* — ,,
- *admittirão* — ,,

Imperative Mood.

Sing.
- *admitte tu* — admit thou
- *admitta elle* — let him admit

Plur.
- *admittâmos nós* — let us admit
- *admitti vós* — admit ye
- *admittão elles* — let them admit

Optative and Subjunctive Moods.

PRESENT.

Sing.
- *que eu admitta* — that I may admit, &c.
- *admittas* — ,,
- *admitta* — ,,

Plur.
- *que nós admittamos* — ,,
- *admittais* — ,,
- *admittão* — ,,

FIRST PRETERIMPERFECT.

Sing.
- *que eu admittira*, or *admittisse* — that I might admit, &c.
- *admittiras*, or *admittisses* — ,,
- *admittira*, or *admittisse* — ,,

Plur.
- *que nós admittiramos*, or *admittissemos* — ,,
- *admittireis*, or *admittisseis* — ,,
- *admittirão*, or *admittissem* — ,,

SECOND PRETERIMPERFECT.

Sing. { eu admittiria   I should or would admit, &c.
        admittirias   ,,
        admittiria   ,,

Plur. { nós admittiriamos   ,,
       admittirieis   ,,
       admittirião   ,,

PRETERPERFECT.

Composed of the participle *admittido* and the present subjunctive of the verb *ter*.

Sing. { que eu tenha admittido   that I may have admitted
        tenhas admit-   thou mayest have
           tido, &c.   admitted, &c.

PRETERPLUPERFECT.

It is composed of the first preterimperfect subjunctive of the verb *ter* and the participle *admittido*.

Sing. { se eu tivera admittido   if I had admitted
        tiveras admittido, &c.   thou hadst admitted, &c.

SECOND PRETERPLUPERFECT.

It is composed of the second preterimperfect subjunctive of the verb *ter* and the participle *admittido*.

Sing. { eu teria admittido   I should have admitted
        terias, &c.   thou shouldst, &c.

FIRST FUTURE.

Sing. { se eu admittir   if I shall admit, &c.
        admittires   ,,
        admittir   ,,

Plur. { se nós admittirmos — if we shall admit, &c.
       admittirdes — ,,
       admittirem — ,,

SECOND FUTURE.

It is composed of the first future subjunctive of the verb *ter* and the participle *admittido*.

Sing. { se eu tiver admittido — if I shall have admitted
        tiveres, &c. — thou shalt, &c.

Infinitive Mood.

PRESENT.

admittir   to admit

PRETERPERFECT.

ter admittido   to have admitted

Participles.

PRESENT.

que admitte   that admits

PRETERIT.

masc. *admittido*, fem. *admittida*   Plur. *admittidos, admittidas*, admitted

FUTURE.

que ha de admittir   that is to admit

GERUNDS.

admittindo   admitting
tendo admittido   having admitted

SUPINES.

para admittir   to admit

Conjugate after the same manner the following verbs :—

Abrir, to open
Conduzir, to conduce
Introduzir, to introduce
Induzir, to induce
Produzir, to produce
Luzir, to shine
Nutrir, to nourish
Reduzir, to reduce, to bring to
Traduzir, to translate
Deduzir, to deduct, &c.

OF THE IRREGULAR VERBS IN *AR*.

There are, in each conjugation, some verbs which do not conform to the common rule, and on that account are called irregulars.

There are but two of the first conjugation, which in some of their tenses depart from the rule of the verb *amar*, viz., *estar* and *dar*. We have already conjugated the first, and the second is conjugated in the following manner :—

Indicative Mood.

PRESENT.

Sing. { *eu dou*   I give
       dás   thou givest
       dá   he gives

Plur. { *nós damos* we give
       dais   you give
       dão   they give

PRETERIMPERFECT.

Sing. { *dava*   I did give, &c. (as in regular verbs of the
       davas, &c.   first conjugation).

PRETERPERFECT DEFINITE.

Sing. { *eu dei*   I gave
       déste thou gavest
       deu   he gave

Plur. { *nós démos* we gave
       déstes   you gave
       dérão   they gave

PRETERPERFECT.

This tense is composed of the participle *dado* and the present indicative of the auxiliary *ter*; as, *tenho dado*, &c. I have given, &c.

PRETERPLUPERFECT.

Composed of the participle *dado* and the imperfect of the auxiliary verb *ter*; as, *eu tinha dado*, &c., I had given, &c.

FUTURE.

Sing. { *eu derei*   I shall *or* will give, &c. (as in the verb *amar*)
       { *darás*, &c.

Imperative Mood.

Sing. { *dá tu*   give thou
      { *dê elle* let him give

Plur. { *demos nós* let us give
      { *dai vós*   give thou
      { *dêem elles* let them give

Optative and Subjunctive Moods.

PRESENT.

Sing. { *que eu dê*   that I may give, &c.
      {   *dês*   ,,
      {   *dê*   ,,

Plur. { *que nós dêmos*   ,,
      {   *deis*   ,,
      {   *dêem*   ,,

PRETERIMPERFECT.

Sing. { *que eu déra*, or *désse*   that I might give, &c.
      {   *déras*, or *désses*   ,,
      {   *déra*, or *désse*   ,,

Plur.	{ que nós déramos, or déssemos	that we might give, &c.
	déreis, or désseis	,,
	dérão, or déssem	,,

SECOND IMPERFECT.

Sing.	{ eu daria	I should give, &c.	Plur.	{ nós daríamos	
	darias	,,		daríeis	
	daria	,,		darião	

The preterperfect, preterpluperfect, and the second preterpluperfect are composed of the participle *dado* and the auxiliary verb *ter*, as in the regular verbs.

FUTURE.

Sing.	{ quando eu der	when I shall give, &c.
	deres	,,
	der	,,
Plur.	{ quando nós dermos	,,
	derdes	,,
	derem	,,

SECOND FUTURE

is composed of the participle *dado*, &c., as the regular verbs.

Infinitive Mood.

PRESENT.

dar, **to give**, &c., as in the regular verbs.

OF THE IRREGULAR VERBS IN *ER*.

I begin with *fazer*, *poder*, and *saber*, because they occur often in conversation.

FAZER, TO DO, *or* MAKE.

Indicative Mood.

PRESENT.

Sing. { *eu faço* — I do
fazes — thou doest
faz — he does

Plur. { *nós fazemos* — we do
fazeis — you do
fazem — they do

IMPERFECT.

Sing. { *eu fazia* — I did, *or* did make, &c.
fazias — ,,
fazia — ,,

Plur. { *nós faziamos*
fazieis
fazião

PRETERPERFECT DEFINITE.

Sing. { *eu fiz* — I made, &c.
fizeste — ,,
fez — ,,

Plur. { *nós fizemos*
fizestes
fizerão

PRETERPERFECT.

Sing. { *eu tenho feito* — I have done, &c.
tens feito, &c. — ,,

PRETERPLUPERFECT.

Sing. { *eu tinha feito* — I had done, &c.
tinhas feito, &c. — ,,

FUTURE.

Sing. { *eu farei* — I shall do, &c. (according to the
farás, &c. — ,, regular verbs.

Imperative Mood.

Sing. { *faze tu*   do thou
       faça elle   let him do

Plur. { *façâmos nós*   let us do
      fazei vós   do you
      fação elles   let them do

Optative Mood.

PRESENT.

Sing. { *que eu faça*   that I may do, &c. (according to the
       faças,   „   regular verbs.)
       faça, &c.   „

PRETERIMPERFECT.

Sing. { *que eu fizera,* or *fizesse*   that I might do, &c.
       fizeras, or *fizesses*   „
       fizera, or *fizesse*   „

Plur. { *que nós fizeramos,* or *fizessemos*   „
       fizereis, or *fizesseis*   „
       fizerão, or *fizessem*   „

SECOND IMPERFECT.

Sing. { *eu faria*   I should do, &c.
       farias   „
       faria   „

Plur. { *nós fariamos*
       farieis
       farião

FUTURE.

Sing. { *quando eu fizer*   when I shall do, &c.
       fizeres   „
       fizer   „

Plur. { *quando nós fizermos*   „
       fizerdes   „
       fizerem   „

SECOND FUTURE.

Sing. { *quando eu tiver feito*   when I shall have done, &c.
       tiveres feito, &c.   ,,

Infinitive Mood.

PRESENT.

fazer   to do

GERUND.

fazendo   doing, *or* in doing.

PARTICIPLE.

feito   made, *or* done.

After the same manner are conjugated *desfazer*, to undo; *contrafazer*, to counterfeit; *refazer*, to do again.

PODER, TO BE ABLE.

Indicative Mood.

PRESENT.

Sing. { *eu posso*   I can, *or* am able
       podes   thou canst
       pode   he can

Plur. { *nós podemos*   we can
       podeis   you can
       podem   they can

IMPERFECT.

Sing. { *eu podia*   I could, *or* was able, &c.
       podias, &c.   ,,

PRETERPERFECT DEFINITE.

Sing. { *eu pude*   I could
       pudeste   thou couldst
       pôde   he could

Plur. { *nós pudémos*   we could
       pudéstes   you could
       pudérão   they could

PRETERPERFECT.

Sing. eu tenho podido, &c.   I have been able, &c.

FUTURE.

Sing. { eu poderei   I shall be able, &c.
       { poderás, &c.   ,,

There is no Imperative.

Optative and Subjunctive Moods.

PRESENT.

Sing. { que eu possa   that I may be able, &c.
       { possas   ,,
       { possa   ,,

Plur. { que nós possâmos   ,,
       { possais   ,,
       { possão   ,,

IMPERFECT.

Sing. { que eu pudera, or pudesse   that I might be able, &c.
       { puderas, or pudesses   ,,
       { pudera, or pudesse   ,,

Plur. { que nós puderamos, or pudessemos   ,,
       { pudereis, or pudesseis   ,,
       { puderão, or pudessem   ,,

SECOND IMPERFECT.

Sing. { eu poderia   I should or would be able, &c.
       { poderias, &c.   ,,

FUTURE.

Sing. { quando eu pudér   when I shall be able, &c.
       { pudéres   ,,
       { pudér   ,,

Plur. { quando nós pudermos   ,,
       { pudérdes   ,,
       { pudérem   ,,

Infinitive Mood.

PRESENT.

poder   to be able

GERUND.

podendo   being able

PARTICIPLE.

podido   been able

SABER, TO KNOW.

Indicative Mood.

PRESENT.

Sing.
- *eu sei* — I know
- *sabes* — thou knowest
- *sabe* — he knows

Plur.
- *nós sabemos* — we know
- *sabeis* — you know
- *sabem* — they know

IMPERFECT.

Sing.
- *eu sabia* — I did know
- *sabias* — thou didst know
- *sabia, &c.* — he did know, &c.

PRETERPERFECT DEFINITE.

Sing.
- *eu soube* — I knew, &c.
- *soubeste* — ,,
- *soube* — ,,

Plur.
- *nós soubemos*
- *soubestes*
- *souberão*

PRETERPERFECT.

Sing. *eu tenho sabido, &c.*   I have known, &c.

FUTURE.

Sing.
- *eu saberei* — I shall or will know, &c. (according to the
- *saberás, &c.* — ,,   regular verbs)

Imperative Mood.

Sing. { *sabe tu* know thou
{ *saiba elle* let him know

Plur. { *saibamos nós* let us know
{ *sabei vós* know you
{ *saibão elles* let them know

Optative and Subjunctive Moods.

PRESENT.

Sing. { *que eu saiba*   that I may know, &c.
{ *saibas*   ,,
{ *saiba*   ,,

Plur. { *que nós saibamos*   ,,
{ *saibais*   ,,
{ *saibão*   ,,

IMPERFECT.

Sing. { *que eu soubera*, or *soubesse*   that I might know, &c.
{ *souberas*, or *soubesses*   ,,
{ *soubera*, or *soubesse*   ,,

Plur. { *que nós souberamos*, or *soubessemos*   ,,
{ *soubereis*, or *soubesseis*   ,,
{ *souberão*, or *soubessem*   ,,

SECOND IMPERFECT.

Sing. { *eu saberia*   I should know, &c.
{ *saberias*   ,,
{ *saberia*   ,,

Plur. { *nós saberiamos*
{ *sabereis*
{ *saberião*

FUTURE.

Sing. { *quando eu souber*   when I shall know, &c.
{ *souberes*   ,,
{ *souber*   ,,

Plur. { *quando nós soubermos*   when we shall know, &c.
       souberdes   ,,
       souberem   ,,

Infinitive Mood.

PRESENT.

saber   to know

GERUND.

sabendo   knowing

PARTICIPLE.

masc. *sabido*, fem. *sabida*, known

OF THE IRREGULAR VERB *TRAZER*, TO BRING.

Indicative Mood.

PRESENT.

Sing. { *eu trago*   I bring   Plur. { *nós trazemos*   we bring
      trazes   thou bringest   *trazeis*   you bring
      traz   he brings   *trazem*   they bring

IMPERFECT.

Sing. { *eu trazia*   I did bring
      trazias, &c. thou didst bring, &c. (according to the regular verbs)

PRETERPERFECT DEFINITE.

Sing. { *eu trouxe*   I brought   Plur. { *nós trouxemos*
      trouxeste   thou broughtest   *trouxestes*
      trouxe   he brought   *trouxerão*

VERBS.

PRETERPERFECT.

Sing. { eu tenho trazido — I have brought, &c.
tens trazido, &c. — "

FUTURE.

Sing. { eu trarei I shall *or* will bring, &c.
trarás "
trará "

Plur. { nós traremos
trareis
trarão

Imperative Mood.

Sing. { traze tu   bring thou
tragã elle let him bring

Plur. { tragamos nós let us bring
trazei vós   bring you
tragão elles let them bring

Optative and Subjunctive Moods.

PRESENT.

Sing. { que eu traga — that I may bring, &c.
tragas   "
traga   "

Plur. { que nós tragamos   "
tragais   "
tragão   "

IMPERFECT.

Sing. { que eu trouxera, *or* trouxesse that I might bring, &c.
trouxeras, *or* trouxesses "
trouxera, *or* trouxesse   "

Plur. { que nós trouxeramos, *or* trouxessemos "
trouxereis, *or* trouxesseis "
trouxerão, *or* trouxessem   "

SECOND IMPERFECT.

Sing. { eu traria — I should bring, &c.
trarias — ,,
traria — ,,

Plur. { nós trariamos
trarieis
trarião

FUTURE.

Sing. { quando eu trouxer — when I shall bring, &c.
trouxeres — ,,
trouxer — ,,

Plur. { quando nós trouxermos — ,,
trouxerdes — ,,
trouxerem — ,,

Infinitive Mood.

PRESENT.

trazer — to bring

GERUND.

trazendo — bringing

PARTICIPLE.

masc. *trazido*, fem. *trazida*, brought

CONJUGATION OF THE IRREGULAR VERB *VER* TO SEE.

Indicative Mood.

PRESENT.

Sing. { eu vêjo — I see
vês — thou seest
vê — he sees, &c.

Plur. { nós vêmos
vêdes
vêem

VERBS.

IMPERFECT.

Sing. { eu via — I did see, &c.
vias — ,,
via, &c. — ,, }

PRETERPERFECT DEFINITE.

Sing. { eu vi — I saw, &c.
viste — ,,
vio — ,, }

Plur. { nós vimos
vistes
virão }

PRETERPERFECT.

Sing. { eu tenho visto — I have seen, &c.
tens visto, &c. — ,, }

FUTURE.

Sing. { eu verei — I shall see, &c.
verás, &c. — ,, }

Imperative Mood.

Sing. | vê tu — see thou
vêja elle — let him see

Plur. { vejâmos nós — let us see
vêde vós — see you
vêjão elles — let them see }

Optative Mood.

PRESENT.

Sing. { que eu vêja — that I may see, &c.
vêjas — ,,
vêja — ,, }

Plur. { que nós vejâmos
vejáis
vêjão }

IMPERFECT.

Sing. { que eu vira, or visse — that I might see, &c.
viras, or visses — ,,
vira, or visse — ,, }

VERBS.

Plur. { que nós víramos, or vissemos — that we might see, &c.
vireis, or visseis — „
vissem — „

SECOND IMPERFECT.

Sing. { eu veria — I should see, &c.
verias — „
veria — „

Plur. { nós veriamos
verieis
verião

FUTURE.

Sing. { quando eu vir — when I shall see, &c.
vires — „
vir — „

Plur. { quando nós virmos — „
virdes — „
virem — „

Infinite Mood.

PRESENT.

vêr — to see

GERUND.

vendo — seeing

PARTICIPLE.

masc. *visto*, fem. *vista*, seen.

In like manner are conjugated the compounds *antevêr*, *prevêr*, and *revêr*.

The verb *prevêr, to foresee,* is conjugated in the present indicative thus:

Sing. { eu prevêjo — I foresee, &c.
prevês — „
prevê — „

Plur. { nós prevêmos
prevêdes
prevêem

CONJUGATION OF THE IRREGULAR VERB *DIZER*, TO SAY.

Indicative Mood.

PRESENT.

Sing. { eu digo / dizes / diz }   I say, &c. / ,, / ,,

Plur. { nós dizemos / dizeis / dizem }

PRETERIMPERFECT.

Sing. { eu dizia / ·dizias, &c. }   I did say, &c. / ,,

PRETERPERFECT DEFINITE.

Sing. { eu disse / disséste / disse }   I said, &c. / ,, / ,,

Plur. { nós dessémos / disséstes / dissérão }

PRETERPERFECT.

Sing. { eu tenho ditto / tens ditto, &c. }   I have said, &c. / ,,

FUTURE.

Sing. { eu direi / dirás, &c. }   I shall, *or* will say, &c. / ,,

Imperative Mood.

Sing. { dize tu / diga elle }   say thou / let him say

Plur. { digâmos nós / dizei vós / digão elles }   let us say / say you / let them say

Optative Mood.

PRESENT.

Sing. { *que eu diga*   that I may say, &c.
         digas, &c.   ,,

IMPERFECT.

Sing. { *que eu disséra,* or *dissésse*   that I might say, &c.
        disséras, or *dissésses*   ,,
        disséra, or *dissésse*   ,,

Plur. { *que nós disséramos,* or *disséssemos*   ,,
        disséreis, or *disseseis*   ,,
        dissérão, or *dissessem*   ,,

SECOND IMPERFECT.

Sing. { *eu diria*   I should say, &c.
        dirias, &c.   ,,

FUTURE.

Sing. { *quando eu dissér*   when I shall say, &c.
        disséres   ,,
        dissér, &c.   ,,

Infinitive Mood.

PRESENT.

dizer   to say

GERUND.

dizendo   saying

PARTICIPLES.

masc. *ditto*, fem. *ditta*, said

Observe that the compounds *desdizer*, to unsay, and *contradizer*, to contradict, are in all points conjugated like *dizer*.

CONJUGATION OF THE IRREGULAR VERB *QUERER*,
TO BE WILLING.

Indicative Mood.

PRESENT.

Sing. { *eu quero* — I will, or am willing, &c.
       queres — ,,
       quer — ,,

Plur. { *nós queremos* — ,,
       quereis — ,,
       querem — ,,

IMPERFECT.

Sing. { *eu queria* — I was willing, &c.
       querias, &c. — ,,

PRETERPERFECT DEFINITE.

Sing. { *eu quiz* — I have been willing, &c.
       quizeste — ,,
       quiz — ,,

Plur. { *nós quizémos* — ,,
       quizéstes — ,,
       quizérão — ,,

FUTURE.

Sing. { *eu quererei* — I shall be willing, &c.
       quererás, &c. — ,,

Imperative Mood.

Sing. { *queiras tu* — be thou willing
       queira elle — let him be willing

H

Plur.	queirâmos nós	let us be willing
	queirais vós	be you willing
	queirão elles	let them be willing

Optative and Subjunctive Moods.

PRESENT.

Sing.	que eu queira	that I may be willing, &c.
	queirás, &c.	,,

IMPERFECT.

Sing.	que eu quizera, or quizesse	that I were willing
	quizeras, or quizesses	thou wert willing
	quizera, or quizesse	he were willing
Plur.	que nós quizeramos, or quizessemos	we were willing
	quizereis, or quizesseis	you were willing
	quizerão, or quizessem	they were willing

SECOND IMPERFECT.

Sing.	eu quereria	I would, or should be willing, &c.
	quererias, &c.	,,

FUTURE.

Sing.	quando eu quizer	when I shall be willing, &c.
	quizeres, &c.	,,

Infinitive Mood.

PRESENT.

querer   to be willing

GERUND.

querendo   being willing

PARTICIPLE:

querido   been willing

Quer is sometimes a conjunction, when repeated in a sentence, and when it is rendered into English by *whether* and *or;* as, *quer o tenhais feito, quer não,* whether you have done that or no. But when it is not repeated and is joined to the particle *se,* it is sometimes rendered into English by *at least;* as, *um se quer,* one at least: and sometimes by *however,* when joined to the particle *que;* as, *como quer que seja,* however it be. In all which cases, it is not to be confounded with the third person singular of the indicative of the verb *querer.*

The verb *querer* is sometimes used with the particle *se* instead of the verb *dever;* as, *as cousas não se querem feitas á pressa,* things must not be done in a hurry.

OF THE IRREGULAR VERB *VALER,* TO BE WORTH.

I shall give no other tenses of this verb than the present indicative, the imperative, and the present of the subjunctive, none but these being irregular.

Indicative Mood.

PRESENT.

Sing. { *eu valho* — I am worth, &c.
       vales — ,,
       vale — ,,

Plur. { *nós valemos* — ,,
       valeis — ,,
       valem — ,,

Imperative Mood.

Sing. { *vale tu* — be thou worth
       valha elle — let him be worth

Plur. { *valhâmos nós* — let us be worth
valei vós — be you worth
valhão elles — let them be worth

Subjunctive Mood.

PRESENT.

Sing. { *que eu valha* — that I may be worth, &c.
valhas — ,,
valha — ,,

Plur. { *que nós valhamos* — ,,
valhais — ,,
valhão — ,,

OF THE IRREGULAR VERB *PERDER*, TO LOSE.

This verb changes the *d* into *c* before the *a* and the *o*, namely, in the first person singular of the present indicative; third person singular, and first and third persons plural of the imperative; and in the whole of the present subjunctive. It is conjugated in the following manner:—

Indicative Mood.

PRESENT.

Sing. { *eu perco* — I lose, &c.
perdes — ,,
perde — ,,

Plur. { *nós perdemos*
perdeis
perdem

Imperative Mood.

Sing. { *perde tu* — lose thou
perca elle — let him lose

Plur.	*percamos nós*	let us lose
	perdei vós	lose you
	percão elles	let them lose

Subjunctive Mood.

PRESENT.

Sing.	*que eu perca*	that I may lose, &c.
	percas	,,
	perca, &c.	,,

The compounds of the verb *ter*—as, *contenho*, I contain; *detenho*, I detain, &c—are conjugated the same as *ter*.

Some verbs of the conjugation ending in *er* are only irregular in the participle passive: as, *escrito*, from *escrever*; *absolto*, from *absolver*.

Those that have the *j* before *o* in the present indicative, change the *j* into *g* in all tenses and persons, in which the *j* would otherwise meet with the vowels *i* or *e*: as, *eleger*, to elect; *eu elejo, tu eleges*, &c., I elect, &c.

IMPERFECT.   PRETERDEFINITE.

elegia, &c.   *elegi, elegeste*, &c., I elected, &c.

The verbs ending in *eio* in the present indicative change that termination into *ia* in the imperfect, and into *i* in the preterdefinite, and are so conjugated.

PRESENT.

Sing.	*eu leio*	I read, &c.	Plur.	*lêmos*
	lês	,,		*lêdes*
	lê	,,		*lêem*

IMPERFECT.

Sing.	*eu lia*	I did read, &c.
	lias, &c.	,,

PRETERDEFINITE.

Sing. { eu li   I read, &c.
       lêste, &c.   ,,

Imperative Mood.

Sing. { lê tu   read thou
       lea elle   let him read

Plur. { leâmos nós   let us read
       lêde vós   read you
       leão elles   let them read

Subjunctive Mood.

PRESENT.

Sing. { que eu lea   that I may read, &c.
       leas   ,,
       lea, &c.   ,,

You must observe that they lose the *i* through all the other moods and tenses. The verb *crer*, to believe, is conjugated in the same manner.

OF THE IRREGULAR VERBS IN *IR*.

Indicative Mood.

PRESENT.

Sing. { eu vou   I go
       vais   thou goest
       vai   he goes

Plur. { nós vamos   we go
       ides   you go
       vão   they go

PRETERIMPERFECT.

Sing. { eu hia   I did go, &c.
       hias   ,,
       hia   ,,

Plur. { nós hiamos
       hieis
       hião

VERBS.

PRETERPERFECT DEFINITE.

Sing. { eu fui — I went
       fôste — thou wentst
       foi — he went

Plur. { nós fômos — we went
       fôstes — you went
       fôrão — they went

PRETERPERFECT.

Sing. { eu tenho ido — I have gone, &c.
       tens, &c. — ,,

PRETERPLUPERFECT.

Sing. { eu tinha ido — I had gone, &c.
       tinhas, &c. — ,,

FUTURE.

Sing. { eu irei — I shall or will go, &c.
       irás, &c. — ,,

Imperative Mood.

Sing. { vai tu — go thou
       va elle — let him go

Plur. { vamos nós — let us go
       ide vós — go ye
       vão elles — let them go

Optative and Subjunctive Moods.

PRESENT.

Sing. { que eu va — that I may go, &c.
       vas — ,,
       va — ,,

Plur. { que nós vámos — ,,
       vades — ,,
       vão — ,,

FIRST PRETERIMPERFECT.

Sing. { que eu fôra, or fôsse — that I might go, &c.
       fôras, or fôsses — ,,
       fôra, or fôsse — ,,

Plur. { *que nós fôramos*, or *fôssemos*   that we might go, &c.
       fôreis, or *fôsseis*   ,,
       forão, or *fôssem*   ,,

SECOND PRETERIMPERFECT.

Sing. { *eu iria*   I should *or* would go, &c.
        irias, &c.   ,,

PRETERPERFECT.

It is composed of the participle *ido* and the present subjunctive of the auxiliary verb *ter*.

PRETERPLUPERFECT.

It is composed of the participle *ido* and the first preterimperfect subjunctive of the auxiliary verb *ter*.

SECOND PRETERPLUPERFECT.

It is composed of the participle *ido* and the second preterimperfect subjunctive of the auxiliary verb *ter*.

FUTURE.

Sing. { *quando eu fôr*   when I shall go, &c.
        fôres   ,,
        fôr   ,,
Plur. { *quando nós fôrmos*   ,,
        fôrdes   ,,
        fôrem   ,,

SECOND FUTURE.

Sing. { *quando eu tiver ido*   when I shall have gone, &c.
        tiveres, &c.   ,,

VERBS.

Infinitive Mood.

PRESENT.

ir   to go

GERUND.

indo   going

PARTICIPLE.

ido   gone

VIR, TO COME.

Indicative Mood.

PRESENT.

Sing. { *eu venho* — I come, &c.
        vens — ,,
        vem — ,,

Plur. { *nós vimos*
        vindes
        vêm

IMPERFECT.

Sing. { *eu vinha* — I did come, &c.
        vinhas — ,,
        vinha — ,,

Plur. { *nós vinhamos*
        vinheis
        vinhão

PRETERDEFINITE.

Sing. { *eu vim* — I came, &c.
        vieste — ,,
        veio — ,,

Plur. { *nós viemos*
        viestes
        vierão

PRETERIMPERFECT.

Sing. { *eu tenho vindo*   I have come, &c.
        tens vindo, &c.   ,,

FUTURE.

Sing. { *eu virei*   I shall come, &c.
        virás, &c.   ,,

Imperative Mood.

Sing. { *vem tu*   come thou
     { *venha elle* let him come

Plur. { *venhâmos nos* let us come
     { *vinde vós*   come you
     { *vênhão elles* let them come

Optative Mood.

PRESENT.

que eu venha, &c.

IMPERFECT.

que eu viera, or *viesse*, &c.

SECOND IMPERFECT.

viria, virias, &c.

Infinitive Mood.

PRESENT.

vir   to come

GERUND.

vindo   coming

PARTICIPLE.

vindo   come

The compounds of *vir*—as, *convir*, to be convenient; *sobrevir*, to happen unexpectedly—are conjugated in the same manner.

OF THE IRREGULAR VERBS *MENTIR*, TO LIE; *SENTIR*, TO FEEL; *SERVIR*, TO SERVE; *FERIR*, TO WOUND.

The verbs change the *i* of the first person singular of the present tense, indicative, into *e* in the other persons of the same tense, as well as in the other tenses and moods, except in the imperative and the present subjunctive. They are conjugated thus:

Indicative Mood.

PRESENT.

Sing. { eu minto   tu mentes   elle mente, &c.
      { eu sinto   tu sentes   elle sente, &c.
      { eu sirvo   tu serves   elle serve, &c.

Imperative Mood.

mente tu, minta elle, mintamos nós, menti vós, mintão elles.
sente tu, sinta elle, sintamos nós, senti vós, sintão elles.
serve tu, sirva elle, sirvamos nos, servi vos, sirvão elles.

Subjunctive Mood.

PRESENT.

Sing. { eu minta   tu mintas, &c.
      { eu sinta   tu sintas, &c.
      { eu sirva   tu sirvas, &c.

The compounds *desmentir, assentir, consentir, dissentir, presentir,* are conjugated like *mentir* and *sentir;* and also the verbs *afferir, referir, conferir, deferir, differir, inferir.*

OF THE IRREGULAR VERBS *AFFLIGIR*, TO AFFLICT; *CORRIGIR*, TO CORRECT; *FINGIR*, TO FEIGN; *UNGIR*, TO ANOINT; *COMPUNGIR, FRIGIR, DIRIGIR, TINGIR, CINGIR*, &c.

These verbs change the *g* of the infinitive mood into *j* in those tenses were the *g* would otherwise meet with the vowel *o*, as in the first person singular of the present indicative, *afflijo;* or *a*, as in the third person of the imperative in both numbers, in the first person plural of the same tense, and in the present subjunctive.

OF THE IRREGULAR VERB *SEGUIR*, TO FOLLOW.

This verb changes the *e* of the infinitive mood into *i* in the first person singular of the present indicative, *eu sigo*, I follow; in the present subjunctive, *que eu siga*, that I may follow; and in the imperative it is conjugated thus: *segue tu, siga elle, sigamos nós, segui vós, sigão elles.*

Observe that the *u* is lost in those tenses where it would otherwise meet with the vowels *o* and *a*, as you see in the examples: and this observation applies also to the verbs *distinguir*, to distinguish; *extinguir*, to extinguish, &c.

The compounds are *perseguir*, to persecute; *conseguir*, to obtain; *proseguir*, to pursue.

OF THE IRREGULAR VERB *OUVIR*, TO HEAR.

This verb changes the *v* of the infinitive mood into *ç* in the first person singular of the present indicative, *eu ouço*, I hear; *tu ouves*, &c.; in the present subjunctive and in the imperative mood it is conjugated thus: *ouve tu, ouça elle, ouçamos nós, ouvi vós, oução elles*, hear thou, &c.

OF THE IRREGULAR VERB *DORMIR*, TO SLEEP.

This verb changes the *o* of the infinitive mood into *u* in the first person singular of the present indicative, thus: *eu durmo, tu dormes, elle dorme*, &c., I sleep, &c. In the present subjunctive, *que eu durma*, &c., that I may sleep; and in the imperative mood it is conjugated thus: *dorme tu, durma elle, durmamos nós, dormi vós, durmão elles*, sleep thou, &c.

OF THE IRREGULAR VERB *FUGIR*, TO FLY AWAY.

This verb is irregular in the present indicative, and is thus conjugated: *fujo, foges, foge, fugimos, fugis, fogem,* I ran away, &c. It is also irregular in the imperative mood, where it is conjugated thus: *foge tu, fuja elle, fujamos nós, fugi vós, fujão elles.* Finally, it is irregular in the present subjunctive; *que eu fuja, fujas,* &c.

It keeps the *u* in all other tenses and moods, as also the *g*.

The verb *surgir*, to arrive, *or* to come to an anchor, has the same irregularity, and makes *surto* in the participle passive.

The verbs *subir, cubrir, encubrir, descubrir, acudir, bullir, sumir, consumir, cuspir, construir, tossir,* &c., have the same irregularity in regard to the letter *u*.

OF THE IRREGULAR VERB *PEDIR*, TO ASK.

This verb is irregular in the first person singular of the present indicative and subjunctive, as well as in the imperative, in which it changes the *d* into *ç*.

Indicative Mood.

PRESENT.

Sing. { *eu peço*   I ask, &c.
       tu pedes   ,,
       elle pede   ,,

Plur. { *nós pedimos*
       vós pedis
       elles pedem

Imperative Mood.

Sing. { *pede tu*   ask thou
       peça elle   let him ask

Plur. { *peçamos nós*   let us ask
       pedi vós   ask you
       peção elles   let them ask

Subjunctive Mood.

PRESENT.

Sing. { que eu peça — that I may ask, &c.
peças — ,,
peça — ,,

Plur. { que nós peçamos
peçais
peção

In like manner is conjugated the verb *medir*, to measure: *eu meço, tu medes*, &c.

OF THE IRREGULAR VERB *VESTIR*, TO DRESS.

Indicative Mood.

PRESENT.

Sing. { eu visto — I dress, &c.
vestes — ,,
veste — ,,

Plur. { nós vestimos
vestis
vestem

Imperative Mood.

Sing. { veste tu — dress thou
vista elle — let him dress

Plur. { vistamos nós — let us dress
vesti vós — dress you
vistão elles — let them dress

Subjunctive Mood.

PRESENT.

Sing. { que eu vista — that I may dress, &c.
vistas — ,,
vista — ,,

Plur. { que nós vistamos
vistais
vistão

In all other tenses and moods it keeps the letter *e*; and in like manner is conjugated the verb *despir*.

OF THE IRREGULAR VERB *SORTIR*, TO FURNISH.

Feijóo says that the *o* of this verb is to be changed into *u* in those tenses where the *t* is followed by *e* or *a*; and that it is to be kept when the *t* is followed by *i*; but in the *Fabula dos Planetas* we read, *surtio effeito*, it took effect; and *Andrade*, 2. *part. Apologet.*, we read, *não sortirão effeito*, where the verb *sortirão* is in the same tense, viz., in the preterperfect definite; therefore nothing can be determined about the irregularity of this verb.

OF THE IRREGULAR VERB *CARPIR*, TO WEEP.

This verb is defective, and is only used in those tenses and persons where the *p* is followed by *i*; as, *carpimos, carpis*, we weep, you weep. Preterimperfect, *carpia, carpias*, &c., I did weep, &c.

OF THE IRREGULAR VERB *REPETIR*, TO REPEAT.

Indicative Mood.

PRESENT.

Sing.			Plur.	
	eu repito	I repeat, &c.		*nós repetimos*
	repetes	,,		*repetis*
	repete	,,		*repetem*

IMPERFECT.

repetia, repetias, &c.

PRETERPERFECT DEFINITE.

repeti, repetiste, &c.

VERBS.

Imperative Mood.

Sing. { repete tu   repeat thou, &c.   Plur. repitamos nós, &c.
       { repita elle   ,,

Subjunctive Mood.

PRESENT.

Sing. { que eu repita   that I may repeat, &c.
       {   repitas, &c.   ,,

IMPERFECT.

que eu repetira, or repetisse, &c.   that I might repeat, &c.

OF THE IRREGULAR VERBS *SAHIR*, TO GO OUT, AND *CAHIR*, TO FALL.

Indicative Mood.

PRESENT.

Sing. { eu saio   I go out, &c.   Plur. { nós sahimos
       {   sahes   ,,   {   sahis
       {   sahe   ,,   {   sahem

PRETERIMPERFECT.

sahia, sahias, &c.

PRETERPERFECT DEFINITE.

sahi, sahiste, &c.

Imperative Mood.

Sing. { sahe tu   Plur. { saiamos nós
       { saia elle   { sahi vós
                               { saião elles

VERBS. 113

Subjunctive Mood.

que eu saia, saias, &c.

This is the common way of writing the irregular tenses of the verb *sahir*, as well as those of the verb *cahir*, viz., *eu caio, tu cahes,* &c., I fall, &c., according to Feijóo.

OF THE IRREGULAR VERB *ORDIR*, TO WARP IN A LOOM.

Feijóo says that this verb changes the *o* into *u* in those persons where it would otherwise meet with the syllables, *da, de, do.*

OF THE IRREGULAR VERB *ADVERTIR*, TO WARN.

Advertir is irregular in the following tenses, only by changing *vir* into *ver*.

Indicative Mood.

PRESENT.

Sing. { *eu advirto* — I warn, &c.
{ *advertes* — ,,
{ *adverte* — ,,

Plur. { *nós advertimos*
{ *advertis*
{ *advertem*

Imperative Mood.

Sing. { *adverte tu* — warn thou, &c.
{ *advirta elle* — ,,

Plur. { *advirtamos nós*
{ *adverti vós*
{ *advertão elles*

I

Subjunctive Mood.

PRESENT.

Sing. { que eu advirta   that I may warn, &c.
       advirtas   ,,
       advirta   ,,

Plur. { que nós advirtamos
        advirtais
        advirtão

CONJUGATION OF THE IRREGULAR VERB *PÔR*, TO PLACE, OR PUT.

Indicative Mood.

PRESENT.

Sing. { en ponho   I put, &c.
       pões   ,,
       põe   ,,

Plur. { nós pômos
        pondes
        põem

PRETERIMPERFECT.

Sing. { eu punha   I did put, &c.
       punhas   ,,
       punha   ,,

Plur. { nós punhamos
        punheis
        punhão

PRETERPERFECT DEFINITE.

Sing. { eu puz   I put, &c.
       puzéste   ,,
       pôz   ,,

Plur. { nós puzémos
        puzéstes
        puzérão

PRETERPERFECT.

It is composed of the present indicative of the auxiliary verb *ter*, and the participle *posto*.

PRETERPLUPERFECT.

Composed of the participle *posto*, and the imperfect of the auxiliary verb *ter*.

FUTURE.

Sing. { eu porei — I shall or will put, &c.
porás — ,,
porá — ,,

Plur. { nós porêmos
poreis
porão

Imperative Mood.

Sing. { põe — put thou, &c.
ponha elle — ,,

Plur. { ponhâmos nós
ponde vós
ponhão elles

Optative and Subjunctive Moods.

PRESENT.

Sing. { que eu ponha — that I may put, &c.
tu ponhas, &c. — ,,

FIRST PRETERIMPERFECT.

Sing. { que eu puzera, or puzesse — that I might put, &c.
tu puzeras, or puzesses, &c. — ,,

SECOND PRETERIMPERFECT.

Sing. { eu poria — I should or would put, &c.
tu porias, &c. — ,,

PRETERPERFECT.

It is composed of the participle *posto*, and the present subjunctive of the auxiliary verb *ter*.

PRETERPLUPERFECT.

Composed of the participle *posto*, and the first preterimperfect subjunctive of the auxiliary verb *ter*.

SECOND PRETERPLUPERFECT.

Composed of the participle *posto*, and the second preterimperfect subjunctive of the auxiliary verb *ter*.

FUTURE.

Sing. { *quando eu puzer*   when I shall put, &c.
        tu puzeres, &c.   "

SECOND FUTURE.

Composed of the participle *posto*, and the future subjunctive of the auxiliary verb *ter*.

Infinitive Mood.

PRESENT.

pôr   to put

GERUND.

pondo   putting

PARTICIPLE PASSIVE.

posto   put

After the same manner are conjugated the verbs derived from *pôr*: as, *compôr*, to compose; *dispôr*, to dispose; *propôr*, to propose, &c.

Some verbs are irregular only in the participle passive: as, *aberto*, from *abrir; escrito*, from *escrever*, &c.

OF NEUTER VERBS.

Neuter verbs are those which make a complete sense of themselves, and do not govern any case after them, like the active verbs: as, *dormir*, to sleep; *andar*, to go; *tremer*, to tremble, &c. There are, however, some neuter verbs which may govern an accusative: as, *dormir um somno profundo*, to sleep soundly; *eu fui andando meu caminho, e não disse uma palavra*, I went my way and said not a word. Neuter verbs may also be defined as those which, in their compound tenses, are seldom conjugated with the verb *ser*, to be; as, I sleep, I tremble, I speak, &c. We may indeed say, *eu tenho dormido*, I have slept, *eu tenho tremido*, I have trembled; but not, I am slept, &c. I said *seldom*, because sometimes neuter verbs may be conjugated with the verb *ser;* as, *ser bem fallado*, to have a good name.

It is necessary to be acquainted with the nature of a neuter verb, to avoid mistakes in the participle, as may be seen in the Syntax of Participles.

OF RECIPROCAL VERBS.

The term Reciprocal is given to such verbs as reflect the action upon the agent, and are conjugated through all their tenses with the conjunctive pronouns *me, te, se,* &c.

EXAMPLE.

Indicative Mood.

PRESENT.

Sing.
- *eu me arrependo* — I repent, &c.
- *tu te arrependes* — ,,
- *elle se arrepende,* &c. — ,,

IMPERFECT.

Sing. *eu me arrependia,* &c. — I did repent, &c.

and so of the rest.

Yet it is to be observed that the conjunctive pronouns *me, te,* &c., may be placed either before or after the verb in the indicative, and consequently we may say, *eu me lembro,* or *eu lembro-me,* I remember; *me lembrei,* or *lembrei-me,* I remembered, &c. But in the imperative they should be placed after the verb, as in the following

EXAMPLE.

Sing. { *lembra-te tu* remember thou, &c.
{ *lembre-se elle* ,,

Plur. { *lembremo-nos nós*
{ *lembrai-vos vós*
{ *lembrem-se elles*

In which example you will observe, also, that the first person plural, which in the other verbs is like the first person plural of the present subjunctive, has the last consonant, *s*, cut off: and so from *lembrêmos,* we cut off the *s* to make *lembrêmo-nos;* and from *arrependâmos,* we make *arrependâmo-nos,* &c. In regard to the infinitive, we may say, *é necessario arrepender-se dos peccados,* it is necessary to repent of sins; *é necessario lembrar-se,* it is necessary to remember; and not *se arrepender,* or *se lembrar.* In like manner we may say *lembrando-me,* remembering, and not *me lembrando.* But the present infinitive may be preceded by the particle *para* (which forms the Portuguese supine), and then the conjunctive pronoun may be placed either before or after it; and we may say *para lembrar-se,* or *para se-lembrar,* to remember, *or* in order to remember.

In the subjunctive mood, you must put the conjunctive pronoun before the present; but you must carefully observe that the conjunctive pronouns must be placed before it when preceded by the particles *se,* if, *que,* that: thus we may say, *que eu me lembrasse, se eu me lembrasse,* that I might remember, &c.; but not *que eu lembrasse me,* &c. But when the first preterimperfect is not preceded by any particle, then you must place the conjunctive pronoun after it; as, *arrependera-me eu disso,* I wish I repented it.

In the second preterimperfect we may place the conjunctive pronouns either before or after it, therefore you may say *arrependeria-me se*, &c., or *eu me arrependeria se*, &c., I should repent if, &c.

In the future you must always place the conjunctive pronouns before it: thus, *quando eu me lembrar*, when I shall remember; but not *quando eu lembrar-me*.

Note. All the verbs active may become reciprocals.

EXAMPLE.

Sing.
- *eu me amo* — I love myself
- *tu te amas* — thou lovest thyself
- *elle se ama* — he loves himself

Plur. *nós nos amamos*, &c. — we love ourselves, &c.

CONJUGATION OF THE RECIPROCAL VERB, *IR-SE*, TO GO AWAY.

Indicative Mood.

PRESENT.

Sing.
- *eu me vou* — I go away
- *tu te vais*, &c. — thou goest away, &c.

PRETERIMPERFECT.

Sing.
- *eu me ia* — I did go away
- *tu te ias*, &c. — thou didst go away, &c.

PRETERPERFECT DEFINITE.

Sing.
- *eu me fui* — I went away
- *tu te fôste*, &c. — thou wentest away, &c.

PRETERPERFECT.

Sing. { *eu me tenho ido*   I am gone away
        tu te tens ido, &c.   thou hast gone away, &c.

PRETERPLUPERFECT.

Sing. { *eu me tinha ido*   I was gone away, *or* I had gone away
        tu te tinhas ido, &c.   thou hadst gone away, &c.

FUTURE.

Sing. { *eu me irei*   I shall *or* will go away
        tu te irás, &c.   thou shalt go away, &c.

Imperative Mood.

Sing. { *vai-te*   go thou away
        va-se   let him go away

Plur. { *vamo-nos*   let us go away
        ide-vos   go away, get away, *or* get you gone
        vão-se   let them go away

Subjunctive Mood.

PRESENT.

Sing. { *que eu me vá*   that I may go away
        que tu te vas, &c.   that thou mayest go away, &c.

FIRST PRETERIMPERFECT.

Sing. { *eu me fôra,* or *me fôsse*   that I might go away
        tu te fôras, or *te fôsses,* &c. { that thou mightest go away, &c.

SECOND PRETERIMPERFECT.

Sing. { *eu me iria*   I would go away
        tu te irias, &c.   thou wouldst go away, &c.

PRETERPERFECT.

que eu me tenha ido, &c.   that I have gone away, &c.

PRETERPLUPERFECT.

que eu me tivera, or *me tivesse ido,* &c.   { that I had gone away, &c.

SECOND PRETERPLUPERFECT.

eu me teria ido, &c.   I should have gone away, &c.

FUTURE.

quando eu me fôr, &c.   when I shall go away, &c.

SECOND FUTURE.

quando eu me tiver ido, &c.   when I shall have gone away, &c.

Infinitive Mood.

PRESENT.

ir-se   to go away

PRETERPERFECT.

ter-se-ido   to have gone away

Participles.

PRESENT.

que se vai   that goes away

PRETERIT.

ido   gone away

FUTURE.

que ha de ir-se   that is to go away

GERUNDS.

indo-se   going away
tendo-se ido   having gone away

SUPINE.

para ir-se   to go, *or* in order to go away

Observe, that in the compound tenses the pronouns, *me, te,* &c., are placed before the auxiliary verb.

2ndly. This verb is also used in speaking of vessels to signify their being leaky; as, *vái-se a cuba,* the tub leaks. It is also used before the gerunds: as, *o inverno vai-se acabando,* the winter is drawing to an end; *elles vão-se preparando,* they are preparing themselves: in which examples the verb is to be rendered into English by *to be,* and without the addition of the adverb *away.* Sometimes it is placed before the present infinitive: as, *ir-se deitár,* to go to bed.

OF THE RECIPROCAL VERB *VIR-SE*, TO COME AWAY.

This verb is to be conjugated like the verb *vir;* but you must place the conjunctive pronouns *me, te,* &c., according to the observations made above.

OF THE RECIPROCAL VERB *AVIR-SE*, TO AGREE.

This is a compound verb, which is to be conjugated by putting the particle *a* before the verb *vir* in all its tenses and moods, attending to the observations already made concerning the conjunctive pronouns, and also in regard to the reciprocal verb *haver-se,* to behave, in the conjugation of which no more is necessary than to add the conjunctive pronouns to the verb *haver.*

IMPERSONAL VERBS.

There are three sorts of impersonal verbs, which have only the third person singular.

The first are properly impersonals of themselves; as,

succede	it happens
basta	it is enough, *or* it suffices
chove	it rains
troveja	it thunders

The second are derived from the active verbs, followed by the particle *se*, which renders them impersonal; as, *ama-se*, they love; *diz-se*, they say; *nota-se*, it is noted. They are also called passive impersonals.

The third, which have a great affinity with reciprocal verbs, are conjugated with the conjunctive pronouns, *me, te, lhe, nos, vos, lhes*; as, *doe-me, doe-te, doe-lhe*, &c.

THE IMPERSONAL VERBS OF THEMSELVES ARE:

convêm, it is convenient
succede, it happens, *or* it falls out
está-me bem, it becomes me
basta, it is enough
chovisca, it mizzles
chove, or *cahe pedra*, it hails
gea, it freezes
neva, it snows
fuzila, or *relampeja*, it lightens
importa, it matters, it concerns
parece, it seems

and the like, which are conjugated with the third person singular of each tense; as,

Indicative Mood.

PRESENT.
chove — it rains

IMPERFECT.
chovia — it did rain

PRETERPERFECT DEFINITE.
choveo — it rained

PRETERPERFECT.
tem chovido — it has rained

PRETERPLUPERFECT.
tinha chovido — it had rained

FUTURE.
choverá — it shall *or* will rain

Imperative Mood.
chôva — let it rain

Optative and Subjunctive Moods.

PRESENT.
que chôva — that it may rain

IMPERFECT.
que chovêra, or *chovêsse* — that it might rain

SECOND IMPERFECT.
choveria — it should rain

FUTURE.
quando chover — when it shall rain

SECOND FUTURE.
quando tiver chovido — when it shall have rained

Infinitive Mood.

PRESENT.
chover — to rain

The particle *se*, which composes the second sort of impersonal verbs, may be placed either before or after them: as, *diz-se*, they say; *sabe-se*, it is known; *sabia-se*, it was known; *logo se soube*, it was immediately known; *se diz*, it is said, &c., but sometimes they make no use of the particle *se*, and only puts the verb in the third person plural; as, *dizem*, instead of *se diz*, they say.

In like manner all the active verbs may become impersonal.

In regard to these verbs, observe, when the noun that follows them is in the singular number, you must put the verb in the singular; if the noun be in the plural, you must put the verb in the plural.

EXAMPLES.

Louva-se o capitão, they praise the captain.
Louvão-se os capitães, they praise the captains.
Vê-se um homem, they see a man.
Vêem-se homens, they see men.

When *lhe* is used after the word *se*, then *lhe* must be rendered into English by *his* or *her;* as, *louva-se-lhe o valor*, they praise his or her courage.

The third sort of impersonal verbs are such as are conjugated with the personal pronouns, *me, te, lhe*, &c., with the third person singular.

EXAMPLES.
Indicative Mood.
PRESENT.

desagrada-me	I am displeased, *or* it displeases me
desagrada-te	thou art displeased
desagrada-lhe	he *or* she is displeased
desagrada-nos	we are displeased
desagrada-vos	you are displeased
desagrada-lhes	they are displeased

IMPERFECT.

desagradava-me, &c.   I was displeased, &c.

PRETERPERFECT DEFINITE.

desagradou-me, &c.   I was displeased, &c.

FUTURE.

desagradar-me-ha, &c.   I shall be displeased, &c.

Optative Mood.

PRESENT.

que me desagrade, &c.   that I may be displeased, &c.

IMPERFECT.

que me desagradára, or desagradasse, &c. } that I were displeased, &c.

SECOND IMPERFECT.

desagradar-me-hia, &c.   I should be displeased, &c.

Conjugate after the same manner—

succede-me, it happens to me, &c.
doe-me, it grieves, *or* it pains me, &c.
parece-me, it seems to me, &c.
he-me preciso, it behoves me, &c.
agrada-me, it pleases me, &c.
lembro-me, I remember, &c.

Many of these impersonal verbs have the third person singular and plural; as,

doe-me a perna, my leg pains me
doem-me os olhos, I have sore eyes
o vosso vestido parece-me novo, your coat appears new to me
os vossos sapatos me parecem muito compridos, your shoes seem to me too long.

OF THE VERB *SER*, TO BE.

The verb *ser* is also used as an impersonal, as will be seen in the following examples: *é tempo de levantar-se*, it is time to get up; *era tempo de ir*, it was time to go, &c., and particularly when it is conjugated with the adjectives *preciso* or *necessario:* as, *é preciso*, or *necessario, fazer isto*, this must be done; *era preciso*, or *necessario, escrever*, it was necessary to write; *eu iria se fosse preciso*, I would go if it should be necessary; *é preciso que eu va*, I must go; *é preciso que eu leia*, I must read; *é preciso que elle coma*, he must eat; *seria preciso que eu fosse*, I should go. You see by the last examples, that when the verb *ser* and the adjective are before the conjunctive mood with the particle *que*, the conjunctive is rendered in English by the infinitive; but if the verb *ser* is followed by the relative pronoun *quem*, it must then be rendered in English in the following manner: as, *eu sou quem tem feito aquillo*, it is I who have done that; *tu és quem tem*, &c., it is thou who hast, &c.; *elle é quem tem*, &c., it is he who, &c.; *nos somos quem temos*, &c., it is we who have, &c.; *vós sois quem tendes*, &c., it is you who have, &c.; *elles são quem têm*, &c., it is they who have, &c.; *el Rei é quem o manda*, it is the King who orders it; *ella é quem o crê*, it is she who believes it; *elles são quem o fizerão?* is it they who have done it? *eu sou quem o fiz*, it was I who did it; *então é quando eu tomo as minhas medidas*, it is then I take my measures; *então é quando eu vi*, it was then I saw, or *only then I saw*. You may observe that *quando*, when, must be made use of in the last examples, although it is not required in English.

OF THE VERB *HAVER*, WHEN IT IS IMPERSONAL.

It is to be thus conjugated—

Indicative Mood.

PRESENT.

ha, or *não ha,* there is *or* there is not, *or* there are *or* there are not.

IMPERFECT.

havia   there was *or* there were

PRETERPERFECT DEFINITE.

houve   there was *or* there were

PRETERPERFECT.

tem havido   there has been *or* there have been

PRETERPLUPERFECT.

tinha havido   there had been

FUTURE.

haverá   there shall be

Imperative Mood.

haja   let there be

Optative and Subjunctive Moods.

PRESENT.

que haja   that there may be

IMPERFECT.

que houvera, or *houvesse*   that there were

SECOND IMPERFECT.

haveria   there would be

PRETERPERFECT.

que tenha havido   if there has been

PRETERPLUPERFECT.

se tivesse havido   if there had been

FUTURE.

quando houver   when there will, *or* shall be

SECOND FUTURE.

quando tiver havido   when there shall have been

Infinitive Mood.

haver   there to be

PRETERIT.

ter havido   there to have been

GERUNDS.

havendo   there being
tendo havido   there having been

Those who learn Portuguese are greatly at a loss how to render the following expressions, *there is not; is there?* although there is nothing more easy. I have explained them at large in the following conjugation.

CONJUGATION OF THE IMPERSONAL VERB, *there is, HA,* WHEN IT MARKS THE PLACE, THROUGH ALL ITS TENSES.

There is (of it)	*ha lá d'isso*
There is not (of it)	*não ha lá d'isso*
Is there (of it?)	*ha lá d'isso?*
Is there not (of it?)	*não ha lá d'isso?*
There was (of it)	*havia lá d'isso*
There was not (of it)	*não havia lá d'isso*
Was there (of it?)	*havia lá d'isso?*
Was there not (of it?)	*não havia lá d'isso?*

There was (of it)	*houve lá d'isso*
There was not (of it)	*não houve lá d'isso*
Was there (of it?)	*houve lá d'isso?*
Was there not (of it?)	*não houve lá d'isso?*
There shall be (of it)	*haverá lá d'isso*
There shall not be (of it)	*não haverá lá d'isso*
Shall there be (of it?)	*haverá lá d'isso?*
Shall there not be (of it?)	*não haverá lá d'isso?*
That there may be (of it)	*que haja lá d'isso*
That there may not be (of it)	*que não haja lá d'isso*
That there were (of it)	*que houvera,* or *houvesse lá d'isso*
That there were not (of it)	*não houvera* or *houvesse lá d'isso*
There would be (of it)	*haveria lá d'isso*
There would not be (of it)	*não haveria lá d'isso*
Would there not be (of it?)	*não haveria lá d'isso?*
If there had been (of it)	*se tivesse havido lá d'isso*
If there had not been (of it)	*se não tivesse havido lá d'isso*
There would have been (of it)	*teria havido lá d'isso*
There would not have been (of it)	*não teria havido lá d'isso*
Would there have been (of it?)	*teria havido lá d'isso?*
Would there not have been (of it?)	*não teria havido lá d'isso?*
When there will be (of it)	*quando houver lá d'isso*
When there will not be (of it)	*quando não houver lá d'isso*

When there will have been (of it)	*quando tiver havido lá d'isso*
When there will not have been (of it)	*quando não tiver havido lá d'isso*
Will there have been (of it?)	*terá havido lá d'isso?*
Will there not have been too much (of it?)	*não terá havido demasiado lá d'isso?*
Through there having been too much (of it)	*por ter havido lá demasiadamente d'isso*
There having been too little (of it)	*tendo havido lá muito pouco d'isso*

When to *there is* or *there is not*, *there are* or *there are not*, *there was* or *were*, or *there was* or *were not*, &c., follows, *is there not? is there? are there not? are there? was*, or *were there not? was*, or *were there?* it is rendered in Portuguese by *é verdade? não é verdade?* or, *é assim? não é assim?* Examples: there is some, is there not? *ha lá d'isso, não é verdade?* there was not any, was there? *não houve lá d'isso, não e assim?* &c.

Most sentences beginning with the word *some* and the verb *to be* are expressed in Portuguese by the impersonal *ha*: as, some friends are false, *ha amigos falsos;* some Christians are unworthy of that name, *ha Christãos que não são dignos de tal nome.*

Observe that *ha* comes before a substantive even of the plural number.

The impersonal *ha* is besides used to denote a quantity of time, space, and number: as, *ha dez annos que morreo,* he has been dead these ten years, *or,* he died ten years ago; *ha trinta milhões d'almas em França,* there are thirty millions of souls in France; *de Paris a Londres ha* 120 *legoas,* Paris is 120 leagues from London.

The question of space is asked thus, *quanto ha de Paris a Londres?* how far is Paris from London?

OF THE IMPERSONAL VERB *HA-SE*, IT IS NECESSARY, or MUST.

This verb answers to the Italian *bisogna* and to the French *il faut*, and always requires to be intercepted with the preposition *de*, thus:—present, *ha-de-se;* preterite, *havia-de-se*—being then followed by the infinitive. It denotes the necessity of doing something, and is rendered in English by *must*, and sometimes by the verb *to be*, through all its tenses, with the words *necessary, requisite, needful*, &c.; and as it denotes the necessity of doing something in general, without specifying who *must*, therefore the agent coming before *must* is *anybody*, according to the subject of the sentence; as,

Ha-de-se fazer aquillo, one, *or* somebody, must do that.
Ha-de-se ir, one, *or* somebody must go.

Sometimes the verb coming after this impersonal is rendered in English by the passive voice; as, *ha-de-se fazer isto*, this must be done.

In the conjugation of this verb, you must use the verb *to be* with the word *necessary*, as I have already said.

EXAMPLE.—Present, *ha-de-se*, it is necessary. Imperfect, *havia-de-se*, it was necessary; and so through all the tenses and moods.

Sometimes the infinitive that follows the particle *de* is placed between the impersonal and its particle *se;* as, *ha-de-achar-se*, it must be found: and sometimes the infinitive precedes the impersonal and this follows the particle *se ;* as, *achar-se-ha,* it will be found : in this case you must not join the particle *de* to it. Observe that the infinitive may be also placed between the imperfect tense of this impersonal verb and its particle *se ;* as, *havia de achar-se,* it was to be found : but when the infinitive precedes both the impersonal and its particle *se,* then you must put the particle *se* before the impersonal, and make use of the imperfect *hia,* and not *havia* ; thus we must say *achar-se-hia,* and not *achar-se havia.*

OF THE DEFECTIVE VERBS *CARPIR*, TO WEEP, AND *SOER*, TO BE WONT.

The verb *carpir* is used only in those tenses and persons where the *p* is followed by an *i ;* as, *carpimos, carpis,* we weep, you weep. Preterimp. *carpia, carpias,* &c., I did weep, &c.

The verb *soer* is only used in the third persons of the present indicative, of the preterimperfect of the same mood, and in the gerund : as, *elle soe,* he is wont; *elles soem,* they are wont. Imperf. *elle soia,* he was wont ; *elles soião,* they were wont. Gerund, *soendo,* being wont.

CHAPTER VI.

OF THE PARTICIPLES.

The participle is a tense of the infinitive, which serves to form the preterperfects and preterpluperfects of all the verbs: as, *tenha amado*, I have loved; *tinha amado*, I had loved.

Amado is a participle, and all the verbs in *ar* form the participle in *ado;* as, *amado, cantado,* &c.

Such participle is likewise a noun adjective. Examples: *Homem amado, mulher amada; livros amados, letras amadas.*

Some participles are frequently abridged; as, *envolto* or *envolvido, corrupto* or *corrompido, enxuto* or *enxugado,* and several others, which the use of authors will point out to you.

The regular verbs ending in *er* or *ir* form the participle in *ido;* as, *vendido, recibido, luzedo, nutrido,* &c.

CHAPTER VII.

OF THE ADVERBS.

The adverb is that which gives more or less force to the verb or the adjective.

The adverb has the same effect with the verb as the adjective with the substantive: it explains the accidents and circumstances of the action of the verb.

There are a great many sorts; as, adverbs of time, place, quantity, &c.

Adverbs of time: as, at present, *presentemente;* now, *agora;* yesterday, *hontem;* to-day, *hoje;* never, *nunca;* always, *sempre;* in the meantime, *entretanto.*

Adverbs of place: as, where, *onde;* here, *aqui;* from whence, *donde;* there, *ali;* from hence, *daqui;* above, *em cima;* below, *em baixo;* far, *longe;* near, *perto.*

Adverbs of quantity: as, how much, *quanto;* how many, *quantos,* or *quantas;* so much, *tanto;* much, *muito;* little, *pouco.*

A great many adverbs are formed from adjectives, changing *o* into *amente*: *santo, santamente,* holily; *rico, ricamente,* richly; *douto, doutamente,* learnedly.

From adjectives in *e* or *l* we likewise form adverbs, by adding *mente* to them; as,

Constante, constantemente, constantly.
Diligente, diligentemente, diligently.
Prudente, prudentemente, prudently.
Fiel, fielmente, faithfully.

In order to assist the memory of those who are learning the Portuguese language, I have here collected a large number of adverbs, which, by frequent repetition, may be easily retained, especially those terminating in *mente.*

A COLLECTION OF ADVERBS.

Abundantemente, abundantly
Com razão, justamente, justly
Absolutamente, absolutely
Antigamente, anciently
De proposito, purposely
Adeus, farewell
Admiravelmente, Maravilhosamente, ás mil maravilhas, admirably
Astutamente, cunningly
Agora, or *por hora,* now at this time
Já, para já, now, immediately

Com condição, upon condition
De parte, aside
De travéz, askance, askew; as, *olhar de travéz*, to look askew, *or* askance
Actualmente, at present
Quasi, pretty near, almost
Então, then
Desde então, since that time
Desde quando? since when
De quando ha? from what time? how long?
De quando em quando, now and then, ever and anon
Quando bem, or *ainda quando*, albeit, although it should be
Quando muito, at the most
Quando menos, at least
Cá, here *or* hither
Lá, there
Ali, there in that place
Ahi, there, expresses the place where stands the person spoken to; as, *ahi onde éstas*, there where you are
Acolá, there
Atraiçoadamente, treacherously
De maravilha, very seldom
A miudo, often
Assim, so

Tão, so
A' pressa, in haste
Facilmente, easily
Ao avesso, or *ás avessas*, the wrong side outward
De improviso, or *improvisamente*, unawares
Livremente, freely
Muito, much
Depressa, quickly
Aqui, here
Até aqui, as far as here, *or* till now, *or* hitherto
D'aqui em diante, henceforward *or* hereafter
Bem, well
A'manhã, to-morrow
A'manhã, pela manhã, to-morrow morning
Depois d'ámanhã, after to-morrow
Ultimamente, lastly
Como, as
Como? how?
Cedo, soon
Tarde, late
Primeiro que, before that
Primeiro que tudo, before all, *or* in the first place
Traz, or *detraz*, behind
Para traz, backward
Isto é, to wit
Em vez, instead
Tambem, also

Tanto que, so much so
Logo que, as soon as
De pensado, wilfully
Acaso, by chance
Fixamente, stedfastly
Finalmente, finally
Muito, very
Atrevidamente, boldly
Feliçemente, happily
Vergonhosamente, shamefully
Nunca, never
Nunca mais, never since
Logo, immediately
Ainda, yet; as, *ainda não veio,* he has not come yet
Ainda, even; as, *seria vergonha ainda fallar d'isso,* it were a shame even to speak of it
Nem se quer, even
Vilmente, basely
Fóra, abroad, out
Já, already
D'um salto, at one jump

De quando em quando, from time to time
Antes, before
Depois, afterwards
Juntamente, together
Inteiramente, entirely
Ao redor, or *em tôrno,* about
De balde, in vain
Loucamente, madly
Mal, ill
Mais, more
Menos, less
Até, until, or even
Sim, yes
Não, no, not
Onde, where
De cór, by heart
A's vezes, sometimes, from time to time
Quando, when
Nada, nothing
Verdadeiramente, truly
Dentro, within
Devagar, softly

CHAPTER VIII.

OF THE PROPOSITIONS.

PREPOSITIONS are indeclinable, and most commonly set before a noun, a pronoun, or verb.

Every preposition requires some case after it, as you will see in the following collection :—

GENITIVE.

Antes do dia, before daybreak
Diante de Deus, before God
Dentro da igreja, within the church
Detraz do palacio, behind the palace
Debaixo da mesa, under the table
Em cima da mesa, upon the table
Alem, besides
Alem dos mares, on that side of the seas
Alem d'isso, besides that, moreover
Alem de que, idem
A'quem, or *d'a'quem dos mares*, on this side of the seas
Ao redor, or *em contorno da cidade*, round about the city
Perto de Londres, near London
A'cerca d'aquelle negocio, concerning that affair
Fóra da casa, out of the house
Fóra de perigo, out of danger
Fóra de si, out of one's wits

Note. This preposition governs also a nominative ; as, *fóra seu irmão*, except his brother, *or* his brother excepted.

De fronte da minha casa, over against my house
De fronte da igreja, facing the church
Depois da cêa, after supper

DATIVE.

Quanto áquillo, with respect to that
Pegado á muralha, close to the wall
Desde o bico do pé até á cabeça, from top to toe

ACCUSATIVE.

Perante o juiz, before the judge
Entre, between, among, *or* amongst
Entre os homens, among men
Sobre a mesa, upon the table
Conforme, or *segundo a lei,* according to the law
Por amor de Deus, for God's sake
Pelo mundo, through the world
Pela rua, through the streets
Pellas terras, through the lands
Por grande que seja, let it be ever so great
Contra elles, against them
Durante, during; as, *durante o inverno,* during the winter

We shall be more particular about prepositions when we examine their construction.

CHAPTER IX.

OF THE CONJUNCTIONS.

A CONJUNCTION is an indeclinable part of speech which serves to join the members and parts of speech together, in showing the dependency of relation and coherency between the words and sentences.

Some conjunctions are copulative, which join, and, as it were, couple two terms together; as, *Portuguezes e Inglezes*, Portuguese and English.

Some are disjunctive, which show separation or division: as, *nem*, nor, neither; *ou*, either, or. Examples: *nem este, nem aquelle*, neither this nor that; *ou este, ou aquelle*, either this or that; *nem mais, nem menos*, neither more nor less; *quer o faça, quer não, tudo para mim é o mesmo*, it is all one to me whether he does it or no; *quer seja verdade, quer não*, whether it be true or not; *nem se quer um*, not even one.

The adversative denote restriction or contrariety: as, *mas*, or *porêm*, but; *comtudo*, yet, however; *mas antes*, or *pelo contrario*, nay.

The conditional conjunctions suppose a condition, and serve to restrain and limit what has just been said: as, *se*, if; *com condição que, dado o caso que*, provided that, or upon condition that, or in case that, &c.

The concessive, which show the assent we give to a thing: as, *embora*, or *seja embora*, well and good; *está feito*, done, agreed.

The casual show the reason of something; as, *porque*, what for, or because, or why.

The concluding denote a consequence drawn from what is before; as, *logo*, or *por consequencia*, therefore, then, or consequently.

The transitive, which serve to pass from one sentence to another: as, *álem disso*, moreover, or besides that; *sobretudo*, or *em summa*, after all, upon the whole, in the main *a proposito*, now I think of it, *or* by the by.

There are others of a different sort: as, *se quer*, or *ao menos*, at least; *ainda que*, although; *de sorte que*, so that; *antes quero pedir que furtar*, I will rather beg than steal;

antes morrerei que dizer-vol-o, I will rather die than tell you; *já que,* since, &c.

To the above-mentioned parts of speech, grammarians have added *Interjections,* which are particles serving to denote some passion or emotion of the mind: but there is another sort, which may be called demonstrative; as, *cá* and *lá,* and *aqui* and *ali.* Examples: *este homem aqui,* this man here; *aquella mulher lá,* that woman there, &c.: and some others continuative, because they denote continuation in the speech; as, *com effeito,* in effect; *álem disso,* besides; *ora vejâmos,* now let us see; *finalmente fômo-nos embora,* and so we went away. To which we may add those invented to imitate the sound of dumb creatures, and the noise which is occasioned by the clashing of bodies against one another; as, *zaz, traz,* &c.

INTERJECTIVE PARTICLES.

OF JOY.

Ha, ha, ha! Ha, ha, ha!
Oh que prazer! Oh joy!

OF GRIEF.

Ay! Alas! ah!
Ay de mim! Poor me!
Meu Deus! My God!

OF PAIN.

Ay! Ay!
Oh! Oh!

TO ENCOURAGE.

Animo! Courage!
Ora vamos! Come, come on!

TO CALL.

Oh! oh lá! Ho! hey! hip!

OF ADMIRATION OR SURPRISE.

Oh, oh lá, ahi! Oh my! Oh dear me!
Apre! Heyday!

OF AVERSION.

Irra! Away!
Nada! Away with! By no means!
Fora! Fie!

FOR MAKING PEOPLE GO OUT OF THE WAY, OR STAND AWAY.

Guardem-se or *arredem-se!* Out of the way, *or* stand away!

FOR SHOUTING.

Viva! Hurrah!

OF SILENCE.

Caluda or *Calai-vos!* Hush! Silence!

OF CURSING AND THREATENING.

Maldito sejais! May you be cursed!

FOR DERISION.

Ah! Ah! oh! oh! oh!

OF WISHING.

Oh prouvéra a Deus! Would to God!
Oxalá! Oh that!
Oh se! Would!

The interjection *Oh!* serves for different emotions of the mind, as admiration, grief, wish, &c., and sometimes is used ironically, but differently uttered, according to the emotion which it expresses.

SOME ABBREVIATIONS USED IN THE PORTUGUESE LANGUAGE.

Ant^o	*Antonio*	Anthony
Seb^m	*Sebastiam*	Sebastian
B^{mo} P^e	*Beatissimo Pâe*	The most blessed Father
Cap^m	*Capitão*	Captain
Comp^a	*Companhia*	Company
Corr^o	*Correio*	Post
D. or D^a	*Dom* or *Dona*	Don or Dona
D^r, D^{or}	*Doutor*	Doctor
D^o D^a	*Ditto, ditta*	Said
Exmo, Exma	*Excellentissimo, ma*	Most excellent
V. Exª	*Vossa excellencia*	Your Excellency
V. S^a	*Vossa senhoria*	Your Lordship
V. A.	*Vossa alteza*	Your Highness
V. M. or V^{ce}	*Vossa mercê*	You
V. P.	*Vossa paternidade*	Your Paternity
V. M^{de}	*Vossa Magestade*	Your Majesty
S.	*Santo*	Saint
Fran^{co}	*Francisco*	Francis
G^{de}	*Guarde*	Save
Snr. Snr^a	*Senhor, ora*	Sir, Lady
Rev^{mo}	*Reverendissimo*	Most Reverend
P^a	*Para*	For
Q^{do}	*Quando*	When
Q^m	*Quem*	Who
Q^{to}	*Quanto*	How much
Supp^e	*Supplicante*	Petitioner
Genl	*General*	General
Ten^{te}	*Tenente*	Lieutenant
V. G.	*Verbi gratia*	For example

And many others that must be learned by use.

PART II.

CHAPTER I.

OF THE DIVISION OF SYNTAX.

SYNTAX is a Greek word, by the Latins called *construction;* it treats of the agreement and construction of words in a sentence. It is divided into three sorts: the first, of Order or Arrangement; the second of Concordance; the third of Government. The Syntax of Order or Arrangement is the proper placing of words in a sentence. The Syntax of Concordance is when the parts of speech agree with one another, as the substantive with the adjective, or the nominative with the verb. The Syntax of Government is when one part of speech governs another.

For the sake of those who, perhaps, have not a grammatical knowledge of their own language, I shall lay down some general rules for the Portuguese construction.

I.—OF THE ORDER OF WORDS.

1. The nominative denotes the subject, and is usually placed before the verb or attribute; it may be either a noun or pronoun: as, *Francisco escreve*, Francis writes; *eu fallo*, I speak.

2. When the action of the verb is attributed to many persons or things, these all belong to the nominative,

and are placed before the verb together with their conjunction: as, *Pedro e Paulo lêm*, Peter and Paul read.

3. The adjectives belonging to the nominative substantive, to which the action of the verb is attributed, are put after the substantive and before the verb: as, *os estudantes morigerados e diligentes estudão*, the obedient and diligent scholars study.

4. If the nominative has an article, this article is always placed before it.

5. Sometimes an infinitive is put for a noun, and stands for a nominative; as, *o dormir faz bem*, sleeping does one good: and sometimes a verb with its case; as, *é acto de humanidade ter compaixão dos afflictos*, to have compassion on the afflicted is an act of humanity.

6. The nominative is sometimes understood; as *amo*, where *eu* is understood: and so of the other persons of the verb.

7. After the nominative comes the verb; and if there is an adverb, it is to be placed immediately after the verb whose accident and circumstances it explains: as, *Pedro ama com extremo a gloria*, Peter is extremely fond of glory.

8. The cases governed by the verb are put after it; they may be one, or many, according to the nature of the action: as, *eu amo a Pedro*, I love Peter; *faço presente de um livro a Paulo*, I make a present of a book to Paul.

9. The preposition is always placed before the case it governs; as, *perto de casa*, near the house.

10. The relative is always placed after the antecedent; as, *Pedro o qual estuda*, Peter who studies.

II.—OF CONCORDANCE.

1. The adjectives agree with their substantives in gender, number, and case: as, *um homem virtuoso*, a virtuous man; *uma bella mulher*, a handsome woman; *sumptuosos palacios*, &c., sumptuous palaces, &c.

2. When two or more substantives singular come together, the adjectives belonging to them must be put in the plural; as, *tanto el rei como a rainha montados a cavallo parecem bem*, both the king and the queen look well when they ride.

3. If the substantives happen to be one in the singular and the other in the plural, or to be of different genders, the adjective common to both agrees in number and gender with the last: as, *elle tinha os olhos e a boca aberta*,* or *elle tinha a boca e os olhos abertos*, his eyes and mouth were opened; *as lagôas e rios estavão congelados*, the ponds and rivers were frozen.

4. But when there is one or many words between the last noun and the adjective, that adjective (common to all) agrees with the masculine noun, though the last noun be feminine; and if the nouns are in the singular, then the adjective must be put in the plural number and masculine gender: as, *o rio e a lagôa estavão congelados*, the pond and river were frozen; *o trabalho, a industria, e a fortuna unidos*, pains, industry, and fortune joined together.

5. Every personal verb agrees with its nominative, expressed or understood in number and person.

---

* Use has made it allowable that the adjective common to both substantives of different genders or numbers may agree only with the last; but the best grammar and practice is to put, in such instances, the adjective in its masculine plural, the same as directed in the 4th rule.

6. The relative *qual* with the article agrees entirely with the antecedent; but without the article and denoting an absolute quality, it agrees with what follows: as, *aquelle coração o qual,* &c., that heart which, &c.; *considerando quaes serão as condições,* &c., considering which would be the conditions, &c.

7. Questions and answers always agree in everything; as, *a que serviço pertence vm^{ce} ? elle respondeo, pertenco ao da rainha,* at whose service are you, sir? he answered, I am at the queen's service.

III.—ON THE DEPENDENCE OF THE PARTS OF SPEECH ON ONE ANOTHER.

1. The nominative being the basis of the sentence, the verb depends on it, as the other cases depend on the verb. The adjective depends on the substantive to which it refers; and the adverb on the verb whose accidents it explains.

2. The genitive depends upon a substantive, expressed or understood, by which it is governed.

3. The accusative depends either on an accusative verb, or on a preposition.

4. The ablative depends on a preposition by which it is governed; as, *parto de Roma,* I go from Rome.

5. The dative and vocative have, strictly speaking, no dependence on the other parts: the dative is common, as it were, to all nouns and verbs; the vocative only points out the person to whom you speak.

I now come to the Construction of the several parts of speech.

CHAPTER II.

OF THE SYNTAX OF ARTICLES.

BEFORE we come to the syntax of the articles, remember that *o, a, os, as*, are articles only when they precede the nouns or pronouns, but not when joined to the verbs.

Those who understand Latin will quickly perceive the difference, if they take notice that every time they render *o, a*, by *illum, illam, illud;* or by *eum, eam, id;* and *os, as*, by *illos, illas, illa;* or by *eos, eas, ea*, they are relative pronouns.

1. The article is used before the names of things which can be spoken of; therefore nouns of substances, arts, sciences, plays, metals, virtues, and vices, having no article before them in English, require the article in Portuguese; as,

O oiro e a prata não podem fazer feliz ao homem, gold and silver cannot make the happiness of man.

A virtude não é compativel com o vicio, virtue cannot agree with vice.

A philosophia é uma sciencia muito nobre, philosophy is a very noble science.

Joguemos as cartas, let us play at cards.

2. The article is not placed before a substantive which is followed by the adjective of number that stands for a surname; as, *Joseph Primeiro*, Joseph the First.

3. When a book, or some part of it, as chapter, page, &c., is quoted, the adjective of number may come either before or after the substantive: but if it comes after, the two words are construed without the article; as, *livro*

primeiro, capitulo segundo, &c., book I., chapter II. If the adjective of number comes before the substantive, it takes the article; as, *o primeiro livro*, the first book.

4. *O* placed before *que* signifies *what* or *which*; as, *faça o que quizer*, let him do what he likes; *o que eu fiz*, which I did.

5. The article is never made use of before proper names of men, women, gods, goddesses, saints.

6. The article is not used in Portuguese before the possessive relative pronouns; as, *de quem é esta casa? é minha, é tua*, &c., whose house is this? it is mine, it is thine, &c.

7. When a mount, mountain, or hill's name is preceded by the word *monte*, it takes neither article nor preposition; as, *o Monte Atlante*, Mount Atlas; *os Montes Pireneos*, the Pyrenees: but after the word *serra*, a ridge of hills, it takes the article; as, *a Serra da Estrella*, Mount Estrella; *a Serra do Potosi*, Mount Potosi; however, they say also, *Serra Liôa*.*

8. The noun of measure, weight, and the number of the things that have been bought, requires the article; as, *o trigo vende-se a tanto o alqueire*, wheat is sold so much a-peck.

A manteiga vende-se a tanto o arratel, butter costs so much a-pound.

Os ovos vendem-se a tanto a duzia, eggs are sold so much -dozen.

9. No article is used with proper names of persons and planets, except *a terra*, the earth; *o sol*, the sun; *a lua*, the moon.

* When *Serra Liôa* is used without the article, it is because it then expresses the district or territory where that ridge of mountains is situate; but, speaking of the ridge or mountain itself, a Portugu se would say, *a Serra Liôa*, with the article.

10. When proper names are used in a determinate sense, that is, when they are applied to particular objects, then they take the article : *o Deus dos Christãos*, the God of Christians ; *o Archimedes de Inglaterra*, the Archimedes of England. The proper names of renowned poets and painters keep also the article; as, *o Camoens, o Pope, o Tasso, o Ticiano*, &c.

11. The preposition *de* is used before nouns following one of these, *sorte, especie, genero*, and any other noun of which they express the *kind, character, quality*, and *nature*, which sort of nouns are usually rendered into English by an adjective, or even by the substantive itself placed adjectively, and making together, as it were, but a compound word : as, *Dôr de cabeça*, the headache ; *uma sorte de terra*, a sort of land ; *fallar de ignorante*, an ignorant speech.

Sometimes the English adjective may be made an adjective in Portuguese, as in the last example, *um fallar ignorante*, an ignorant speech ; but not unfrequently the Portuguese express the English adjective by a substantive of the same signification with *de* before the other noun, though they have an adjective of the same nature as the English ; as, *o diabo da perseguição*, the devilish persecution : and sometimes the adjective is used by them substantively, or the substantive is understood ; *o preguiçoso de meu filho*, my lazy son ; *a velha de sua mãi*, his *or* her old mother. Finally they also make use of the definite article : as, *o monstro do homem*, or *da mulher*, the monstrous man, *or* women ; *a pobre da rapariga*, the poor girl, &c.

12. Nouns are used without an article in the following cases :—

1st. In the title of a performance, and in the middle of sentences, where they characterise in a peculiar manner the person or thing spoken of, in which case the English use the particle *a* ; as,

Discurso sobre as obrigações da religião natural, a discourse concerning the obligations of natural religion.

Primeira parte, the first part.

O Conde de Clermont, principe do Sangue, morreo, &c., the Count of Clermont, a prince of the blood, died, &c.

O S^{to} Antonio, navio de noventa peças, the St. Anthony, a ninety-gun ship.

2ndly. In sentences of exclamation : as,

As mais bellas flores são as que menos durão ; qualquer chuva as desmaia, o vento as murcha, o sol as queima, e acaba de secar ; sem fallar d'uma infinidade de insectos que as perseguem e deitão a perder : natural e verdadeira imagem da belleza! the most beautiful flowers last but a very short time ; the least rain tarnishes them, the wind withers them, the sun scorches them, and completes the drying of them up ; without mentioning an infinite number of insects that spoil and hurt them : a natural and true image of beauty !

3rdly. When nouns of number are used in an indefinite sense ; as, *mil soldados de a cavallo contra cem infantes*, a thousand horse against a hundred foot.

Tenho lido dous poetas, I have read two poets, that is, any two out of all that ever existed.

But before a noun of number, in a definite sense, it would take an article ; as,

Tenho lido os dous poetas, I have read both poets ; because this plainly indicates a definite two, of whom some mention has been already made.

Os cem infantes que combateram contra os mil de a cavallo, que, &c., the hundred foot that fought with the thousand horse that, &c.

4thly. After the verb *ser*, when it signifies *to become*,

and after *ser tomado por*, to be accounted ; *passar por*, to pass for : as, *elle será doutor com o tempo*, he will become a doctor in time ; *elle passa por marinheiro*, he passes for a sailor.

When the adjective is used substantively, it must have the neuter article *o* before it :

O verde offende menos a vista que o vermelho, green hurts the eye less than red.

There are also some adverbs preceded by the neuter article *o ;* as the following : *o melhor que eu puder*, the best I could ; *o menos que for possivel*, the least possible.

Articles are repeated in Portuguese before as many nouns (requiring the article) as there are in the sentence ; as,

O ouro, a prata, a saude, as honras, e os deleites não podem fazer feliz ao homem que não tem sciencia nem virtude, gold, silver, health, honours, and pleasures, cannot make a happy man without wisdom and virtue.

The article *o* is put before the word *senhor*, sir, *or* my lord ; as,

O senhor duque, my lord duke ; *o senhor presidente*, my lord the president ; *os senhores*, the gentlemen ; *dos senhores*, of the gentlemen.

The feminine article *a* must be prefixed to *senhora*, my lady, *or* madam ; as, *a senhora duqueza*, or *condessa de*, &c., my lady duchess, *or* countess of, &c.

The article is never used in Portuguese as it is in English, before *mais*, more, or *menos*, less, in the following sentences : *quanto mais vivemos, tanto mais aprendemos*, the longer we live, the more we learn ; *quanto mais um hydropico bebe, tanto mais sêde têm*, the more a dropsical man drinks the more thirsty he is ; *quanto mais pobre é o homem, tanto menos cuidados têm*, the poorer a man is, the less care he has, &c.

Sometimes the English particle *to*, before infinitives, is rendered in Portuguese by the article *o ;* as, *é facil o dizer, o ver*, &c., it is easy to say, to see, &c.

In a word, *the natural associators with articles* are those *common appellatives* which denote the several genera and species of beings, or those words which, though indefinite, are yet capable, through the article, of becoming definite. Therefore *Apollonius* makes it part of the pronoun's definition, to refuse coalescence with the article : and it would be absurd to say, *o eu*, the I ; or, *o tu*, the thou ; because nothing can make those pronouns more definite than they are.

Note. When the adjective *um, uma*, is used as an article in Portuguese, it denotes individuals as unknown; but the articles *o, a*, denote individuals as known. Example : Seeing an object pass by which I never saw till then, a beggar with a long beard, for instance, I say : *Ali vai um pobre com uma barba comprida*, there goes a beggar with a long beard. But the man departs and returns a week after ; then I must say, *Ali vai o pobre da barba comprida*, there goes the beggar with the long beard.

CHAPTER III.

OF THE SYNTAX OF NOUNS.

AND FIRST, OF THE SUBSTANTIVES.

WHEN two or more substantives come together, without a comma between them, they all govern each the next in the genitive, the first governing the second, the second the third in the same case, and so on (that is, the first is always followed by the preposition *de*, or by the article before the next noun); but that genitive can never come in Portuguese before the noun that governs it as in English.

A philosophia de Newton, Newton's philosophy.

As guardas do principe, the prince's guards.

A porta de casa, the house-gate.

Eis aqui a casa do companheiro do irmão de minha mulher, here is my wife's brother's partner's house.

When two substantives singular are the nominative of a verb, the verb must be put in the plural; as, *meu irmão e meu pai estão no campo*, my brother and my father are in the country.

If the nominative is a collective substantive, the verb is always put in the singular; as, *toda a cidade assistió*, all the city was present.

OF THE SYNTAX OF ADJECTIVES.

Of adjectives, some are put before the noun, and some after; and others may be put indifferently, either before or after.

The possessive pronouns, *meu*, *teu*, *seu*, &c., and adjectives of number, come before the substantive, as in English. Examples: *Meu pai*, my father; *a sua casa*, his house; *duas pessoas*, two persons; *o primeiro homem*, the first man.

But when an adjective of number stands for a surname, or is joined to a proper or Christian name, it comes after the substantive, without the article; as, *João V.*, John the Fifth.

THE FOLLOWING ADJECTIVES COME AFTER THE SUBSTANTIVE.

1st. Verbal adjectives and participles: as, *um homem divertido*, a comical, a merry man; *uma mulher estimada*, a woman esteemed.

2ndly. Adjectives referring to nations: as, *um mathematico Inglez*, an English mathematician; *um alfaiate Francez*, a French tailor; *musica Italiana*, Italian music.

3rdly. Adjectives of colour: as, *um vestido negro*, a black suit of cloths; *um capote vermelho*, a red cloak, &c.

4thly. Adjectives of figure: as, *uma mesa redonda*, a round table; *um campo triangular*, a triangular field, &c.

5thly. Adjectives expressing some physical or natural quality: such are, *quente*, hot; *frio*, cold; *humido*, wet; *corcovado*, hunchbacked, &c.

Most other adjectives are placed before or after the substantive: as, *santo*, holy; *verdadeiro*, true, &c.

If the substantive has three or more adjectives belonging to it, they must be placed after it with the conjunction *e* before the last, which must likewise be observed, even when there be but two adjectives. The Portuguese do not say, *uma desagradavel enfadonha obra*, but, *uma obra desagradavel e enfadonha*, a disagreeable tedious work, &c.

Of adjectives, some always require either a noun or verb after them, which they govern; as, *digno de louvor*, praiseworthy; *digno de ser amado*, worthy to be loved; *capaz de ensinar*, capable to teach; and these have always the particle *de* after them.

Some will be used in an absolute sense without being attended by any noun or verb; as, *prudente*, wise; *incuravel*, incurable, &c.

Others may be construed both with or without a noun, which they govern: *ella é uma mulher insensivel*, she is a woman without any sensibility; *ella é insensivel ao amor*, she is insensible to love.

The following adjectives, which require the preposition *de* before the next infinitive, govern the genitive case. Observe, that some of them require, in English, the preposition *at* or *with* after them.

Digno, worthy; as, *elle é digno de louvor*, he is worthy of praise. This adjective is sometimes followed by *que;* as, *digno que seu nome fosse*, &c., her name deserved to be, &c.

Indigno, unworthy; as, *indigno da estimação que faço d'elle*, unworthy of the esteem which I have for him.

Capaz, capable; *incapaz*, incapable: as, *capaz* or *incapaz de servir a propria patria*, capable *or* incapable of serving one's country.

Notado, charged; as, *notado de avareza*, charged with avarice.

Contente, glad; as, *estou contente do successo que elle teve*, I am glad *or* overjoyed at his success.

Cançado, tired; as, *cançado de estudar*, tired of studying.

Dezejoso, greedy; as, *dezejoso de gloria*, greedy of glory, &c. And likewise adjectives signifying fulness, emptiness, plenty, want, desire, knowledge, remembrance, ignorance, or forgetting.

All adjectives signifying inclination, advantage and disadvantage, profit or loss, pleasure or displeasure, due submission, resistance, likeness, govern the dative case: as, *insensivel ás affrontas*, insensible to affronts; *ser inclinado á alguma cousa*, to be inclined to something; *nocivo á saude*, hurtful to health.

Adjectives signifying dimensions: as, *alto*, high, tall;

largo, wide, broad ; and *comprido*, long, come after words of the measure of magnitude, both in English and Portuguese ; but they are preceded by *de* in Portuguese : as, *dez pés de largo*, ten feet broad ; *seis pés de comprido*, six feet long, &c. They also turn the adjective of dimension into its corresponding substantive, with the preposition *de*, and preceded by the measure : as, *seis pés de altura*, six feet high ; *dez pés de largura*, ten feet broad.

Adjectives signifying experience, knowledge, or science, require *em*, or *no*, *na*, *nos*, *nas*, after them : as, *versado nos livros*, versed in books ; *experto na medicina*, expert in medicine.

Cardinal nouns require the genitive case after them ; as, *um dos dois*, one of the two.

The ordinal nouns, as well as collective and proportional nouns, likewise require the genitive after them : as, *o primeiro dos réis*, the first of the kings ; *uma duzia de ovos*, a dozen of eggs, &c.

OF THE SYNTAX OF COMPARATIVES AND SUPERLATIVES.

The comparative is not made of the positive in Portuguese, as in Latin and English, but by adding *mais*, more, or *menos*, less, which govern *que*, signifying *than :* as, *o todo é mais que a parte*, the whole is greater than a part ; *o seu amante é mais bello, mais moço, e mais rico que ella*, her lover is handsomer, younger, and richer, than she is ; *eu acho-o agora menos bello do que quando o comprei*, I now find it less handsome than when I bought it.

The simple comparatives *mais* and *menos*, followed by a noun of number, have *de* after them : as, *ainda que elle tivesse mais de cem homens*, though he had above a hundred men ; *elle tem mais de vinte annos*, he is above twenty.

When the comparison is made by *so as, as much as*, they must be rendered by *como*.

EXAMPLES.

O meu livro é tão bello como o vosso, my book is as handsome as yours; *um principe não é tão poderoso como um rei*, a prince is not so powerful as a king.

They put sometimes *muito* and *pouco* before the simple comparatives *mais* and *menos* : as, *elle é muito mais grande*, he is taller by much; *elle é pouco mais grande*, he is taller by little, &c.

CHAPTER IV.

OF THE SYNTAX OF PRONOUNS.

WE have sufficiently explained the pronouns in the First Part; and, to avoid any further repetition, shall only observe that,

1st. The English make use of the verb *to be*, put impersonally through all its tenses in the third person, before the personal pronouns, *I, thou, he, she, we, you, they*; it it I, it is he, &c. In Portuguese the verb *to be*, on this occasion, is not impersonal; as they express, it is I, by *sou eu;* it is thou, *es tu;* it is he, *é elle;* it is we, *somos nós;* it is ye, *sois vós;* it is she, *é ella;* it is they, masc., *são elles;* it is they, fem., *são ellas:* and in like manner through all the tenses; as, it was I, *era eu;* it was we, *eramos nós*, &c.

2ndly. The Portuguese seldom make use of the second

person singular, except when through a great familiarity among friends; or a father and mother to their children; or to servants.

Observe here, that when an adjective comes after vm^{ce}, *v. s.*, *v. e.*, &c., it does not agree in gender with vm^{ce}, *v. s.*, &c., but with the person we speak to, or we speak of: thus we say to a lady, vm^{ce} *é muito bella*, you are very beautiful; and to a man, vm^{ce} *é muito bom*, you are very good.

3rdly. *Nós* is generally used by a king, a governor, or a bishop, in their writings, and then it signifies in English, *we;* as, *nós mandamos*, or *mandamos*, we command: but *nos* before or after a verb in Portuguese signifies *us* in English; as, *elle nos disse*, he told us; *dai nos tempo*, give us time.

4thly. *Vós* is applied when speaking to God or to a multitude.

5thly. The conjunctive pronouns are joined to verbs, and stand for the dative and accusative cases; as, *deu-me*, he gave me; *ama-me*, love me: but the personal pronouns are used instead of them when they are preceded by a preposition, and not immediately followed by a verb; *elle fallou contra mim*, he spoke against me.

6thly. When *o, a, os, as,* are joined to the present tense, infinitive mood, they change the last *r* of it into *lo, la,* &c., thus: *para ama-lo*, to love him; *para ve-la* or *ve-las*, to see her *or* them, &c.; and when they are joined to the preterperfect tense, indicative mood, of the verb *fazer*, and some others that have that tense ending in *iz;* they change the last *z* of them into *lo, la,* &c.; as, *fi-lo*, I did it; *elle fe-lo*, he did *or* made it, &c.: but when they are joined to the future tense, indicative mood, of any verb with the auxiliary verb *haver*, then they change the terminations *rei, rás,* &c., of the futures into *lo, la,*

SYNTAX OF PRONOUNS.

&c.; as, *fa-lo-hei*, I will do it; *ama-lo-hei*, I will love him, &c.*

REMARKS ON THE PRONOUNS.

1st. *Him* or *it*, which follows the verb in English, must be expressed in Portuguese as in the following examples:—

When *him* or *it* in English follows the verb in the first person of the singular number, it must be expressed in Portuguese by *o* before or after the verb. Example: I call him *or* it, *eu o chamo*.

When *him* or *it* in English follows the verb in the first person of the singular number, it may be expressed in Portuguese either by *o* before the verb, or after it, omitting the last consonant of the verb. Example: thou callest him *or* it, *tu o chamas*, or *cháma-lo-tu*.

When *him* or *it* is joined with the third person singular of a verb, it may be expressed by *o* before or after the verb. Example: he calls him *or* it, *elle o chama*, or *elle chama-o*.

When *him* or *it* is with a verb in the first person plural, it may be expressed in Portuguese either by *o* before the verb or *lo* after it; omitting the last consonant, as in the second case. Example: we call him *or* it, *nós o chamamos*, or *nós chamamo-lo*.

---

* In regard to all that is said concerning the change of terminations into *lo, la, los, las,* we beg to observe that the modern and best writing in such cases, where the relatives *o, a, os, as*, are to be appended to verbs ending in *r, s*, or *z*, is to change, for the sake of harmony, all those letters into *l*, and then add the relative, connecting by an -. The *l* being then but the substitute for those three letters is thus better placed where they stood: so the forms *chámal-o*, thou callest him *or* it; *fazel-a*, to make it; *fal-os*, makes them; *nomeail-as*, you name them, &c., are only better sounding transformations for *chámas-o, fazer-a, faz-os, nomeais-as*.

When *him* or *it* is after a verb in the second person plural, it is expressed in Portuguese either by *o* before the verb, or *lo* after it, omitting the last consonant, &c. Example: you call him *or* it, *vós o chamais*, or *vós chamai-lo*.

When *him* or *it* follows the verb in the third person plural, it may be expressed in Portuguese either by *o* before the verb, or *no* after it. Example: they call him *or* it, *elles o chamão*, or *elles chamão-no*.*

2ndly. *Her* or *it* after a verb in English is expressed in Portuguese by *a*, according to the rules given above.

3rdly. *Them* after a verb is expressed in Portuguese by *os* for the masculine, and by *as* for the feminine, according to the gender and the rules proposed.

4thly. The words *o, a, os, as*, must always be put after the gerunds, but not before the infinitives. Examples: seeing him, we must not say *o vendo*, but *vendo-o*, because *vendo* is a gerund.† To see him, instead of saying *para*

---

* Let the student remark that the *no, na, nos, nas*, in cases like this, are not the same as the combination of the preposition *em* with the articles, which assumes the like forms; the *n* is here employed only to avoid hiatus, nearly as the Greeks, for the same purpose, used sometimes their *ν*, corresponding to our *n*. The best writing, therefore, is that now used by some writers for the sake of distinction, of marking the *n* with an ', thus, *chamão-n'o*; or, as others do, isolating it by hyphens, thus, *chamão-n-o*, in like manner as the French add their *t* in *l'a-t-il vu?*

† When, however, *o, a, os, as*, and the gerund are to be used, preceded by the preposition *em*, in the acceptations of *as soon as, immediately after, the moment*, then those pronouns are placed before the gerund and after the said preposition: as, *em o vendo*, as soon as I (*or* thou, *or* he, *or* she, *or* you, *or* they) see (seest, sees, &c., *or* saw, sawest, &c., *or* have seen, hast seen, &c., *or* shall see, shalt see, &c., *or* shall have seen, &c.) him; *em a encontrando*, immediately after I (*or* thou, *or* he, &c.) meet (meetest, met, have met, shall meet, shall have met, &c.) her; *em os comendo*, the moment I (*or* thou, &c.) ate (*or* have eaten, shall eat, &c.) them.

ver-o, you must say *para o ver*, or *para vê-lo*, because it is in the infinitive.

5thly. The words *lo, la, los, las*, must always be put after the verbs. Example: to see him, you must say *para vel-o*, or *para o ver*, and not *para lo ver*. The same words must follow also the adverb *ei:* as, *ei-lo aqui*, here he is; *ei-lo ali*, there he is; *ei-las aqui*, here they are; *ei-la ali*, there she is; *ei-las ali*, there they are. They follow likewise the persons of the verbs: *eu fi-lo, tu fizeste-lo, elle fe-lo, nós fizemo-lo,* &c., I made it, &c.

I have been speaking of the words *o, a, os, as, lo, la, los, las*, and not of the articles, *o, a, os, as;* because when those words precede, and sometimes when they follow the verbs, they are not articles, but relative pronouns. They are articles only when they precede nouns or pronouns.

CHAPTER V.

OF THE SYNTAX OF VERBS.

THE verbs through every tense and mood (except the infinitive) ought to be preceded by a nominative case, either expressed or understood, with which they must agree in number and person. The nominative is expressed when we say *eu amo, tu cantas;* understood when we say *canto, digo,* &c.

The Portuguese, as well as English, use the second person plural, though they address themselves but to a single person.

EXAMPLES.

Meu amigo, vós não tendes razão, my friend, you are in the wrong.

And if we would speak in the third person, we must say, *vm^{ce} tem razão*, sir, you are in the right.

The verb active governs the accusative; as, *amo a virtude*, I love virtue.

The passive verb requires an ablative after it; as, *os doutos são envejados pelos ignorantes*, the learned are envied by the ignorant.

There is in Portuguese another way of making the passive, by adding the relative *se* to the third person singular or plural; as, *ama-se a Deus*, God is loved.

Where there are two nominatives singular before a verb, it must be put in the plural.

When a noun is collective, the verb requires the singular, not the plural; as, *a gente está olhando*, the people are looking.

SYNTAX OF THE AUXILIARY VERB.

The verb *ter* is made use of to conjugate all the compound tenses of verbs; as, *tenho amado, tinha amado*, I have loved, I had loved.

Ter signifies also to possess, to obtain; as, *tenho dinheiro*, I have money; *têm muita capacidade*, he has a great deal of capacity.

Haver, in account-books and trade, expresses credit, or discharge.

Haver is also taken impersonally in Portuguese, and signifies in English *there be;* as, *ha muito ouro no Mexico*, there is a great quantity of gold in Mexico.

Haver se, made reciprocal, is the same as *to behave, to*

act; as, *houve-se o governador com tal prudencia, que,* &c., the governor behaved with such wisdom, that, &c.

We have already observed the difference between *ser* and *estar*.

The verb *estar* is also used to conjugate the other verbs, chiefly expressing action; as, *estou lendo, estou escrevendo,* I am reading, I am writing.

Estar with the preposition *em,* in, or with *no, na, nos, nas,* signifies, *to be present in a place* ; as, *estou no campo,* I am in the country.

Estar with the preposition *para* denotes the inclination of doing what the following verb expresses, but without a full determination ; as, *estou para me ir para Londres,* I have a mind to go to London.

Estar with the preposition *por,* and the infinitive mood following, means, that the thing expressed by the verb is not yet done: as, *isto está por escrever,* this is not yet written ; *isto está por alimpar,* this is not yet cleaned. *Estar por alguem* signifies to agree with one, or to be of his opinion.

Note. See, in the Third Part, the different significations of the verbs *estar* and *haver.*

When *ser* signifies the possession of a thing, it governs the genitive: as, *a rua é d'el-rei,* the street belongs to the king ; *esta casa é de meu pai,* this house belongs to my father.

Em ser is taken for a thing to be whole or entire, without any alteration or mutilation ; as, *as fazendas estão em ser,* the goods are not sold.

OF THE SYNTAX OF VERBS ACTIVE, PASSIVE, ETC.

When two verbs come together, with or without any nominative case, then the latter must be in the infinitive mood; as, *quer vm^{ce} aprender a fallar o Inglez?* will you learn to speak English?

All verbs active govern the accusative; but if they are followed by a proper name of God, man, or women, or any noun expressing their qualities or title, then they govern the dative case: as, *conheço a seu pai*, I know his father; *Acharão a João no caminho*, they found John in the road.

All verbs of gesture, movement, going, remaining, or doing, as also the verbs that have the word that goes before and the word that comes after, both belonging to one thing, require the nominative after them: as, *Pedro vai errado*, Peter goes on wrong; *o pobre dorme descançado*, the poor sleep without care. Also the verb in the infinitive mood has the same case, when verbs of wishing and the like come after them: as, *todos dezejão ser ricos*, everybody wishes to be rich; *antes quisera ser douto que parecel-o*, I had rather be learned than be accounted so.

After verbs the Portuguese express *yes* and *no* by *que sim* and *que não*. Examples: *creio que sim*, I believe yes; *creio que não*, I believe not; *digo que sim*, I say yes; *cuido que não*, I think not; *aposto que sim*, I lay yes; *queireis apostar que não?* have you a mind to lay not?

Verbs signifying grief, compassion, want, remembrance, forgetting, &c., must have the genitive: as, *pêsa-me muito da morte de seu irmão*, I am very sorry for the death of your brother; *elle morre de fôme*, he perishes of hunger; *lembre-se do que me disse*, remember what you said to me; *compadeçi-me das suas desgraças;* I pitied him for his misfortunes; *esqueci-me de tudo isto*, all this I forgot.

The reciprocals of jeering, boasting, and distrusting, govern also the genitive; as, *jactar-se, gloriar-se, picar-se, envorgonhar-se*, &c.

All verbs active govern the dative when the substantive represents a person; as, *eu conheço a vm^{ce}*, &c., I know you, &c.

The following verbs belong to this rule :—

Jogar, to play: as, *jogar as cartas*, to play at cards; *jogar aos centos*, to play at piquet; *jogar ao xadrez*, to play at chess, &c.

Obedecer, desobedecer, agradar, comprazer: as, *eu obedeço a Deus e a el-rei*, I obey God and the king; *comprazeó em tudo aos soldados*, in all he pleased the soldiers.

Mandar, when it signifies to command an army, company, &c., requires the accusative, but, when anything else, the dative: as, *elle mandava a cavallaria*, he commanded the horse; *o governador mandou a todos os moradores que se retirassem para suas casas*, the governor ordered all the inhabitants to retire into their houses.

Ir, to go; as, *vou a Paris*, I go to Paris.

Assistir, ajudar, soccorrer, to help; *assistir ao officio divino*, to assist at divine service.

Saudar, to salute *or* greet; as, *elle sauda a todos*, he salutes everybody.

Fallar, to speak; *satizfazer*, to satisfy; *servir*, to serve; *favorecer*, to favour; *ameaçar*, to threaten.

The verbs of pleasing, displeasing, granting, denying, pardoning, govern the dative case.

The impersonals *acontecer, succeder, importar, pertencer*, and the like to these, often have two personal datives: as, *a mim me succedeo*, it happened to me; *a elle lhe convom*, it suits him, or it is convenient for him; *a elle não lhe importa*, it does not concern him, &c.

All active verbs require the accusative; and the Latin verbs which govern the accusative of the thing, and the dative of the person, govern generally the same in Portuguese: as, *escreve o que digo a teu irmão*, write to your brother what I say.

Verbs of asking, teaching, arraying, must have an

accusative of the doer or sufferer, and sometimes neuter verbs will have an accusative of the thing: as, *gozar saude,* to enjoy health; *peço este favor,* I ask this favour; *elle toca muito bem a flauta,* he plays very well on the flute; *curar uma doença,* to cure a sickness.

Passive verbs, and the greatest part of the reciprocal verbs, require the ablative, with, *de, do, da, dos, das, por,* or *pelo, pela, pelos, pelas:* as, *fui chamado por el-rei,* I was called by the king; *reterei-me da cidade,* I retired from the city; *elle foi amado do povo,* he was loved by the people. Except *acostar-se,* which requires a dative, preceded by *a ; encostar-se,* which sometimes will have a dative and sometimes an ablative, preceded by *em, no, na, nos,* or *nas ; meter-se, sentar-se, introduzir-se,* &c., which must have the ablative with the preposition *em, no, na, nos, nas.*

Verbs joined to a noun which they govern must have the infinitive with *de ;* as, *tenho vontade de rir,* I am inclined to laugh.

The price of anything bought, or sold, or bartered, must have the accusative with *por.*

The verb *pôr-se,* when it signifies *to begin,* requires the infinitive, with the particle *a ;* as, *pôr-se a chorar,* to begin to cry.

Verbs of plenty, filling, emptying, loading, unloading, require the ablative: as, *esta terra abunda de trigo,* this country abounds with corn; *elle está carregado de miserias,* he is loaded with calamities.

Verbs denoting custom, help, beginning, exhortation, invitation, require the infinitive with the particle *a :* as, *ajudar a semear,* to help to sow; *convidou-me a cear,* he invited me to supper.

Verbs that signify distance, receiving, or taking away, will have the ablative; as, *a Madeira dista de Marrocos* 320 *milhas,* Madeira lies 320 miles from Morocco

SYNTAX OF VERBS. 169

Verbs signifying receiving, or taking away, generally require the ablative of the person; but they sometimes require an accusative, particularly the verb *receber*, when it signifies *to welcome* or *to entertain*: as, *elle recebe todos com muito agrado*, he gives his company a hearty reception, he makes them very welcome.

Verbs denoting obligation govern the infinitive with the preposition *a;* as, *eu o obrigarei a fazer isto*, I will oblige him to do it.

Verbs of arguing, quarrelling, fighting, &c., must have the ablative with *com;* as, *pelejou mais de uma hora com seu irmão*, he quarrelled more than one hour with his brother.

After the verb *ser*, to be, *para* is made use of as well as *a*: the first is employed to denote the use or destination of anything; as, *esta penna é para escrever*, this pen is to write with. But the particle *a* is used to denote only the action; as, *elle foi o primeiro a fugir*, he was the first to run away.

Verbs of motion to a place always govern the dative; as, *vou á comedia*, I go to the play; though the verb *voltar*, to return, may also have an accusative, with the preposition *para*. But verbs of motion from a place govern the ablative with, *de, do, da, dos, das;* as, *venho do campo*, I come from the country. If the motion is through a place, then they govern the accusative, with *por;* as, *passarei por Londres*, I will come by the way of London.

OF THE USE AND CONSTRUCTION OF THE TENSES.

Although I have spoken at large upon the tenses in the First Part, I would further observe—

1. That the infinitive of the auxiliary verb *haver* is

used together with the pronouns *lo, la, los, las,* instead of the future indicative ; as, *ouvil-o-hei,* I will hear him : and then the *r* of the infinitive is changed into *lo, la, los, las.**
Sometimes the infinitive of the auxiliary verb *haver* is used with the pronouns conjunctive, *me, te, se,* &c., instead of the same future : as, *dar-lhe-hei,* I will give him ; *enfadar-se-ha,* he will be angry.

2. That when we find the particle *if,* which in Portuguese is expressed by *se,* before the imperfect indicative, we must generally use the imperfect subjunctive in Portuguese. Examples : *se eu tivesse,* if I had ; *se eu pudesse,* if I could. But sometimes the imperfect indicative is used ; as, *disse-lhe que se queria,* &c., he told him that if he was willing, &c.

3. That the first imperfect subjunctive in Portuguese is also used in a sense that denotes the present, especially in sentences of wishing ; as, *quizera que Domingo fizesse bom tempo,* I wish it would be fine weather on Sunday. But if the same tense is preceded by *ainda que,* although, then it must be rendered into Portuguese by the second imperfect subjunctive, or by the imperfect indicative ; as, *eu não a quizera, ainda que ella tivesse milhoens de seu,* though she were worth several millions, I would not have her ; *ainda que elle consentisse n'isso, não se podia fazer,* although he would consent to it that could not be done. Lastly, when the first imperfect subjunctive is preceded by *se,* it is sometimes rendered into Portuguese by the second imperfect subjunctive ; as, *se elle viesse,* if he should come.

The English are apt to put the first imperfect of the subjunctive where the Portuguese make use of the second ;

---

* At present the form used in such cases is to change the final *r* of the verb into *l,* and add the articles or pronouns, *o, a, os, as* &c., connecting them by an -, so, *ouvil-o-hei,* &c.

as, I had been in the wrong, *não teria tido razão :* and though they may say, *não tivera tido razão,* they may not say, *não tivesse tido razão,* to express the English of *I should have been in the wrong,* or *I had been in the wrong.*

Note, that to express in Portuguese, *though that should be,* we must say *quando isso fosse,* and not *seria.*

The Portuguese use the future tense subjunctive after the conjunction *if,* when they speak of a future action, but the English, the present indicative. Examples : to-morrow, if I have time, *amanhã se tiver tempo,* and not *se tenho ;* if he come we shall see him, *nós o veremos se elle vier.*

A conjunction between two verbs makes the last of the same number, person, and tense as the first. Examples : the king wishes and commands, *el-rei quer e ordena ;* I see and I know, *eu vejo e conheço.*

Sometimes the present is made use of instead of the preterdefinite in narrations ; as, *ao mesmo tempo que hia andando o encontra, o despoja, e o ata a uma arvore,* as he was going, he meets him, strips him, and ties him to a tree.

When the Portuguese use the infinitive with the third person plural, they add *em* to it, and it is generally preceded by *por,* for, and *para,* in order to, that, *or* to the end that : as, *elles forão enforcados por furtarem,* they were hanged for robbing ; *para serem informados,* to the end that they may be informed ; *para poderem dizer,* that they may be able to say.

Observe that when the Portuguese put *por* before the first future subjunctive, they speak of a time past ; as, *por fallardes,* because you have spoken. But when they put *para* before it, then they speak of a time to come ; as, *para fallarmos,* to give us an opportunity for speaking, in order to speak.

OF MOODS.

All the tenses of the indicative mood may be employed without any conjunction before them; although they admit of some. Besides the conjunction *que*, those that may be made use of are *se, como*, and *quando;* with some distinction in respect to *se*, because this conjunction is seldom used before the future tense, and then it is governed by a verb signifying ignorance, doubt, or interrogation: as, *não sei se hão de vir*, I do not know whether they will come; *estou em duvida, se os inimigos passarão o rio*, I doubt whether the enemy will pass the river; *não pergunto se partirá*, I do not ask whether he will set out.

The optative or subjunctive in Portuguese has always some sign annexed: as, *oxalá, prouvera a Deus, ó se!* would to God, God grant, &c.; *que para, que*, &c., that, &c.

The particle *que* is not expressed in the present tense of this mood, but it is understood in sentences of wishing or praying; as, *Deus o faça bom*, let God amend him.

When *que* is between two verbs, the last is not always put in the subjunctive, because, though some say, *créio que venha*, I believe he comes, I think it is better to say, *creio que vem;* but when there is a negative, the verb following *que* must be put in the subjunctive: as, *não creio que venha*, I do not believe he will come; *não creio que venha tão cedo*, I do not believe he will come so soon.

When the verbs *crer*, to believe, *saber*, to know, are use interrogatively, and followed by the particle *que*, the next verb is put in the indicative, when the person who asks the question makes no doubt of the thing which is the object of the question; as if, knowing that peace is made, I want to know if the people whom I converse with know it too, I should express myself thus: *sabeis vós que está feita a paz?* do you know that peace is made? But if I have it only by a report, and doubt of it, and want to be informed of it, I must ask the question thus: *sabeis vós que a paz esteja feita?* and not *sabeis vós que está feita a paz?*

Observe also, that the present subjunctive of *saber* is elegantly used when it is attended by a negative and the particle *que* in this phrase, *não, que eu saiba,* not that I know of.

All the verbs used impersonally with the particle *que* require the subjunctive: as, *é preciso que elle venha,* he must come; *convem que isto se faça,* it is convenient that this be done. You must only except such sentences as express any positive assurance, or certainty; as, *é certo que vem,* it is certain that he comes; *sei que está em casa,* I know he is at home.

From these observations it follows that all the verbs not expressing a positive assurance, or believing, but only denoting *ignorance, doubt, fear, astonishment, admiration, wishing, praying, pretension,* or *desire,* govern the subjunctive mood after *que*: as, *duvido que possa,* I doubt if it be in his power; *temo que morra,* I am afraid he will die; *admiro-me que consinta n'isso,* I wonder he agrees to it, &c.; to all which they add *oxalá,** signifying *God grant,* which is used in Portuguese before all the tenses of the optative or conjunctive, as well as *praza a Deus,* may it please God, or *prouvera a Deus,* might it please God.

When *que* is relative, and there is a verb in the imperative or in the indicative, with a negative or interrogation before it, it likewise governs the subjunctive: as, *não ha cousa que mais me inquiete,* there is nothing that disturbs me more; *ha cousa no mundo que me possa dar tanto gosto?* is there anything in the world that could give me more pleasure? *allegai-lhe tantas razoens que o possão per-*

* An Arabic word derived from *Oh, Allah!*

suadir, give him so many reasons that he may be persuaded.

The present subjunctive is sometimes rendered into English by the second pretcrimperfect subjunctive, when it is followed by a verb in the future tense; as, *ainda que eu trabalhe, nunca hei de me cançar*, though I should work, I never should be tired.

The Portuguese use specially the same present subjunctive for the future; as in those sentences and others, like:—

Não duvido que venha, I do not doubt but he will come.

Duvido que o faça, I doubt that, *or* whether he will do it.

Therefore carefully avoid those faults which foreigners are so apt to make, in considering rather the tense which they want to turn into Portuguese, than the mood which the genius of the language requires.

The present indicative is also used for the future, the same as in English. Example: *jantais hoje em casa?* do you dine at home to-day?

OF THE PARTICLES GOVERNING THE OPTATIVE OR SUBJUNCTIVE.

The conjunction *que*, that, generally requires the subjunctive after it; but *antes que, primeiro que*, before that, always require it.

Que makes all the words to which it is joined become conjunctives; as, *para que*, to the end that; *bem que, ainda que*, &c. *Posto que*, although; *até que*, till; *quando, como quer que*, commonly govern the subjunctive. But *com que assim* governs the indicative; as, *com que* or *com que assim virá amanhã*, so he will come to-morrow.

In Portuguese, to express *though* or *although*, if it is by *ainda que,* you may put either the subjunctive or indicative after it. Examples: *ainda que seja homem honrado,* though he is an honest man; *ainda que elle faz aquillo,* though he does that. But if you render *although* or *though* by *não obstante,* then you must use the infinitive. Examples: though he is an honest man, *não obstante ser elle homem honrado;* though he does this, *não obstante fazer elle isto.*

The impersonal verbs generally govern the subjunctive with *que;* but with this distinction, when the impersonal is in the present tense, or future, of the indicative mood, then it requires the present subjunctive mood: but when the impersonal, or any other verb taken impersonally, is in any of the preterites indicative, then it governs the imperfect, perfect, or pluperfect of the subjunctive, according to the meaning of the sentence; as, *importa muito que el-rei veja tudo,* it is of great moment that the king may see all; *foi conveniente que o principe fosse com elle,* it was convenient that the prince should go with him.

The present subjunctive is likewise construed when the particle *por* is separated from *que* by an adjective; as, *por grande, por admiravel, por douto que seja,* though he be great, admirable, learned.

An imperative often requires the future of the subjunctive; as, *succeda o que succeder,* or *seja o que fôr,* happen what may.

The imperfect subjunctive is repeated in this phrase, and others, like *succedesse, o que succedesse,* happen what may.

The future of the subjunctive mood follows generally these, *logo que, quando, se, como,* &c.: as, *logo que chegar iremos a passeiar,* as soon as he comes, we will go and take a walk; *quando viér estaremos promptos,* when he comes we shall be ready.

Observe, that *quando* and *logo que* may also be construed with the indicative mood: as, *quando el-rei vê tudo não o enganão,* when the king sees everything, he is not deceived; *logo que chegou, fallei com elle,* as soon as he came, I spoke with him.

OF THE INFINITIVE MOOD.

In Portuguese there is not a general sign before the infinitive, as in English the particle *to;* but there are several particles used before the infinitive, denoting the same as *to* does in English, and they are governed by the preceding verbs or nouns. These particles are the following: *a, para, de, com, em, por, até, depois de;* and the article *o,* when the infinitive serves as a nominative to another verb; as, *o dizer e o fazer são duas coisas,* saying and doing are two different things.

A coming between two verbs denotes the second as the object of the first: as, *a tardança das nossas esperanças nos ensina a modificar os nossos dezejos,* the delay of our hopes teaches us to modify our desires; *elle começa a discorrer,* he begins to reason.

Para denotes the intention or usefulness; as, *a adversidade serve para experimentar a paciencia,* adversity serves to try one's patience. *Para* after an adjective denotes its object; as, *está prompto para obedecer,* he is ready to obey.

De is put between two verbs, if the first governs the genitive or ablative; and when the substantive or adjective governs either of these two cases, *de* must go before the following verbs, or infinitive: as, *venho de ver a meu pai,* I have just seen my father; *é tempo de hir-se,* it is time to go away; *el-rei foi servido de mandar,* the king has been pleased to order.

The infinitive is on several occasions governed by prepositions or conjunctions; as, *sem dizer palavra*, without speaking a word; where you may observe it is expressed in English by the participle present: as, *nunca se cança de jogar*, he is never weary of playing; *diverte-se em caçar*, he delights in hunting; *elle está dôente por trabalhar demasiado*, by working too much he is sick; *perde o seu tempo em passeiar*, he loses his time in walking; *hei-de ir-me sem me despedir?* shall I go away without taking my leave?

The infinitive is also used passively; as, *não ha que dizer, que ver*, &c., there is nothing to be said, seen, &c.

The gerund of any verb active may be conjugated with the verb *estar*, to be, after the same manner as in English: as, *estou escrevendo*, I am writing; *elle estava dormindo*, he was asleep, &c.

CHAPTER VI.

OF THE SYNTAX OF PARTICIPLES AND GERUNDS.

THE participle in the Portuguese language generally ends in *do* or *to*; as, *amado, visto, dito*, &c.

The active participles that follow the verb *ter*, to have, must end in *o*; as,

Tenho visto el-rei, I have seen the king.
Tenho visto a rainha, I have seen the queen.
Eu tinha amado os livros, I had loved books.
Eu tinha levado as cartas, I had carried the letters.

We meet with authors who sometimes make the parti-

ciples agree with the thing of which they are speaking;
as, in *Camoens*, canto 1, stanza xxix. :

> *E porque como vistes, tem* passados.
> *Na viagem tão asperos perigos,*
> *Tantos climas e céos* exprimentados, &c.

And canto 2, stanza lxxvi. :

> *São offerecimentos verdadeiros,*
> *E palavras sinceras não dobradas,*
> *As que o rei manda aos nobres cavaleiros,*
> *Que tanto mar e terras tem* passadas.

If it be a neuter verb, the participle ought always to end in *o*. Example:

El-rei tem jantado, the king has dined; *a rainha tem céado*, the queen has supped; *os vossos amigos tem rido*, your friends have laughed; *minhas irmãs tem dormido*, my sisters have slept.

When the active participle appears to precede an infinitive, it must be terminated in *o*; as, *o juiz lhe tinha feito cortar a cabeça*, the judge has caused his head to be cut off.

The passive participles which are joined with the tenses of the verb *ser*, to be, agree with the substantive that precedes the verb *ser*; as, *o capitão foi louvado*, the captain was praised; *a virtude é estimada*, virtue is esteemed; *os preguiçosos são censurados*, the lazy are blamed; *as vossas joias forão vendidas*, your jewels were sold.

The Portuguese generally suppress the gerunds *having* and *being* before the particles: as, *dito isto*, having said so; *acabado o sermão*, the sermon being ended. This manner of speaking is called by grammarians the ablative absolute.

The participle of the present tense in Portuguese has

singular and plural, but one termination serves for both genders: as, *um homem temente a Deus*, a man fearing God; *uma mulher temente a Deus*, a woman fearing God; *homens tementes a Deus*, a people fearing God.

There are many participles which are used substantively; as, *ignorante, amante, ouvinte, estudante,* &c., an ignorant, a lover, an auditor or hearer, a scholar, &c.

It is better to place the nominative after the gerund than before; as, *estando el-rei na comedia*, the king being at the play.

CHAPTER VII.

OF PREPOSITIONS.

I. A PREPOSITION is a part of speech which is put before nouns, and sometimes before verbs, to explain some particular circumstance.

Prepositions may be divided into separable and inseparable. An inseparable preposition is never found but in compound words, and signifies nothing of itself. A separable preposition is generally separated from other words, and signifies something of itself.

The inseparable prepositions are:

Ab and *abs;* as, *abrogar*, to abrogate; *abster-se*, to abstain.

Arce, or *archi;* as, *arcebispo*, an archbishop; *archiduque*, an archduke.

Ad; as, *adventicio*, adventitious.

Am; as, *ambiguo*, ambiguous; *amparo*, protection, shelter.

Circum; as, *circumstancia,* circumstance.

Co; as *cohabitar,* to live together, to cohabit.

Des serves to express the contrary of the word it is joined to; as, *desacerto,* mistake; *desfazer,* to undo; *desenganar,* to undeceive, are the contrary of *acerto, fazer,* and *enganar.*

Dis; as, *dispôr,* to dispose; *distinguir,* to distinguish; *distribuir,* to distribute.

Ex; as, *extrahir,* to extract.

In has commonly a negative or privative sense, denoting the contrary of the meaning of the word it precedes; as, *incapaz,* unable; *infeliz,* unhappy; *inacção,* inaction, &c.: but sometimes it is affirmative, as in Latin.

Observe that *in* before *r* is changed into *ir;* as, *irregular,* irregular, *irracional,* irrational: before *l* into *il;* as *illegitimo,* illegitimate: before *m, in* is changed into *im;* as *immaterial,* immaterial.

Ob; as, *obviar,* to obviate.

Pos; as, *pospôr,* to postpone.

Pre; as, *preceder,* to go before; *predecessor,* an ancestor.

Pro; as, *propôr,* to propose; *prometter,* to promise.

Re is a particle borrowed from the Latin, which generally denotes iteration, or backward action: as, *reedificar,* to rebuild; *repercutir,* to strike back.

So; as *socorrer,* to help, to succour.

Sor; as *sorrir,* to smile.

Sos; as, *soster,* to support.

Soto; as, *sotopôr,* to put or lay under.

Sub or *sob;* as, *subalterno,* subaltern; *subscrever,* to subscribe; *sobpena, sobcolor,* &c.

The Arabic article *al,* which is common to all genders and both numbers, is found in the beginning of almost all the words that remain in the Portuguese language from the Arabic, and it is the surest way to distinguish them. But the Portuguese articles are added to the Arabic nouns, without taking off their article, *al*: as, *a almofada*, the cushion; *o Alcorão*, the Koran, &c.

The Greek preposition *anti* enters into the composition of a great many Portuguese words, which cannot be set down here. It is enough to observe that it signifies generally opposite; as in *Antipodas*, Antipodes; *antipapa*, anti-pope. And sometimes it signifies before; as in *antiloquio*, a preface, introductory remarks; but in this last sense it is derived from the Latin preposition *ante*.

OF SEPARABLE PREPOSITIONS.

II. It is absolutely impossible ever to attain to the knowledge of any language whatever, without thoroughly understanding the various relations denoted by the prepositions, and the several cases of nouns which they govern; both which relations and cases being arbitrary, vary and differ much in all languages. This only instance will evince it: the English say, *to think of a thing;* the French, *to think to a thing;* the Germans and Dutch, *to think on* or *upon a thing;* the Spaniards and Portuguese, *to think in a thing*, &c. Now, it will avail an Englishman but little to know that *of* is expressed in Portuguese by *de*, if he does not know what relations *em* and *de* denote in the language; since the Portuguese say, to think *in* a think, and not *of* a thing: therefore we will treat here of each of them, and of their construction separately.

1st. *A*, or rather *ao, ás, aos* (at, in, on, &c.), deno the place whither one is going; as,

Eu vou a Londres, I go to London.

Voltar a Portugal, to return or go to Portugal.

A, in this sense, is a preposition, but in the following observations it is a particle.

2ndly. *A* denotes time: as, *chegar a tempo,* to arrive in time; *a todo hora,* at all hours.

3rdly. *A* denotes the mode of being or of doing of people; as also their posture, gesture, or action: as,

Estar á sua vontade, to be at one's ease.

A direita, on the right hand; *á esquerda,* on the left hand.

Viver á sua vontade to live to one's mind, as one likes.

Andar a pé, ou a cavallo, to go on foot or on horseback.

Montar a cavállo, to ride on horseback.

Correr á redea sôlta, to ride full speed.

Trajar á Franceza, to dress after the French mode.

Viver á Ingleza, to live after the English fashion.

Andar a grandes passos, to walk at a great rate.

Andar a passos lentos, to walk very slowly.

4thly. *A* denotes the price of things; as, *a oito xelins* at eight shillings. It denotes also the weight: but as the nouns signifying weight are generally used in the plural number, *s* is added to *a*, when it is placed before nouns of the feminine gender, and *os* when it precedes nouns of the masculine gender: thus, *ás onças,* by the ounce; *aos arrateis,* by the pound, &c. *A* denotes also the measure: as, *medir a palmos,* to span or measure by the hand extended.

When *a* is preceded by *d'aqui,* and followed by a noun of time, it denotes the space of time after which something is to be done; as, *el-rei partirá d'aqui a tres dias,* the king will set out three days hence.

5thly. *A* denotes the tools used in working, as likewise the games one plays at: as, *abrir ao buril*, to grave: where *o* is added to *a;* *trabalhar á candea,* to do anything by candle-light; *á agulha*, with the needle.

Andar á vela, to sail *or* to be under sail.

Jogar a pella, to play at tennis.

Jogar as cartas, to play at cards; here *s* is added to *a;* the noun being of the feminine gender and plural number.

Jogar aos centos, to play at piquet; here *os* is added to *a*, as preceding a noun signifying a game, of the masculine gender and plural number.

6thly. *A* signifies sometimes *as*. Example: *está isto a seu gosto?* is this as you like it? And sometimes it signifies *after:* as, *a seu modo*, after his *or* her way. It signifies also *in;* as, *ao principio*, in the beginning; but then *o* is added to it.

7thly. *A* is also put before infinitives, preceded by another verb; as, *ensinar a cantar*, to teach to sing. It is also placed between two equal numbers, to denote order; as, *dois a dois*, two by two; *quatro a quatro*, four by four: and sometimes it is preceded by a participle or adjective, and followed by an infinitive mood.

8thly. *A* is a particle of composition, with many nouns, verbs, and adverbs, of which it often increases the meaning; as, *adinheirado*, very rich, that has a great deal of money: but it generally expresses in verbs the action of the nouns they are composed of; as, *ajoelhar*, to kneel down, which is formed from *a* and *joelho*, knee; *abrandar*, to appease; *alargar*, to enlarge; from *brando*, soft; *largo*, wide, &c.

9thly. *A*, when it is preceded by the verb *ser*, and followed by the personal pronouns, signifies *in the stead of;* as, *se eu fosse a vós, faria aquillo*, if I were you (in your place), I would do that.

10thly. When *a* is placed before *casa*, and the sense implies *going to*, it is rendered into English by *to*, but the word *casa* is left out; as, *elle foi á casa do governador*, he went to the governor's. You must observe that *a* in this sense is a preposition.

11thly. *Ao pé* signifies *near;* as, *ponde um ao pé do outro*, place, put, or set them near one another. Sometimes *mesmo* comes before *ao pé*, to express still more the nearness of a thing, and *mesmo ao pé* is rendered into English by *hard by, just by*, &c.; as, *a sua casa está mesmo ao pé da minha*, his house is just by mine.

12thly. When the noun *respeito* is preceded by *a* it is used in the same sense as *em comparação*, but requires one of these particles, *do, da, dos, das*, after it, and signifies *in comparison of, in regard to, in respect of;* as, *isto é nada a respeito do que posso dizer*, this is nothing to other things that I can say.

13thly. When *a* comes before a neuter verb, it marks a dative; and after an active verb, an accusative case.

A before the word *proposito* is used in familiar discourse; as, *a proposito, esquecime de dizer-vos o outro dia*, now I think of it, I forgot to tell you the other day.

14thly. *Ao revez*, or *ás avessas*, are also used as prepositions, attended by *de, do, da*, &c., and it signifies *quite the reverse*, or *contrary;* as, *elle faz tudo ao revez*, or *ás avessas, do que houvera de ser, ou do que lhe dizem*, he does everything quite the reverse of right, or contrary to what he is bid.

15thly. *A* before *troco* signifies *provided that*. It is also used before the word *tiro;* as, *a tiro de peça*, within cannon-shot.

16thly. *Cara a cara, corpo a corpo*, signify face to face, body to body. *Tomar uma cousa a boa ou a má parte*, signifies *to take a thing well or ill*.

Such are the chief relations denoted by the particle *a*, The others must be learned in construing and reading good Portuguese books.

1st. *De*, or rather *do, da, dos, das* (of, from, &c.) denote, first, the place one comes from: as, *sahir de Londres*, to go out of London; *vir de França, das Indias*, &c., to come from France, from the Indies, &c.

2nd. *De* between two nouns denotes the quality of the person expressed by the first noun; as, *um homem de honra*, a man of honour: or the matter which the thing of the first noun is made of; as,

Uma estatua de marmore, a statue of marble.

Uma ponte de madeira ou de pedra, a wood or stone bridge.

Observe, that two nouns so joined with *de* are commonly rendered into English by two nouns likewise, but without a preposition, or rather by a compound word, whose first noun (whether substantive or adjective) expresses the matter and quality, manner, form, and use of the other: as, a stone bridge, *uma ponte de pedra*; a dancing-master, *um mestre de dança*.

3rd. *De, do, da, dos, das*, are used after the participles of the preterite, with *ser*; as, *ser amado, ou bem visto do povo, dos sabios*, &c., to be loved by the people, by the learned, &c.

Do serves for the masculine, *da* for the feminine, and *de* for both.

4th. *De* sometimes signifies *by*; as, *de noite*, by night; *de dia*, by day.

5th. *De* before *em* and many nouns of time denotes the regular interval of the time after which something begins again; as, *eu vou vel-o de dois em dois dias*, I go to see him every other day: and before nouns of place and adverbs repeated with *em* or *para* between, *de* denotes the passing from one place or condition to another; as, *correr de rua em rua*, to run from street to street; *de mal para peor*, from bad to worse.

6th. *De* after some verbs signifies *after* or *in;* as, *elle portou-se d'esta sorte*, he behaved in *or* after this manner.

7th. *De* is used before an infinitive, and is then governed by some preceding noun and verb: as, *capaz de ensinar*, capable of teaching; *digno de ser amado*, worthy to be loved, &c.; *procurar de fazer*, to endeavour to do; *authoridade de prégar*, the power *or* authority of preaching, &c.

8th. *De* is sometimes rendered into English by *on;* as, *pôr-se de joelhos*, to kneel down on one's knees.

9th. *De* between two nouns denotes the use which a thing is designed for: as, *azeite de candea*, lamp-oil; *arma de fogo*, a fire-arm; *moinho de vento*, a windmill.

This relation is expressed in English by two nouns, making a compound word; the first of which signifies the manner, form, and use, denoted by the Portuguese preposition: as, *cadeira de braços*, an arm-chair *or* elbow-chair; *vela de cera*, a wax-candle, &c.

10th. *De* denotes sometimes the qualities of things; as, *meias de tres fios*, stockings with three threads. Sometimes it denotes also the price; as, *panno de dezoito xelins*, eighteen-shilling cloth.

11th. *De* is sometimes rendered into English by *upon;* as, *viver* or *sustentar-se de peixe*, to live upon fish. Sometimes it is rendered into English by *with;* as, *morrer de frio*, to starve with cold.

12th. *De* sometimes signifies *for* or *out of;* as, *saltar de alegria*, to leap for joy; *de modesto*, out of modesty.

13th. *De* signifies sometimes *at;* as, *zombar de alguem*, laugh at one.

14th. *De* is sometimes left out in English; as, *gozar de uma cousa*, to enjoy a thing.

15th. *De*, followed by two nouns of number and the preposition *até* between them, is rendered into English by *between;* as, *um homem de quarenta até cincoenta annos*, a man between forty and fifty.

16th. *De*, preceded by the preposition *diante*, is left out in English: as, *diante de mim*, before me; *diante de Deus*, before God.

17th. *De*, when it is placed before *casa*, and the sense implies *coming from*, is rendered into English by *from;* but the word *casa* sometimes is left out in English, and sometimes not; as, *venho de casa* (meaning my house), I come from home, from my house: but *venho da casa da Senhora C.* must be rendered into English thus, *I come from Mrs. C.'s.*

Finally, *de* is used before several words: as, *de bruços*, lying all along on the ground; *de madrugada*, early in the morning; *de veras*, in earnest, seriously; *de verão*, in summer; *homem de palavra*, a man as good as his word; *de costas*, backwards, *or* on one's back; *andar de pé*, to be sickly without being bed-ridden; and many others which must be learned by use.

ANTES.

III. *Antes*, before, shows a relation of time, of which it denotes priority; and is always opposite to *depois*, after; as, *antes da creação do mundo*, before the creation of the world.

Primeiro is also used as a preposition; as, *elle chegou primeiro que eu*, he arrived here before me.

DIANTE.

IV. *Diante*, before, shows a relation of place, and it is always opposite to *detraz*, behind. It signifies also sometimes *em* or *na presença* : as, *ha arvores diante de sua casa*, there are trees before his house ; *ponde aquillo diante do fogo*, set *or* put that before the fire ; *prégar diante d'el-rei*, to preach before the king.

Diante is also sometimes an adverb, and may be used instead of *adiante ;* as, *ir diante*, or *adiante*, to go before ; but in the following phrase you must say, *não vades tão adiante*, and not *diante*, do not go so far ; *por diante* is to be rendered into English by *on* in the following phrase, *ide por diante*, go on.

DEPOIS.

V. *Depois*, after, denotes posteriority of time, and is used in opposition to *antes* : as, *depois do diluvio*, after the deluge ; *depois do meio dia*, afternoon.

Depois is also used with an infinitive ; as, *feito aquillo*, or *tendo feito aquillo*, or *depois de fazer aquillo*, after having done that : and it is also made a conjunction with *que*, governing the indicative ; as, *depois que teve feito aquillo*, after he had done that.

DETRAZ.

VI. *Detraz*, behind, denotes posteriority both of place and order, and it is said in opposition to *diante* : as, *a sua casa está detraz da vossa*, his house is behind yours ; *elle vinha detraz de mim*, he walked after me.

EM.

VII. *Em*, or *no, na, nos, nas* (in, into, within, &c.), denote a relation both of time and place. The many various significations in which these prepositions are used must be accurately observed, and much regard had to them in practice.

No and *na* are sometimes rendered into English by *a ;* as, *duas vezes no dia, na semana*, &c., twice a-day, a-week, &c.

No, na, &c., are always used before nouns denoting the place wherein something is kept; as, *está no gabinete*, it is in the closet; *na papeleira*, in the bureau; *nas gavetas*, in the drawers; *na rua*, in the street, &c.; but sometimes they are rendered into English by *upon ;* as, *cahir no chão*, to fall upon the ground.

Em, no, na, &c., signify commonly *in ;* as, *em Londres*, in London; *está na graça d'el-rei*, he is in favour with the king: but in some cases it has a very particular meaning; as, *estar em corpo*, which signifies literally *to be in body*, but the true sense of it is *to be without a cloak*, so that the body is more exposed to view without an upper garment. *Estar em pernas*, litterally *to be in legs*, signifies *to be bare legged ;* that is, the legs exposed without stockings. *Estar em camisa* is said of one that has only the shirt on his back.

When this preposition *em* is before an infinitive, then it is an English gerund; as, *consiste em fallar bem*, it consists in speaking well: but when it is found before a gerund, it signifies *as soon as ;* as, *em acabando irei*, as soon as I have done, I will go.

Nos nossos tempos is rendered into English by *now-a-days*.

Em is used in sentences that imply a general sense; as, *elle está em miseravel estado*, he is in a wretched condition; and not, *no miseravel :* but if the sentence implies a particular sense, you must make use of *no, na,* &c.; as, *no miseravel estado em que elle está*, in the wretched condition wherein he is; and not *em miseravel*. You must observe in this last example and the like, that *em* is to be used before *que*, and not *no, na*, &c., which are to be placed only before *qual :* therefore you must not say, *no miseravel estado no que elle está ;* but *no miseravel estado no qual elle está*.

Em, construed with pronouns without an article, makes a sort of adverb, rendered into English by a preposition and a noun; thus, in this sentence, *nós iremos em coche*, we shall go in a coach, *em coche* is an adverb of manner, which shows how we shall go; but *no coche* denotes something besides: as, if a company were considering how they shall ride to a place, somebody would say, *vós ireis na cadeirinha, e nós no coche*, you shall go in a chair, and we in a coach; *no coche* would be said in opposition to *na cadeirinha*, and both respectively to some specified chair and coach; or else they should say, *vós ireis em cadeirinha, e nós em coche*. But in this other sentence, *eu deixei o meu chapeo no coche*, I left my hat in the coach, it would be improper to say *em coche*, because some particular coach is meant, and that which has driven me here or there, or which has been spoken of.

We say *de verão, no verão*, or *em o verão; de inverno, no inverno*, &c., in summer, in winter, &c.

Em is also rendered into English by *at;* as, *em todo tempo*, at all times.

Em is used, and never *no, na*, &c., before proper names of cities and authors: as, *elle está em Londres*, he is in London; *nós lêmos em Cicero*, we read in Cicero. But they say, *no Porto*, in Oporto.

Em, and *no, na*, &c., are construed with the names of kingdoms; as, *em* or *na Inglaterra*, in England: but *no, na*, is most commonly construed with names of provinces; as, *no Alentejo, na Beira*, &c., in Alentejo, in Beira, &c.

Em is sometimes rendered into English by *into;* as, *Narciso foi transformado em flor*, Narcissus was metamorphosed into a flower: and sometimes by *to;* as, *de rua em rua*, from street to street.

No, na, are sometimes rendered into English by

against; as, *dar com a cabeça na parede,* to dash one's head against the wall.

No, na, &c., are also rendered into English by *in,* and sometimes by *into;* as, *ter um menino nos braços,* to hold a child in one's arms; *entregar alguma coisa nas mãos de alguem,* to deliver a thing into somebody's hands.

Em is used before the word *travez;* as in this phrase, *pôr-se de mal em travez com alguem,* to fall out together.

Em, before a noun of time, denotes the space of time that elapses in doing something; as, *el-rei foi a Hanover em tres dias,* the king went to Hanover in three days that is, he was no longer than three days in going.

Em is sometimes used after the verb *hir,* to go; as, *vai em graça de Deus,* he goes with the blessing of God.

Em before *quanto,* and sometimes without it, is rendered into English by *while* or *whilst;* as, *em quanto vós fazeis aquillo, eu farei isto,* while you do that, I shall do this : but if they are followed by a noun of time with an interrogation, then they must be rendered into English by *in how much,* or *many;* as, *em quanto tempo?* in how much time? Observe, that *em quanto a mim, a ti, a elle,* &c., are rendered into English by *for what concerns me, thee, him,* &c.

No serves for the masculine, *na* for the feminine, and *em* for both.

Em signifies *as*: as, *em sinal da sua amizade,* as a token of his friendship; *em premio,* as a reward.

The prepositions *em, no, na,* &c., and *dentro,* have very often the same signification, therefore they may sometimes be used one instead of the other: as, *está na gaveta,* or *dentro da gaveta,* it is in the drawer; *está na cidade,* or *dentro da cidade,* he is in town.

Em before the words *favor, utilidade, consideração, razão,* and the like, signifies *in behalf of, on account of,*

&c., as, *em razão das bellas acçoens que elle tem feito*, in consideration of the great things he has performed.

Observe, that they very often make an elision of the last vowels, *o*, *a*, of the preposition *no*, *na*, where there is a vowel in the beginning of the next word; as, *n' agoa*, instead of *na agoa :* they also cut off the *e* of the preposition *em*, and change the *m* into *n*, as you may see in *Camoens*, canto 2, stanza xxxii., *n'algum porto*, instead of *em algum porto*, wherein you must observe that *n'* is to be rendered into English by *to* or *into*.

COM.

VII. This preposition signifies *with*, and it denotes conjunction, union, mixing, assembling, keeping company: as, *casar uma donzella com um homem honrado*, to marry a maid with an honest man; *hir com alguem*, to go with some one; *com a ajuda de Deus*, by God's help, &c.

Observe, that most of the adverbs formed of the adjectives are turned into Portuguese by the preposition *com* and the substantive: as, *atrevidamente*, boldly; *com atrevimento*, with boldness; *elegantemente*, elegantly; *com elegancia*, with elegance; *cortezmente*, politely; *com cortezia*, with politeness, &c.

The last consonant, *m*, is very often cut off, even before the noun of number, *um*, one; and so they say *c'um*, instead of *com um*, as may be seen in *Camoens*, canto 2, stanza xxxvii.

With me, with thee, with himself, &c., are rendered into Portuguese by *commigo, comtigo* or *comvosco, comsigo, com nosco, comvosco, comsigo*.

When *com* is preceded by *para*, it signifies towards, and sometimes *over* in English: as, *sejamos piedosos para com os pobres*, let us be merciful towards the poor; *ter grande poder para com alguem,* to have great influence over somebody's mind.

Com before the word *capa* is used metaphorically, and then it signifies *under colour,* or *pretext.*

PARA.

VIII. *Para* is rendered into English by *for;* but it signifies also *to,* when it is found before the infinitive, and denotes the intention, or purpose in doing something: as, *este livro é para meu irmão,* this book is for my brother; *esta penna é para escrever,* this pen is to write; *Deus nos fez para amal-o,* God made us for to love him; *o comer é necessario para conservar a vida,* eating is necessary for preserving life.

Para que is rendered into English by *for what;* as, *para que é isto?* for what is this? and sometimes by *that,* or *in order that;* as, *para que venha ver-me,* that he may come and see me. But *porque* signifies *why, for what, upon what account;* as, *porque não vindes?* why do you not come? but when it is not followed by an interrogation, it signifies *because.*

Para serves likewise before the verbs, to denote what one is able to do in consequence of his present disposition: as, *elle é bastante forte para andar a cavallo,* he is strong enough to ride; *elle tem bastante cabedal para sustentar-se,* he has means enough to maintain himself; *a occasião e muito favoravel para nos não servirmos della,* the occasion is too favourable to let it slip.

Para expresses also the capacity or incapacity of doing anything: as, *elle é homem para tudo,* he is a man fit for anything; *é homem para pouco,* he is good for little; *é homem para nada,* he is good for nothing.

This preposition is also used to denote the end or

motive of doing anything: as, *trabalho para o bem publico*, I work for the public good; *um hospital para os pobres*, an hospital for the poor.

Para is a preposition of time: as, *isto me basta para todo o anno*, this is sufficient for me for all the year; *estão unidos para sempre*, they are united for ever; *para dois meses era muito pouco*, for two months it was too little.

Para is sometimes preceded by the adverb *lá*, and followed by a noun of time, and then it is rendered into English by *against* or *towards;* as, *lá para o fim da semana*, against the end of the week, *or* towards the end of the week.

Para is sometimes rendered into English by *considering*, or *with respect to:* as, *este menino está muito adiantado para o idade que tém*, or *para o pouco tempo que estuda*, this child is very forward for his age, *or* considering the little time he has learned; *para ser Inglez falla muito bem*, he speaks very well considering that he is an Englishman.

Para signifies sometimes *just* or *ready to;* as, *elle está para partir*, he is just going away, he is ready to go.

Para is also used before the word *graças*: as, *elle não é para graças*, he takes no jest; *elle não está para graças*, he is out of humour, *or* he is in an ill-humour.

Para onde? signifies *whither? to what place?*

Para que? or *para que fim?* signifies *to what end* or *purpose?* *Para cima* signifies *upward.*

Para uma e outra parte signifies *to both sides, places,* or *parts.*

Para is also rendered into English by *towards*, and is said of places; as, *para o oriente*, towards *or* to the east.

Para onde quer que signifies *whither* or *to what place thou wilt, anywhere.*

Para outra parte signifies *towards another place.*

Para commigo, towards me.
Para o diante signifies *for the time to come.*
De mim, para mim, signifies *for what concerns me.*

Para is used by *Camoens*, canto 2, stanza xxiv., before the preposition *detraz,* and signifies *backwards.*

Para between two nouns of number is rendered into English by *or*, and sometimes by *and :* as, *um homem de quarenta para cincoenta annos*, a man between forty and fifty ; *dista de quatro para cinco legoas*, it is about four or five leagues distant.

POR.

IX. *Por, pelo, pela, pelos,* or *pelas,* signifies *for :* as, *por amor de vós*, for your sake ; *por seis semanas*, for six weeks ; *palavra por palavra*, word for word.

Polo and *pola*, instead of *pelo* and *pela*, are out of use.

Por sometimes denotes that the thing is not yet done : as, *esta obra está por acabar*, this work is not yet done.

Por, by, for, over, through : as, *alcancei-o por empenho*, I obtained it by protection ; *eu vou por dinheiro*, I am going for money ; *passeio pelos campos*, I walk through the fields ; *por tudo o reino*, all over the kingdom.

When *por* is before an infinitive, and followed by a negative, in the latter part of the sentence, it is rendered into English by *although* or *though :* as, *por ser devota*, or *por devota que seja, não deixa de ser mulher*, though she is a religious woman, yet she is a woman ; *por ser pobre*, or *por pobre que seja, não deixa de ser soberba*, though she has no fortune, she is nevertheless, *or* for all that, proud. Here the negative together with the verb *deixar* are rendered into English by the verb *to be*, and the particles *nevertheless, yet*, &c. Sometimes the words *nem por isso* are used before the verb *deixar*, but the sense is the same.

Por followed by an adjective and the particle *que*, with a verb in the subjunctive mood, is rendered into English by *ever so :* as, *por grande que elle seja*, let him be ever so great ; *por pouco que seja*, ever so little.

Por before *menos* signifies *far less than*, or *under ;* as, *vm^{ce} não o terá por menos de vinte libras*, you shall not have it under twenty pounds.

Por before *quanto*, with an interrogation, signifies, *for how much*, *at what rate ?* But if there be no interrogation, as in the following and the like sentences, then it is to be rendered into English by *for ever so much ;* as, *não o faria por quanto me dessem*, I would not do it for ever so much.

Por before *cima* signifies *upwards*, and before *baixo* is rendered into English by *downwards ;* as, *o remedio obra por cima e por baixo*, the medicine operates, *or* works, upwards and downwards.

Por before *pouco, muito, bem*, &c., and followed by *que*, makes a sort of conjunction governing the subjunctive, and is rendered into English by *if*, followed by *ever* or *ever so little, much, well*, &c., as, *por pouco que erreis*, if you do amiss ever so little *; por bem que eu faça*, if I do ever so well, &c.

Por before *mim* signifies sometimes *as for* or *for my part :* as, *por mim estou prompto*, as for me, *or* for my part, I am ready ; *por mim podeis dormir se quizerdes*, as for me, you may sleep.

Por, pelo, pela, &c., denote the efficient cause of a thing, as also the motive and means, or ways of doing it ; in all which significations they are rendered into English by *by, through, out of, at*, &c.; as,

A Asia foi conquistada por Alexandre, Asia was conquered by Alexander.

Vós fallais d'isso só por inveja, it is out of envy only you speak of it.

Elle entrou pela porta, mas sahio pela janella, he got in at the door, but he got out at the window, &c.

Por denotes place, after the verbs *ir* and *passar;* as, *por onde ireis vós?* which way shall you go?

Eu passarei por França, I will go through France; *por onde passou elle?* which way did he go?

Por construed with nouns without an article, denotes most times *distribution of people, time,* and *place;* and it is rendered into English by *a,* or *every,* before the noun: as,

Elle deu tanto por cabeça, he gave so much a-head.

Tanto por soldado, por anno, por mez, por semana, &c., so much a-soldier, a-year, a-month, a-week; *a razão de vinte por cento,* at the rate of twenty per cent.

Elle pede tanto por legoa, he asks so much a league, *or* every league.

Por between two nouns without an article, or between two infinitives without a preposition, denotes the choice which one makes between two things, alike in their nature, but different in their circumstances; as,

Casa por casa antes quero esta que aquella, since I must have one of these two houses, I like this better than that; *morrer por morrer, melhor é morrer combatendo que fugindo,* when a man must die it is better to die fighting than running away.

Pelo meio is rendered into English by *through;* as, *pelo meio dos campos,* through the fields.

Por meio is rendered into English by *by;* as, *elle alcançou o seu intento por meio de astucias,* he has compassed his ends by devices.

Por turno signifies *in one's turn.*

Por before the infinitive is used instead of *para* by the best Portuguese writers, and *porque* instead of *para que;* as may be seen particularly in *Camoens,* canto 2, stanzas vii. and viii., and in the following example: *por não* or *para não repetir o que já temos dito*, not to repeat what we have already said.

Por is sometimes rendered into English by *for, upon the account of, for the sake*, &c.: as, *elle fará isto por amor de vós*, he will do this upon your account, *or* for your sake; *deixarão-o por morto*, he was left for dead; *eu tenho-o por meu amigo*, I take him to be my friend; *todos os homens de bem são*, or *estão, por elle*, all honest people are for him, or are on his side; *por quem me tomais vós?* for whom do you take me?

We have already observed that *porque*, without an interrogation, signifies *because*; but it has the same signification in the following sentence, and the like: *porque elle é mentiroso segue-se que tambem eu o seja?* because he is a liar, does it follow therefore that I am one?

Por isto, or *por ista razão*, signifies *therefore*.

O porque signifies the reason, the cause, or the subject; as, *sabe-se o porque?* is it known upon what account?

Por modo de dizer signifies *as one may say, if I* or *we may say*, &c.

Por diante signifies *before;* and *por detraz* signifies *behind*.

Por ventura signifies *perhaps*.

Pelo passado signifies *formerly, in time past, heretofore*.

Por nenhum caso, by no means.

Por mar e por terra, by sea and land.

Um por um signifies *one by one*.

Por is sometimes rendered into English by *in;* as, *elles são vinte por todos*, they are twenty in all.

When the verb *passar* is followed by *por* then the word *alto* signifies *to forget;* as, *passou-lhe aquillo por alto*, he forgot that: but speaking of goods it signifies *to smuggle*.

Por joined with the verb *ir* signifies *to fetch* and *to go for:* as, *vai por vinho,* go fetch some wine ; *vai pelo medico,* go for the physician.

Por is commonly used before substantives : as, *por exemplo,* for example ; *por commodidade,* for conveniency ; *por costume,* for custom's sake : and many others, that may be learned by use.

You must observe that *pelo* serves for the masculine, *pela* for the feminine, and *por* for both.

CONTRA.

X. *Contra,* against, contrary to, denotes opposition ; as, *que diz vm^{ce} contra isto?* what do you say against this? It signifies also, *over against, opposite to.*

Pró e contra signifies in English *pro and con.*

DESDE.

XI. *Desde* denotes both time and place and enumeration of things, and is commonly followed in the sentence by the preposition, *até,* to ; then *desde* denotes the term *from whence,* and *até,* that of *hitherto* : as,

Desde o principio até o fim, from the beginning to the end.

Elle foi a pé desde Windsor até Londres, he walked from Windsor to London.

Eu tenho visto todos desde o primeiro até o ultimo, I have seen them all from the first to the last ; *fôrão todos mortos desde o primeiro até o ultimo,* they were all slain to a man.

Desde a creação do mundo, from *or* since the creation.

Desde o berço, ou infancia, from the cradle, from a child.

Desde já, even now ; as, *desde já prevejo,* I even now foresee.

Desde agora, from this time forward.

Desde então, from that time ever since.

Desde que, as soon as, since.

Desde quando? how long since, *or* ago?

Rio navegavel desde a sua nascente, a river navigable at its very rise.

ATÉ.

XII. *Até* signifies *till, even, to,* &c., as you may see in the following examples:—

Até onde? how far?

Até Roma, as far as Rome.

Até quando? till when, *or* how long?

Até que eu viva, as long as I live.

É um homem de tanta bondade, que até os seus inimigos são obrigados a estimal-o, he is so good a man that even his enemies have a value for him.

Até os mais vís homens tomavão a liberdade de, &c., the very worst of men took such a liberty as to, &c.

Até que, until, till.

Até ás orelhas, up to the ears.

Elle vendeo até a camisa, he has sold the very shirt off his back.

Até agora, or *até aqui*, till now, *or* hitherto.

Até aqui (speaking of a place), to this place, hither, so far.

Até la, to that place, so far.

Até que isto se faça, till it be done.

Até então, till then, till that time.

Até is also used before an infinitive; as, *gritar até enrouquecer*, to bawl oneself hoarse.

Rir até não poder mais, to split one's sides with laughing.

Dar de comer a alguem até o fartar, to fill *or* cram one with food till he bursts.

Até á primeira, till our next meeting, till we meet again.

POR CIMA.

XIII. *Por cima*, above, over, denotes superiority of place; as,

Morar por cima de alguem, to live or lodge above somebody.

A balla lhe passou por cima da cabeça, the ball went over his head.

Por cima de tudo, upon the whole.

PARA CIMA.

XIV. *Para cima*, above, denotes superiority of age, and is sometimes put at the end of the sentence; as,

Elles alistaram todos os que tinhão de dez annos para cima, they enlisted everybody above ten.

ACIMA.

XV. *Acima*, above, denotes rank, and some moral subjects; as,

Acima d'elle, above him, or superior to him.

Estar acima de tudo, to be above the world.

Uma mulher que está acima de tudo, não se lhe dá do que o mundo diz d'ella, a woman who is above the public censure, does not care what people say of her.

EM CIMA.

XVI. *Em cima*, upon; as, *em cima da mesa*, upon the table.

Em cima de tudo isto, or only *em cima*, signifies *and besides all that, over and above all that.*

DE CIMA.

XVII. *De cima*, when it is an adverb, signifies *from above;* but when a preposition, it is rendered into English by *from, off,* or *from off;* as,

Tira aquillo de cima da mesa, take that from off the table.

Elle nunca apartou os seus olhos de cima d'ella, he never turned his eyes from her.

Cahir de cima das arvores, to fall off the trees.

DEBAIXO.

XVIII. The preposition *debaixo*, under, below, *or* from under, signifies subjection to a sway or government, and an epoch; as, *debaixo do imperio de Augusto*, under the empire of Augustus.

Debaixo, as a preposition of place, marks out inferiority of position; as,

Tudo o que ha debaixo dos céos, all there is under heaven.

Ter uma almofada debaixo dos joelhos, to have a cushion under the knees.

Estar debaixo de chave, to be under lock and key.

Debaixo is sometimes rendered into English by *upon;* as, *affirmar uma cousa debaixo de juramento*, to swear a thing, to declare upon oath.

ABAIXO.

XIX. This preposition is rendered into English by *under, inferior,* or *next:* as, *assentou-se abaixo d'elles*, he sat inferior to *or* under them; *assentou-se abaixo de mim*, he sat next inferior to me ; *abaixo d'el-rei elle é o primeiro,* he is the next man to the king.

This preposition is sometimes put at the end of the following phrases : *de telhas abaixo,* here below in this lower world ; *de cabeça abaixo,* headlong.

FÓRA.

XX. *Fóra,* out, without, except, but, denotes exclusion and exception. It requires generally a genitive before a noun of time or place ; but it governs also the nominative : as,

Fóra do reino, out of the kingdom.
Fóra da cidade, out of town.
Fóra de tempo, out of season.
Procura-o fóra de casa, look for him without doors.
Elles sahiram todos, fóra dous ou tres, they all went out, except *or* but two or three.

Elle lhe permite tudo, fóra o ir ás assembleas, he indulges her in everything but in going to assemblies.

Elle tem todos os poderes, fóra o de concluir este negocio, he has full powers except of concluding this business.

Fóra is sometimes preceded by *tão,* and then it is to be rendered into English by *so far ;* as, *elle está tão fóra de soccorrer os seus alliados, que se declara contra elles,* he is so far from assisting his allies, that he declares himself against them.

Fóra is sometimes rendered into English by *besides ;* as, *fóra d'aquelles que,* &c., besides those that, &c. : and sometimes by *beyond ;* as, *fóra de medida,* beyond measure.

Fóra de horas, signifies *beyond the hour,* or *very late.*

Pôr alguem fóra da porta, or *mandar alguem pela porta fóra,* to turn one out of doors.

DE FRONTE.

XXI. This preposition governs the genitive, and signifies *over against*. It is followed by *de, do, da*, &c.; as,

De fronte da sua casa está um outeiro, over against his house is a hill.

Eu estava de fronte d'elle, I was over against him.

SEM.

XXII. *Sem* signifies *without;* as,

Sem dinheiro, without money.

Sem duvida, without doubt.

Sem dar a entender, or *sem fazer conhecer*, without giving to understand.

Sem mais nem menos, without any reason, *or* provocation.

Estar sem amo, to be out of place.

Sem que algum acto precedente possa derrogar o presente, any former act to the contrary of the present notwithstanding.

Sem governs also the infinitive, which is rendered into English with the participle; *fallar sem saber*, to speak without knowing.

It is also a conjunction with *que*, governing the subjunctive; as,

Enfada-se sem que lhe digão nada, he is angry without anybody saying anything to him.

Não era eu já bastantemente infeliz, sem que procurasseis de acrescentar a minha infelicidade? was I not miserable enough before, but you must still labour to make me more so?

Lembro-me sem que me digais, I remember without your telling.

Elle virá sem que mandem por elle, he will come without sending for him.

CONFORME, or SEGUNDO.

XXIII. *Conforme*, or *segundo*, according to, conformable to, govern the nominative, and never the dative, as in English; as,

Elle foi tratado conforme o seu merecimento, he was treated according to his deserts.

Conforme o meu parecer, in my judgment, in my opinion.

In common conversation *conforme* is used adverbially, and rendered into English as follows:

Isso é conforme, or only *conforme*, that is right, may be, that is according.

Conforme a occasião o pedir, according as there may be need.

SOBRE.

XXIV. *Sobre* signifies *upon:* as, *sobre a mesa*, upon the table; *sobre o rio*, upon the river.

Sobre tudo, or *sobre todas as coisas*, over all, above all, above all things, above anything, especially; as, *sobre tudo tende cuidado na saude*, but, above all things, mind your health.

Pôr alguem sobre si, or *dar-lhe o primeiro lugar*, to place one above himself.

Ir sobre uma cidade, to march against a town.

Ir sobre alguem, to fall, *or* to rush upon one.

Ir sobre seguro, to go upon sure grounds.

Sobre a noite, about *or* towards the evening.

Sobre o verde, somewhat green.

Sobre a minha palavra, upon my word.

Sobre palavra, upon parole.

Mandar carta sobre carta, to send letter upon letter.

Elle recebeo a carta sobre o jantar, he had just dined when he received the letter.

Elle dorme sobre o jantar, he sleeps immediately after dinner.

Sobre isto, or *sobre estas coisas*, is sometimes rendered into English by *more than that*, or *besides that*; as,

Elle o roubou, e sobre isto matou-o, he robbed him, and more than that, he killed him.

Sobre que is rendered into English by *though*, or *although*; as,

Este negocio sobre que é difficultoso não é impossivel, although this is a hard affair, yet it is not impossible.

Sobre is rendered into English sometimes by *besides*; as,

Sobre as miserias da guerra, elle teve a desgraça, &c., besides the miseries of the war, he had the misfortune of, &c.

Estar sobre si, or *andar sobre si*, signifies *to stand upon one's guard*.

Eu vos escreverei sobre esta materia, I will write to you about this matter.

ÁCERCA.

XXV. *Ácerca* signifies *about*: as, *ácerca d'isto lhe disse*, about this I told him; *ácerca de lá ir lhe respondi*, about going there I answered him.

PERTO, JUNTO, AO PÉ, PEGADO.

XXVI. *Perto*, near, by, about, denotes proximity of place and time, and governs the genitive case; as, *aquillo está muito perto do lume*, that is very near the fire; *perto das oito horas*, about eight o'clock.

Perto do rio, near the river.

Estamos perto do Natal, we are near Christmas.

Ao pé requires also the genitive case; as,

Assentai-vos ao pé de mim, sit down by me, *or* near me; *ao pé do rio,* near the river, &c.

Note, that *junto,* near *or* near by, and *pegado,* hard by, require the dative case; as,

Junto á cidade, near the town.

Pegado ao palacio, hard by the palace.

LONGE.

Longe, far, a great way off, governs the genitive, and the particle *de,* or *do, da,* &c.; as,

Longe de casa, far from home.

Longe d'aqui, far from hence.

DE LONGO, *or* AO LONGO.

This preposition requires the genitive case; as,

Ao longo da praia, along the coast.

Ao longo da costa, do prado, &c., along the coast, the meadow, &c.

OF FURTHER PARTICLES.

AINDA, AINDA QUE, POSTOQUE *or* QUANDO BEM, AINDA ASSIM *or* COMTUDO.

Ainda signifies *yet;* as, *elle ainda não veio,* he is not come yet. It signifies also *even;* as, *seria vergonha ainda fallar d'isso,* it were a shame even to speak of it; *nem ainda por cem libras,* not even for a hundred pounds.

Ainda que signifies *though or although*: as, *ainda que vós sois mais velho do que elle,* though you be older than he; *ainda que assim fosse,* though it were so.

Ainda que is very often followed by *comtudo*, yet for all that; as, *ainda que elle não tivesse necessidade d'isso, comtudo*, &c., though he had no need of it, yet, &c.

Ainda assim, or *comtudo*, is sometimes rendered into English by *nevertheless*, or *for all that;* as, *ainda assim sempre elle foi louvavel*, he was praiseworthy for all that.

JÁ DESDE, JÁ QUE, and JÁ POR QUE.

Já desde is rendered into English by *even from;* as, *já desde o principio*, even from the beginning.

Já que signifies *since;* as, *já que isso assim é*, since it is so.

The particle *que* sometimes is not placed immediately after *já;* as, *já ha dois annos que morreo*, he died two years since *or* ago.

Já ha muito tempo que sahistes de casa, it is a long time since you went from home.

Já por que is repeated in the same sentence, and then the first is rendered into English by *first; because ;* and the second by *secondly, because ;* as, *já por que era cego, já por que era coixo*, first, because he was blind, and secondly, because he was lame.

DEPOIS QUE.

Depois que is rendered into English by *after;* as, *depois que eu tinha entrado*, after I was gone in.

COM QUE.

Com que is only a note either of introduction or connexion; as,

Com que havia um homem doente, &c., now a certain man was sick; sometimes they add to it the particle *assim*, and then it is to be rendered into English by *and so*.

OU.

Ou signifies *or* or *either:* as, *ou bom, ou máo*, either good or bad; *mais ou menos*, more or less; *ou elle queira ou não*, whether he will or not,

QUER.

Quer, when a particle, must be repeated, and the first is rendered into English by *either* or *whether*, and the second by *or*: as, *quer elle queira quer não*, whether he will or not; *quer vós o tenhais feito, quer não*, whether you have done that, or not.

SE QUER, or AO MENOS.

Se quer, or *ao menos*, &c., signifies *at least, however:* as, *se vós não quereis ser por elle não sejais se quer contra elle*, if you do not choose to be for him, at least do not oppose him; *dai-lhe se quer com que sustentar-se*, give him, however, a subsistence; *o nosso primeiro fim é livrar-nos de todos os males, ao menos dos maiores*, our chief end is to be freed from all evils, at least the greatest.

Nem se quer um is rendered into English by *not even one;* as, *forão todos mortos, e nem se quer um escapou*, they were all slain to a man.

QUANDO MUITO.

Quando muito, at most, at furthest, is generally used before the nouns of time and price: as, *elle estará aqui dentro em um mez quando muito*, he will be here in a month at furthest; *dez libras quando muito*, ten pounds at most.

TANTO.

Tanto, so much, is sometimes followed by *como*, and then it is rendered into English by *as well as, as much as*, &c.

Amo-te tanto como a mim mesmo, I love thee as well as myself.

Elle teme tanto como qualquer de vós, que lhe resulte algum dano, he is afraid of harm as much as any of you.

Cuidei que a estimasse tanto como a si mesmo, I thought he esteemed her as much as he did himself.

Elles vêem tanto de dia como de noite, they can see as well by day as by night.

Eu tive tanto como vós, I had as much as you.

Outro tanto is rendered into English by *the double, twice as much*, or *as much ;* as,

Eu alcancei outro tanto mais por isso, I had as much more for it ; *eu posso fazer outro tanto*, I can do as much.

Tanto mais is followed by *que*, and rendered into English by *and the more so as ;* as,

Eu estou prompto para ir com vm^{ce} um dia d'estes á comedia se vm^{ce} quizer ; tanto mais que se deve representar uma nova peça ; I am ready to go with you some day or other to the play, if you will give me leave ; and the more so, as a new piece is to be acted.

Tanto que, or *logo que*, is rendered into English by *as soon as ;* as, *tanto que eu o vi*, as soon as I saw him.

Tanto melhor is rendered into English by *so much the better*.

Tanto is sometimes preceded by *com*, and followed by *que*, and is rendered into English by *so, provided that :* as, *com tanto que o façais*, provided that you do it ; *com tanto que me não faça mal*, so he does me no harm.

Tanto quanto is rendered into English by *as much as;* as, *tanto quanto posso*, as much as I can.

TÃO.

Tão, so, is generally followed by *como;* as,

Este não é tão bom como o outro, this is not so good as the other; *eu sei isso tão bem como vós*, I know it as well as you.

Tão is sometimes followed by *que*, and is rendered into English by *so, such, to that degree;* as,

Elle é tão prudente que não tem igual, he is so wise that he has not his equal; *não sou tão louco que o creia*, I am not so simple as to believe it; *faz tão grande vento que*, &c., the wind is so high that, &c., *or* the wind blows to that degree, &c.

COMO.

Como is rendered into English by *as, like, how*, &c., as may be seen in the following expressions:—

Como? how?

Dizei-me como lhe hei de fallar? tell me how I may speak to him.

Como assim? how so?

Como! what!

Como quer que, whereas.

Como quer que seja, howsoever, in what manner or fashion soever.

Seja como fôr, be it as it will.

Como isto assim é, since it is so.

Como, as it were, *or* almost.

Como se, as if, *or* even as if; as, *como se elles tivessem já vencido*, as if they had already overcome.

Como tambem, as well as.

Rico como elle é, as rich as he is.

Como sois meu amigo quero, &c., as, *or* because, you are my friend, I will, &c.

Dizei-me o como, tell me how.

Eu sei como fazer para que elle venha, I know how to make him come.

Como elle lá não esteja, eu irei, provided he is not there, I will come.

ASSIM.

Assim, so, thus, is rendered into English as in the following expressions :—

Pois é assim de veras? de veras que é assim, is it even so? it is even so.

Assim seja, or *seja assim,* so be it, *or* be it so.

Assim é, it is so.

Para assim dizer, as it were.

Assim sou eu louco que, &c., I am not so foolish as to, &c.

Assim Deus me salve, as I hope to be saved.

Tanto assim, so that.

Assim é que vós, &c., is this your way, &c.

Assim como assim, after all, nevertheless, *or* for all that; as, *em vão dilatais a vossa jornada, assim como assim é preciso que vades,* it is in vain for you to put off your journey, you must go thither nevertheless, *or* for all that, you must go after all.

Assim como, as well as, *or* as soon as.

Basta assim por agora, enough for the present.

Assim na paz, como na guerra, both in time of peace and war.

Assim, assim, so so, indifferent.

Assim quizera elle como póde, he can if he will.

Assim is sometimes followed by *que,* and is rendered into English by *how, what;* as, *assim que quer isto dizer?*

how now ! what do you mean by this ? And sometimes it is followed by *como ;* as, *assim como o sol eclipsa os outros planetas, da mesma sorte,* &c., as the sun eclipses the other planets, so, &c.

SE.

Se, if : as, *se elle vier,* if he comes ; *se me amasses,* should you love me ; *se elle fosse homem de honra,* were he but an honest man ; *se soubessem quem eu sou todos dirião,* &c., were it told who I am, every one would say, &c. ; *se é verdade que,* &c., if so be that, &c.

The reciprocal verbs as well as those that are used impersonally, may have two *se* successively : as, *se se for,* if he goes away ; *se se falla d'isso,* if they speak of it.

Se is sometimes rendered into English by *whether;* and when it is repeated, the second is rendered into English by *or ;* as,

Quizera saber se a culpa é nossa, se vossa, I would know whether it is our fault or yours.

ALIÁS.

Aliás is sometimes rendered into English by *else ;* as, *entrai, porque aliás fecharei a porta,* come in, or else I will shut the door ; *porque aliás serião os vossos filhos immundos,* else were your children unclean. And sometimes it is rendered into English by *otherwise, in other things* or *respects.*

EMBORA.

Embora is rendered into English by *prosperously, auspiciously ;* but sometimes it is a particle merely expletive, and answers to the Italian *pure :* as *dizei muito embora o que quizerdes,* say what you please : the Italian says, *dite pur quel che vi piáce,* you may say what you please.

Muito embora seja assim, well, let it be so.

Embora is sometimes rendered into English by *away;* as, *vai-te embora,* go away.

SENÃO.

Senão signifies *if not, did not, were it not that, but that;* as,

Senão tivesse medo de meu pai, did I not fear my father.

Se elle não tivesse vergonha de confessar, were he not ashamed to confess.

The following expressions, in which they make use of this particle, may be rendered into English by *but, for,* and some other variations.

Senão fosse por elle, but for him, *or* had it not been for him.

Senão fosse por vós, had it not been for you, without you, without your help, hindrance, &c.

Senão fosse por mim, elle morreria de fome, were it not for me, he would starve.

Senão is sometimes rendered into English by *but;* as, *nem elles têm outro intento, senão,* &c., nor do they aim at anything else, but, &c.

Ninguém disse assim senão Cicero, nobody said so but Cicero.

Senão may be also expressed by *mais que,* in the following sentence and the like:

Elle não faz senão jogar, or *elle não faz mais que jogar,* he does nothing but play.

NÃO, NÃO PORQUE.

Não, *not* or *no*, when followed by *porque*, is rendered into English by *not that, not but that*: as, *não porque lhe faltasse engenho*, not but that he had wit; *não porque não fosse justo, mas porque*, &c., not but that it was right, but because, &c.; *não porque a coisa seja impossivel, mas porque*, &c., not that the thing is impossible, but because, &c.

TAMBEM, or OUTROSI.

Tambem, or *outrosi*, signifies *also, too, likewise*; as, *vós assim o quereis e eu tambem*, you will have it so and I too.

PARA QUE, PORQUE.

See the prepositions *para* and *por*.

POIS.

This particle is very much used by the Portuguese, and is rendered into English several ways, as in the following examples:—

Pois ide, e vinde logo, go, then, and come back presently.

Pois não sou eu capaz de fazel-o? what, am I not capable of doing it?

Pois or *pois então que quer dizer isto?* well, and what is the meaning of this?

Pois or *pois então que hei de fazer?* what shall I do then?

Pois eu digo que elle está dentro, why, he is here within, I say.

Pois porque me vigiais? why, then, do you watch me?

Elle tem cabeça; pois tambem um alfinete a tem, he has got a head and so has a pin.

Pois before *não*, and preceded by an interrogation, denotes a strong assertion, and is rendered into English by *without doubt, yes, surely, to be sure*, &c., as, *virá elle? pois não!* will he come? yes, to be sure!

ANTES or MAIS DEPRESSA.

These particles are sometimes rendered into English by *rather* or *sooner*: as, *antes* or *mais depressa quizera morrer*, I would rather die; *antes quizera viver só que na vossa companhia*, I would sooner live alone than be in your company. Sometimes *antes* is rendered into English by *before*: as, *ide-vos antes que elle venha*, go away before he comes; *antes que eu morra*, before I die.

MAS ANTES, PELO CONTRARIO, MAS PELO CONTRARIO.

These particles are rendered into English by *on the contrary, on the other hand, nay*: as, *mas antes, mas pelo contrario*, or *pelo contrario isto é muito differente*, nay, it is quite another thing; *mas antes, pelo contrario*, &c., *elle é avarento*, nay, on the contrary, he is a covetous man.

PARA MELHOR DIZER.

This phrase is rendered into English by *nay*: as, *elle tem já bastante, ou para melhor dizer, mais do necessario*, he has already enough, nay, too much; *a isto é que nós chamamos direito das gentes ou para melhor dizer, da razão*, this is what we call the law of nations, which may be called more properly the law of reason.

QUE.

We have already observed that *que* is a particle which most conjunctions are composed of: as, *ainda que*, although; *de sorte que*, so that, &c.

The particle *que* sometimes is the sign of the third person of the imperative, as *let* in English: as, *que falle*, let him speak; *que rião*, let them laugh.

Que is used between two verbs, to determine and specify the sense of the first: as, *eu vos asseguro que assim é*, I assure you that it is so; *duvido que assim seja*, I doubt whether it is so or not.

Que is also used after *hora* in the beginning of a sentence, and followed by a verb in the subjunctive, to denote by exclamation one's surprise, aversion, and reluctance to something; in which case there is a verb grammatically understood before *que;* as, *hora que se esquecesse elle de si mesmo!* I wonder, or is it possible for him to have forgotten himself!

The expression of admiration is sometimes expressed without any verb: as *que gosto; e ao mesmo tempo, que pena !* how much pleasure and trouble at once !

Que is sometimes repeated; as,

Que bellos livros que tendes, what fine books you have got; *que bella que é a virtude!* how beautiful is virtue !

Que is sometimes followed by *de ;* as, *que de penas ha no mundo!* how many troubles there are in the world !

Que is used after nouns denoting time, and is sometimes rendered into English by *when*, or *since*, &c., and sometimes left out; as,

O dia que elle partio, the day when he set out.

Quanto tempo ha que estais em Londres? how long have you lived in London?

Ha dez annos que faz a mesma cousa, he has done the same thing these ten years.

Ha dez annos que morreo, he died ten years ago.

Que is sometimes rendered into English by *because,* as in *Camoens,* canto 2, stanza xvi., *que levemente um animo,* and sometimes by *that, to the end that, in order to ;* as in *Camoens,* canto 2, stanza xvii., *que como vissem, que no rio,* &c.

Que before *se* in the beginning of a sentence, is a redundancy not expressed in English ; as, *que se vós dizeis que,* if you say that, &c.

Que is used after the conjunction *apenas,* scarcely or hardly, and is rendered into English by *when :* as, *apenas acabou de fallar, que logo morreo,* he had scarcely done speaking, when he expired.

Que sometimes is preceded by *de sorte, de maneira, de geito,* and then it is rendered into English by *so that, in such a manner, insomuch that ;* as, *eu o farei de sorte que fiqueis contente,* I will do it so that, *or* in such manner that, you shall be contented.

DE VERAS.

De veras signifies *in earnest ;* but sometimes it is rendered into English by *indeed :* as, *de veras ; não o posso crêr,* indeed ! I can hardly believe it.

HORA.

Hora or *ora* is an interjection that serves to encourage, as we have seen above ; but when it is repeated, it is rendered into English by *sometimes, awhile, another while :* as, *ora está bem, ora está mal,* sometimes he is well, sometimes ill ; *elle ora está de um parecer, e ora de outro,* he is now of one opinion, and next moment of another. *Por ora* signifies *now, for the present.*

CHAPTER VIII.

OF THE PORTUGUESE ORTHOGRAPHY; AND OF CAPITALS AND STOPS.

I. PROPER names, as well as surnames, always begin with a capital.

II. The names of nations, kingdoms, and provinces also begin with a capital: as, *França*, France; *Inglaterra*, England, &c.

III. All names of dignities, and degrees, and honours, require a capital; as, *Rei*, *Bispo*, &c., King, Bishop, &c.

IV. At the beginning of a sentence, as well as of a verse, the first letter is always a capital.

The names of arts and sciences, as well as those of kindred, begin with a capital.

OF STOPS.

The use of stops, or points, is to divide words in a sentence.

The Portuguese have six stops, or pauses, viz.:—

1. The *ponto final*, the same as our period or full stop (.), and is used at the end of a sentence, to show that the sentence is completed.

2. The *dois pontos*, which is our colon (:), and is the pause made between two members of a period; that is, when the sense is complete, but the sentence not ended.

3. The *ponto e vírgula* is our semicolon (;), and denotes that short pause which is made in the subdivision of the members or parts of a sentence.

4. The *ponto de interrogação*, the point of interrogation, thus (?).

5. *Ponto de admiração*, the point of admiration, thus (!).

6. The *virgula*, the same with our comma (,), and is the shortest pause or rest in speech, being used chiefly to distinguish nouns, verbs, and adverbs, as also the parts of a shorter sentence.

The conjunction *e*, the relative *qual*, and the disjunctions *ou* and *nem*, require a comma before them.

The Portuguese make use also of a parenthesis, thus (); but they have discontinued the use of the diæresis, called by their printers *crema* (··);* they use also the *angulo*, thus, ^, called by the printers *caret*.

The apostrophe, or, as they call it, *viracento*, is used in this as in other languages, being designed only for the more pleasant and easy pronunciation of words, by cutting off an antecedent vowel; as, *d' armas, d' elvas*, and not *darmas, delvas*, &c.

OF THE ACCENTS.

The accent is a sound of the voice by which we pronounce some syllables shorter, and others longer.

I intend to speak here only of the accents the Portuguese ought to make use of, according to Madureira, in his *Portuguese Orthography*.

The Portuguese, indeed, are acquainted with three accents, but they ought to make use of only two, namely, the acute, which descends from the right to the left (´), and the circumflex, thus (^).

1. The acute serves to prolong the pronunciation, and is put, according to Madureira, on the last syllable of the

---

* The diæresis was formerly used in the Portuguese orthography; so much so that it has even three names in that language from its classical times, viz., *diéresis, ápices, cimalhas*.

ORTHOGRAPHY. 221

third person singular of the future tense; as, *amará, lerá,* &c.

2. On the penultima of the preterpluperfect tense of the indicative mood; as, *amára, ensinára,* &c.

3. The acute accent ought to be put also on the penultima of the third persons of the present tense of the verbs *renunciar, pronunciar, duvidar,* &c.—thus, *renuncía, pronuncía, duvída,* &c.—that they may be distinguished from the nouns *renuncia, pronuncia, duvida,* &c. The same accent is also put on *está, nó,* to distinguish them from *ésta,** this, and *no,* in the.

The vowel *o* has two sounds, according to the two accents that may be put upon it: one open, when it is marked with the acute accent, and is pronounced like *o* in *store;* the other close, when it is marked with the circumflex accent, and then is pronounced like *u* in *stumble.*

There are many nouns and adjectives which are accented in the singular with the circumflex, and in the plural with the acute; and the adjectives that have two terminations, particularly those ending in *oso, osa,* must be accented, in the singular, with the circumflex in the masculine, and with the acute in the feminine; as,

Fôgo, fire; plural, *fógos.*
Fôrno, oven; plural, *fórnos.*
Ôlho, eye; plural, *ólhos.*
Ôvo, egg; plural, *óvos.*
Ôsso, bone; plural, *óssos.*
Pôço, well; plural, *póços.*
Pôrco, hog; plural, *pórcos.*
Rôgo, prayer; plural, *rógos.* And also *fôjo, tôrno, formôso, sequiôso, suppôsto, pôvo, tôrto, copiôso,* &c.

---

* It must not be forgotten that the accents are not commonly marked in most of these terms, and the others given as examples; but they are put here to designate the right pronunciation.

The following keep the circumflex accent in both numbers : *bôlo, bôlos ; bôjo, bôjos ; bôto, bôtos ; côco, côcos ; chôro, chôros ; côto, côtos ; fôrro, fôrros; gôrdo, gôrdos ; gôsto, gôstos ; gôzo, gôzos ; lôbo, lôbos ; môço, môços ; nôjo, nôjos ; pôtro, pôtros ; tôlo, tôlos ; ferrôlho, ferrôlhos ; rapôso, rapôsos ; arrôz, arrôzes ; algôz, algôzes*, &c.

On the contrary, the following keep the acute accent in both numbers : *cópo, cópos ; módo, módos ; nósso, nóssos ; vóssos*, &c.

When the circumflex accent is put on the *e*, then the *e* is pronounced like the French *é ;* but when *e* is accented with the acute accent, then the *é* is to be pronounced like the *è* open in French ; and is exceedingly sonorous and long. See the pronunciation of the vowel *e*.

Nouns ending in *az, iz, oz, uz*, must have the acute accent on the vowel before the *z ;* as, *rapáz*, a boy ; *nóz*, a walnut ; *alcaçúz*, liquorice : but you must except *arrôz*, rice ; *algôz*, a hangman.

Nouns ending in *ez* generally have the circumflex accent : as, *mêz*, a month ; *marquêz*, a marquis, &c.

SOME OBSERVATIONS UPON THE PORTUGUESE ORTHOGRAPHY.

Both the Portuguese orthographers and best authors vary so much in their rules and ways of writing, that it is impossible for any grammarian to explain clearly this part of the Portuguese Grammar, it requiring no less authority than that of the Royal Portuguese Academy. However, not totally to set aside so material a part of the Grammar, I shall present the learner with the following observations :—

I. When the Latin words from which the Portuguese

are derived begin with a *b*, the Portuguese likewise must begin with it; therefore you must write and pronounce the *b* in the following words, *bom, bondade, bem, bento,* &c., because they are derived from *bonus, bonitas,* &c. But you must except *bainha, bexiga, bairro,* which begin with a *b*, though they are derived from *vagina, vesica, vicus*.

II. Likewise, if the Latin words begin with a *v*, the Portuguese words derived from them must also begin with it; as, *vida, viver, varrer, ver, vinho,* &c., from *vita, vivere, verrere, videre, vinum,* &c.

Though *b* ought to be pronounced only by closing the lips, and *v* by touching the superior teeth with the inferior lips; yet, by a certain affinity between these two letters, in speaking there is a great confusion in the pronunciation of them in the province of *Entre Douro e Minho;* and this confusion has not been peculiar to the Portuguese language, for Nebrixa says, in his *Castilian Orthography*, that in his time some Spaniards could hardly make any distinction between these two letters.

III. The *p* found in some words originally Latin, is changed in Portuguese into a *b;* as, *cabra, cabello, cabeça,* &c., from *capra, capillus, caput,* &c.

IV. The *y*, as Bluteau says, must be made use of in words having a Greek origin; as, *syllaba, Chrysopeia, pyramide, polygono, hydrographia, hydropico, physica, hyperbole, hypocrita, Apocrypho,* &c.

V. The *ph* are used in the Portuguese in some words taken from the Greek; as, *philosophia, philologia, Philadelphia, epitaphio,* &c.

VI. The *r* in Portuguese has two pronunciations: one soft, expressed by a single *r*, as in *arado*, a plough, and after the consonants *b, c, d, f, g, p, t;* and another hard, in which two *r*'s are used; as in *barra, carro,* &c. But you must observe:—

1. That in the beginning of a word two *r*'s must never be used, because then the *r* is always pronounced hard in Portuguese; as in the words *remo, rico, roda,* &c.

2. When the consonants *l, n, s,* are before the *r,* either in a single or a compound word, this letter must never be doubled, because then its sound is always strong; as in *abalroa, enriquecer, honra, Henrique, Israelita,* &c.

3. The *r* after a *b* is also pronounced hard in compounds with the prepositions *ab, ob, sub,* and yet is not doubled; as in *abrogar, obrepção, subrepção,* &c.

VII. The *s* is never doubled in the beginning of words, nor after the consonants; therefore you must write, *sarar, saber, falsamente, falso, manso,* &c.

The *s* is pronounced like *z* between two vowels, in words derived from the Latin, as well as in those that end in *osa* and *oso;* as, *musa, caso, riso, amoroso, cuidadoso, casa,* &c. You must also observe that *coser* signifies *to sew,* but *cozer* signifies *to boil* or *bake.*

VIII. *Th* are generally used in words derived from the Greek; as, *amphitheatro, atheisto, theologo, lethargo, methodo,* &c., but are pronounced like *t.*

Th are also used in the Portuguese preposition *athé,* though some write it thus, *até.*

IX. When *pt* are found in Latin words, it must be kept in the Portuguese derived from them; as, *apto, inepto, optimò,* &c., from *aptus, ineptus, optimus,* &c.

The same must be observed in regard to *ct.*

X. *Ch* are sounded like *k,* in words derived from the Greek; as, *archanjo, archiduque, Chrysostomo, chrysol, chrysologo, Christovão, monarchia,* &c. These words must be written with *ch,* in order to preserve to the eye their etymology.

Note, that *ch* in words that are not derived from the Greek are pronounced like *ch* in the English words *church,*

ORTHOGRAPHY. 225

chin, much; but as some confound the *ch* with the *x*, and begin with *x* those words that should begin with *ch*, I have thought it necessary to make a collection of them.

WORDS BEGINNING WITH
CHA.

Chá	Chancela	Charameleiro
Chãa	Chancelaria	Charco
Chaça	Chanceler	Charneca
Chacina	Chançoneta	Charneira
Chaço	Chanqueta	Charola
Chacota	Chantagem	Charpa
Chafariz	Chantrado	Charro
Chaga	Chantre	Charrua
Chalupa	Chão	Chasco
Chama	Chapa	Chasona
Chamalote	Chapado	Chatim
Chamar	Chapeado	Chato
Chamariz	Chapeleta	Chavão
Chambão	Chapéo	Chavascal
Chamejar	Chapim	Chave
Chamiça	Chapinhar	Chavalha
Chaminé	Chapuz	Chaveta
Chamuscar	Charamela	Chavinha
Chança		

CHE.

Chêa, *or* Cheia	Cheirar, *and its*	Cherivia
Chefe	*derivatives*	Cherne
Chegar		

CHI.

Chiar	Chibo	Chichorro
Chibarro	Chicharos	Chichelos

Q

Chicoria	Chilrar	Chiqueiro
Chicote	Chimbeo	Chispa
Chifra	Chincar	Chispar
Chifrar	Chincheiro	Chiste
Chifre	Chinchorro	Chita
Chilindrão	Chinela	

CHO.

Choça	Chócca	Chorro
Choca	Chocolate	Chover
Chocalhar	Chofrado	Choupa
Chocalho	Chofre	Choupana
Chocar	Chóldabólda	Choupo, *or* Chôpo
Chocarrear	Choque	Chouriço
Choccarice	Chorar	Choutar
Choco	Chorrilho	

CHU.

Chuça	Chufa	Churume
Chupamel	Chumaço	Chusma
Chupar	Chumbar	Chuva
Chuchurriar	Chumbo	Chuveiro
Chuço	Churrião	

CHY.

Chyar.

The following words begin with *ce* and not *se* :—

CEA.

Cêa	Ceado	Cear

CEB.

Cebola	Cebolal	Cebolinho

CED.

Cedavím	Ceder	Cedro
Cedela	Cedilho	Cedula
Cedenho	Cedo	

CEG.

Cega	Cego	Cegude
Cegar	Cegonha	Cegueira

CEI.

Ceifa	Ceirão	Ceivar
Ceifão	Ceirinha	

CEL.

Colada	Celeuma	Celicola
Celebração	Celga	Celidonia
Celebrar	Celha	Cella
Célebre	Celho	Celleiro
Celeste	Celibado	Celleireiro
Celestial	Celibato	Celtas
Celestrina		

CEM.

Cem · · · Cemiterio

CEN.

Cenaculo	Censor	Cento
Ceno	Censura	Centoculo
Cenobio	Censurado	Centopea
Cenobitico	Censurar	Central
Cenotaphio	Centauro	Centro
Cenoura	Centena	Centuplo
Cenrada	Centeal	Centuria
Cenreira	Centesimo	Centurião
Censo	Centeyo	Ceo

CEP.

Cêpa	Cêpo	Ceptro
Cepilho		

CER.

Cêra	Cereijal	Certa
Ceraferario	Ceremonia	Certo
Cerbero	Ceremonial	Certão
Cêrca	Cerieiro	Certeza
Cercado	Cérne	Certidão
Cercador	Cernelha	Certificar
Cercadura	Cerol	Cerva
Cercar	Ceroulas	Cerval
Cérce	Cerqueiro	Cerveja
Cerceado	Cerração	Cervilhas
Cercear	Cerralheiro	Cerviz
Cercilho	Cerralho	Ceruda
Cerco	Cerrar	Ceruleo
Cerdoso	Cerrar-se	Cervo
Cerebro	Cêrro	Cerzir
Cereijas		

CES.

Cesar	Cessão	Cestinho
Cesarea	Cessação	Cesteiro
Cesma	Cessar	Cesto
Cesmaria	Cesta	Cesura
Cesmeiro	Cestinha	

CEV.

Ceva	Cevadel	Cevadouro
Cevada	Cevadeira	Cevar

CEZ.

Cezão	Cezimbra

ORTHOGRAPHY.

N.B. *Cerrar* signifies *to shut* or *shut up;* but *serrar* signifies *to saw*, to cut timber or other matter with a saw.

The following words must have *ci*, and not *si*, in their beginning :—

CIA.
Ciar-se Ciatica

CIB.
Ciba Cibalho Ciborio

CIC.
Cicatriz Cicero Cicioso

CID.
Cidadão Cidadoa Cidrão
Cidadãos Cidra Cidreira
Cidade Cidrada

CIE.
Ciencia

CIF.
Cifar Cifra Cifrar

CIG.
Cigana Cigarra Cigurelha
Cigano Cigude

CIL.
Cilada Cilhar Cilicio
Cilhas Cilicia Cilladas

CIM.

Cima	Cimeyra	Cimitarra
Cimalha	Cimento	Cimo
Cimbalo		

CIN.

Cinca	Cingidouro	Cintillar
Cincar	Cingir	Cintura
Cincho	Cingulo	Cinza
Cinco	Cinnamomo	Cinzeiro
Cincoenta	Cinta	

CIO.

Cio	Cioso	Ciosa

CIP.

Cipó	Cipreste	Cipriano

CIR.

Cira	Circulo	Circumstancia
Ciranda	Circuito	Circumstantes
Cirandagem	Circumcidar	Cirio
Cirandar	Circumcisão	Cirugia
Circo	Circumferencia	Cirugião
Circulação	Circumspecto	Cirzir
Circular	Circumspecção	

CIS.

Ciscar	Cismatico	Cisterciense
Cisco	Cisne	Cisterna

CIT.

Citação	Citerior	Citharedo
Citado	Cithara	Citrino

CIU.
Ciume   Ciumes

CIV.
Civel   Civil   Civilidade

CIZ.
Cizania   Cizento   Cizirão

XI. No Portuguese word begins with ç.

The ç is used after p in those Portuguese words that have in their Latin root pt : as, *descripção, accepção,* &c., from *descriptio, acceptio,* &c.

OF DOUBLE LETTERS.

It is to be generally observed that the consonants are doubled in those Portuguese words whose Latin roots have likewise the same double consonants : as, *accelerar, accento, occidente,* &c., from *accelero, accentus, occidens,* &c.; *affligir, affluencia, affirmação,* &c., from *affligo, affluentia, affirmatio,* &c., as will be seen in the following collection.

B

is to be doubled in *abbade, abbacial, abbadia, abbadessa, abbreviatura, abbreviar.*

C

is to be doubled in the following words, and some of their derivatives.

Abstracção	Accentuar	Accessivel
Acção	Accepção	Accesso
Accento	Accessão	Accessorio

Accidental	Construcção	Inspecção
Accidente	Contracção	Instrucção
Accelerada	Correcção	Intellecção
Accelerado		Interjecção
Accelerar	Decocção	Intersecção
Acclamação	Deducção	Introducção
Acclamar	Dejecção	
Accomodação	Desoccupação	Manuducção
Accomodado	Desoccupado	
Accomodar	Desoccupar	Objecção
Accumulação	Detracção	Obstrucção
Accumulado	Dicção	Occasião
Accumular	Diccionario	Occasionar
Accusação	Direcção	Occaso
Accusado	Distracção	Occidental
Accusador		Occidente
Accusar	Eccentrico	Occiduo
Accusativo	Ecclesiastico	Occisão
Adstricção	Erecção	Occurrer
Afflicção	Evicção	Occultamente
Attracção	Exacção	Occultado
	Extracção	Occultar
Baccho		Occulto
Bocca	Facção	Occupação
Boccaça	Ficção	Occupado
Boccadinho	Fracção	Occupar
Boccado		Occurrencia
Boccal	Impeccabilidade	Occurrente
	Impeccavel	
Circumspecção	Inaccessivel	Peccado
Coacção	Indicção	Peccador
Cacção	Inducção	Peccadora
Collecção	Infecção	Peccante
Constricção	Infracção	Peccar

ORTHOGRAPHY. 233

Predicção	Seccar	Successor
Preoccupar	Secco	Succintamente
Producção	Secção	Succinto
Projecção	Seccura	Succo
Protecção	Sôcco	Successo
Putrefacção	Soccorrer	Succubo
	Soccorro	
Rarefacção	Subtracção	Transacção
Reconducção	Succeder	Traducção
Refecção	Successão	
Refracção	Successo	Vacca
Reseccçaão	Successivo	Vaccada
Restricção	Successivel	Vaccum

D.

This letter is doubled in the following words: *addição, addicionado, addicionar, additamento, additar.*

F

is to be doubled in

Affabilidade	Affeado	Affeminado
Affavel	Affear	Affeminar-se
Affadigado	Affeamento	Afferradamente
Affadigar	Affectadamente	Afferrado
Affagado	Affectado	Afferrar
Affagar	Affectar	Afferretoado
Affagos	Affecto	Afferretoar
Affamado	Affectuoso	Afferrolhar
Affamar-se	Affeição	Afferventado
Affastado	Affeiçoado	Afferventar
Affastar	Affeiçoar	Affervorado
Affazendado	Affeite	Affervorar
Affazer-se	Affeitar	Affiado

Affiar	Afforamento	Differença
Affidalgado	Afformentar	Differençar
Affidalgar-se	Afformoscado	Differenças
Affigurado	Afformoscar	Differente
Affigurar	Affoutado	Differentemente
Affilhada	Affoutar	Difficil
Affilador	Affouteza	Difficuldade
Affilar	Affouto	Difficultar
Affinado	Affracar	Difficultosamente
Affinar	Afframengado	Difficultoso
Affincado	Affréguesado	Diffusão
Affincar	Affreguesar-se	Diffusamente
Affirmadamente	Affronta	Diffuso
Affirmador	Affrontado	
Affirmar	Affrontamento	Effectivamente
Affistular-se	Affrontar	Effectivo
Affixar	Affrontosamente	Effeito
Afflamar-se	Affrontoso	Effeituar
Afflicção	Affroxadamente	Efficazmente
Afflicto	Affroxado	Efficacia
Affligir	Affroxar	Efficaz
Affluencia	Affugentado	Efficiente
Affocinhar	Affugentar	Effigie
Affogado	Affumado	
Affogador	Affumar	Offender
Affogar	Affundado	Offerecer
Affogamento	Affundar-se	Offuscar
Affogueado	Affundir-se	
Affoguear	Affuzillar	Suffocar
Afforado		Suffragio, *and some*
Afforador	Diffamado	*others*
Afforar	Diffamar	

G

This letter is to be doubled in

Aggravante	Aggressor	Exaggerar
Aggravar	Exaggeração	Suggerir
Aggravado	Exaggerador	Suggestão
Aggravo	Exaggerado	Suggerido

L

is to be doubled in

Aballado	Alliviar	Aquella
Aballador	Allucinação	Aquelle
Aballar	Allucinar	Aquillo
Aballo	Alludir	Armellas
Aballisado	Allumiar	Arrepellado
Aballisador	Allusão	Arrepellão
Aballisar	Amantellado	Arrepellar
Acafellador	Amarello	Atropellado
Acafelladura	Amarellecer-se	Atropellar
Acafellar	Amarellidão	Avillanado
Acallentado	Amollado	
Acallentar	Amollar	Bacellado
Acapellado	Amollecer	Bacêllo
Affillado	Amollecido	Barbella
Affillador	Amollentar	Barrella
Affillar	Ampolla	Bella
Allegação	Annullação	Bellamente
Allegado	Annullar	Bello
Allegar	Appellação	Belleza
Allegoria	Appellante	Belleguim
Allegorico	Appellar	Bellico
Allegorisar	Appellidar	Bellicoso
Alleluia	Appellido	Belligero

Belluino	Cella	D'elle
Bulla	Celleiro	D'elles
Bullario	Clavellina	Degollado
	Codicillo	Degollação
Calliope	Colla	Degollar
Camillo	Collado	Degolladouro
Cavillação	Collar	Distillação
Cavillosamente	Colleira	Distillador
Caballina	Collação	Distillar
Cadella	Collateral	Donzella
Cadellinha	Colecção	Duello
Callo	Collecta	
Camartello	Collectivo	Ebullição
Cambadella	Collector	Ella
Cancella	Collega	Ellas
Capella	Collegiada	Elle
Capellão	Collegial	Elles
Capellada	Collegio	Elleboro
Capellania	Colligar	Ellipse
Capêllo	Colligir	Elliptico
Capillar	Collyrio	Emolliente
Castella	Collo	Emollir
Castello	Collocação	Enallage
Casullo	Collocar	Encapellado
Casulla	Colloquio	Encapellar
Cavalla	Compellir	Encastellado
Cavallaria	Compostella	Encastellar
Cavalleiro	Constellação	Encelleirar
Cavallo	Corollario	Equipollencia
Cebolla	Covello	Equipollente
Cebollal	Courella	Escabellado
Cebollinho		Escabello
Chancellér	D'ella	Escudella
Chancellaria	D'ellas	Escudellão

Estillação	Gallico	Illuminativo
Estillado	Gallinha	Illusão
Estillar	Gallinhaço	Illuso
Estillicidio	Gallinheira	Illustração
Estrella	Gallinheiro	Illustrar
Estrellado	Gallinhola	Illustre
Excellencia	Galliopoli	Illustrissimo
Excellente	Galliota	Illyrio
Expellir	Galliza	Imbella
	Gallo	Impellir
Falla	Gamella	Incapillato
Fallacha	Gazella	Infallivel
Fallacia	Gella	Inintelligivel
Fallador		Intervallo
Fallar	Hellesponto	
Fallecer	Hendecasyllabo	Janella
Fallecido	Hollanda	Janelleira
Fallencia	Hypallage	Janellinha
Fallido		Jarmello
Ferdizello	Illação	
Flagellante	Illaquear	Libello
Flagello	Illativo	Lordello
Folle	Illegitimo	Lousella
Folliculo	Illeso	
Fontello	Illiçar	Malfallante
	Illiciador	Mallogrado
Gabella	Illicitamente	Mamillar
Gallado	Illicito	Marcella
Galladura	Illocavel	Marcellina
Gallar	Illudido	Marcello
Gallego	Illudir	Martellada
Gallia	Illuminação	Martellar
Gallicado	Illuminado	Martello
Gallicar	Illuminar	Martellinho

Medulla	Palla	Pusillanime
Mellifluo	Palladio	
Mello	Pallante	Quartella
Metallico	Pallas	
Millenario	Palliado	Rabadella
Millesimo	Palliar	Rabellado
Mirandella	Pallidez	Rebellão
Miscellania	Pallido	Rebellar-se
Molle	Pallio	Rebellião
Molleira	Panella	Rella
Molleza	Paradella	Rodofolle
Mollice	Parallaxe	Rodopello
Mollidão	Parallelo	Rosella
Mollificante	Parallelogramo	Ruella
Mollificar	Pelle	
Mollinar	Pellesinha	
Monosyllabo	Pellica	Sella
	Pellicula	Sellado
Nella	Phillis	Sellador
Nellas	Pimpinella	Sellagão
Nelle	Pollegada	Sellar
Nelles	Pollegar	Selleiro
Nigella	Pollez	Sello
Novella	Pollução	Sentinella
Novelleiro	Polluto	Sibylla
Nulla	Polysyllabo	Sigillo
Nullidade	Portella	Sigillado
Nullo	Postilla	Sobrepelliz
Nuzellos	Pousafolles	Sugillação
	Prunelle	Syllaba
Odivellas	Pulmella	Syllabatico
Ollaria	Pupilla	Syllabico
Olleiro	Pupillo	Syllogisar
Ouguella	Pusillanimidade	Syllogismo

ORTHOGRAPHY. 239

Tabella	Tunicella	Vellicação
Tabellião	Tullio	Vellicar
Tabellioa		Vello
Titillação	Vacillação	Velloso
Titillar	Vacillante	Velludo
Tôlla	Vacillar	Verdesella
Tollice	Valla	Villa
Tôllo	Vallado	Villania
Torcicollo	Vallar	Villaãmente
Tranquillidade	Valle	Villão
Tranquillo	Vassallagem	Vitella
Trella	Vassallo	Vitellino
Trisyllabo	Vallcidade	

Note. Annular signifies to annul; but *annular* is an adjective, and signifies *annular*, or in the form of a ring.

M.

is to be doubled in

Accommodar	Commodo	Emmadeirar
	Commover	Emmadeixar
Commemoracão	Commum	Emmagrecer
Commenda	Communger	Emmanquecer
Commensurar	Communicar	Emmassar
Commentar	Communidade	Emmudecer
Commerciar	Commutar	Engommar
Commetter	Consummar	Epigramma
Comminação		
Commiseração		
Commissão	Desaccommodar	Flamma
Commissario	Descommodo	Flammante
Commoção	Dilemma	Flammula

Gemma	Immoderadamente	Inflammar
Gomma	Immodesto	
Grammatica	Immodico	Mamma
	Immolar	Mammar
Immaculada	Immortalisar	
Immanente	Immortificado	Recommendar
Immarcessivel	Immovel	
Immaterial	Immudavel	Somma
Immaturo	Immundo	Sommar
Immediatamente	Immunidade	Summa
Immemoravel	Immutavel	Summario
Immenso	Incommodo	Summidade
Immensuravel	Incommunicavel	Symmetria, *and*
Immobilidade	Incommutavel	*some others.*

Note. *M* and not *n*, is always made use of before *b, m, p.*

N.

is likewise doubled in several verbs compounded with *an, en, in, con;* as, *annelar, annexa, annão, annata, annel, anna, Anno, annular, connexão, connexo, depennar, empennar, ennastrar, ennegrecer, innato, innagavel, innocencia, manna, Marianna, panno, penna,* when it signifies a pen, *tyranno,* and some others.

P.

This letter is to be doubled in words beginning with *p*, compounded with the Latin prepositions *ad, ob, sub;* as, *apparato, apparecer, oppor, opprimir, suppor, Philippe, pappa,* &c.

Note. *Pappa* signifies *pap,* or a sort of food for children, but *papa* signifies *the Pope.*

R.

The *r* is doubled in such words as are strongly pronounced in the middle; as, *guerra, arrancar, arredar, arrimar, arruinar, carregar, carro,* &c.

S.

The *s* is to be doubled in the Portuguese superlatives, because it is doubled in the Latin roots; it is also doubled in the following words:—

Abbadessa	Assobiar	Necessitar
Accesso	Assolar	N'isso
Aggressor	Assombrar	Nossa
Amassar	Assoprar	Nosso
Appressar	Assustar	
Arremessar	Atravessar	Osso
Assaltar		
Assanhar	Condessa	Passar
Assar		Passear
Assegurar	Essa	
Assessor	Esse	Remessa, *and many*
Assignar		*others.*
Assim	Ingresso	
Assistir	Isso	

T.

T is doubled in the following words and their derivatives:—

Attemperar	Attenuar	Attribuir
Attenção	Attonito	Attributo
Attender	Attracção	Attrição
Attentar	Attractivo	Attrito
Attenuação	Attrahir	

Commetter	Intrometter	Remetter
		Remetter
Demittir	Omittir	
		Setta
Enfittar	Permittir	Settenta
	Prometter	
Fitta		Trasmittir

OF THE QUANTITY OF SYLLABLES AND THEIR SOUND.

OF WORDS THAT MAKE THEIR PENULTIMA IN *a*.

Note. Observe what we have before mentioned concerning the accents.*

All words ending in *abo, aba, aco, aca, acho, acha, aço, aça, ado, ada, afo, afa, ago, aga, agem, agre, alho, alha, alo, ala*, have the penultima long; as, *diábo, mangába, macáco, macáca, caváca, mingácho, garnácha, madraço, linhaça, amádo, punhada,* (except *ralâmpago, antropófago, lêvado,* and *cágado,* (which are short in the penultima), *abáfo, abafa, saramágo, adága* (except *estômago, âmago, amâraco,* which are short), *tralâlho, toálha, bedálo* (except *anômalo, bufalo, escândalo,* which are short), *tanchágem, vinágre.*

Words ending in *amo, ama, anho, anha, ano, ana,* have their penultima long; as, *escâmo, courâma, costânho, arânha, engâno, pestâna;* except *pâmpano, tímpano, bígamo.*

Words ending in *apo, apa, aque, aro, ara,* have their

---

* Through the remainder of this chapter the proper accents are expressly marked, for the sake of example; not that the words usually appear so accentuated.

penultima long; as, *guardinápo, solápa, basbaque, empáro, seára*; except *cántaro, púcaro, láparo, báfaro, lúparo, pífaro, pícaro, cámera, támara, pássaro, Lázaro, bárbaro, cócaras*, &c.

Words ending in *aro, arra, arto, ata, avo, ava, axo, axa*, make the penultima long; as, *bizárro, bizárra, biscáto, patarata, escrávo, escráva* (except *côncava* and *bisavó*), *cartáxo, tarráxa*.

OF WORDS THAT MAKE THEIR PENULTIMA IN *e*.

All words ending in *ebo, eba, edo, eda, efa*, have their penultima long; as, *mancêbo, mancêba, azêdo, azêda, sanéfa*.

Words ending in *efe* are long; as, *magaréfe*: as well as those ending in *eco, eca, eço, eça;* as, *bonéco, bonéca, cabêço, cabêça*.

Words ending in *ego, ega*, are long: as, *morcêgo, socêgo, relêgo, entrêga, allega;* except *cónego, tráfego, côrrego, sófrego, pêcego, fôlego, bátega, cócegas*.

Words ending in *ejo, eja, elo, ela*, are long; as, *caranguêjo, bocêjo, igrêja, Alentéjo, envéja, martélo, guerréla*.

Words ending in *emo, ema, eno, ena*, are long: as, *suprêmo, postêma, acêno, açucêna;* except *apózema*.

Note. The penultima is short in the word *ingreme*.

Words ending in *epo, epa, epe, eque, ero, era*, are long: as, *decépo, carépa, julépe, moléque, sevéro, sevéra, tempêro,* when a noun, and *tempéro*, when a verb; except *áspero, próspero*.

Words ending in *eso, esa, ezo, eza, eto, eta, ete, evo, eva, eve*, are long; as, *acêso, acêsa, desprêzo, grandêza,* and *despréso* (when a verb), *entremêto, galhêta, ramalhête, bofête atrêvo, atrêva, atrêve*.

OF WORDS THAT MAKE THEIR PENULTIMA IN *i*.

Words ending in *ibo, iba, ibe, icho, icha, iche, ico, ica, iço, iça, ice, ido, ida, ifo, ifa, ife,* have the penultima long; as, *estríbo, arríba, arríbe, esguícho, esguícha, azevíche, paníco* (a sort of stuff), *botíca;* except *mecânico, ecuménico, crítico, político, pânico* (panic), and some others borrowed from the Greek and Latin. In *iço, iça,* &c.; as, *roliço, preguiça, velhíce, marído, medída;* except *hómido, pállido, hórrido,* and some others derived from the Latin. In *ifo, ifa,* &c.; as, *borrífo, alcatífa, patífe.*

Words ending in *igo* and *iga* are long; as, *amígo, amíga;* except *pródigo, pródiga.*

Words ending in *ijo* and *ija*, are long; as, *aflíjo, artemíja.*

Words ending in *ilho, ilha,* are long; as, *atílho, baetílha.* Others ending in *ilo, ila;* as, *gorgomílo, perfíla, desfíla.*

Words ending in *imo, ima,* have the penultima long; as, *opímo, cadímo, esgríma, lastíma* (when a verb); except *lástima* (when a noun), *Jerónimo, péssimo,* and all the superlatives, *anónimo,* and some others.

Words ending in *inho, inha, ino, ina, ipo, ipa, ipe,* have the penultima long; as, *constípo, constípa, Euripo, acipípe.* Others in *iquo, iqua, ique, iro, ira, ire;* as, *iníquo, iníqua, lambíque, retíro, mentíra, suspíro.*

Words ending in *iso, isa, izo, iza, ito, ita, ivo, iva, ixo, ixa,* are long in the penultima; as, *avíso, camísa, juízo, ajuíza, altívo, altíva, prolíxo, prolíxa, apíto, cabríto;* except *púlpito, vómito, decrépito, espírito, débito,* and some others.

RULES FOR SUCH WORDS AS MAKE THEIR PENULTIMA IN O.

Words ending in *obo, oba, obe, obro, obra, obre,* have their penultima long; as, *lôbo, lôba, arróba, arróbe, glôbo, alcóva, óbro, óbra, côbre, dôbro.*

Words ending in *ocho, ocha, oco, oca, oço, oça, odo, oda, ode, oso, osa, ose,* have the penultima long; as, *agarrócho, garrócha, carócha, biôco;* except *altiloco, massaróco, minhóca, almôço, môça* (a girl), *móça* or *móssa* (a notch), *almóço* (when a verb), *carróço, lôdo, bôda, bóde, póde* (the third person singular of the present indicative of the verb *poder*), *pôde* (the third person singular of the preterperfect definite of the same verb), *galhófa, bôfe.*

Words ending in *ofro, ofra, ofre,* are long; as, *alcachófra, cófre, enxófre.*

Words ending in *ogo, oga, ogue,* are long; as, *affógo, affoga, affógue, desafógo* (when a verb), and *desafôgo* (when a noun).

Words ending in *ojo, oja,* have the penultima long; as, *despójo* (when a verb), *nôjo, despôjo* (when a noun).

Words ending in *olo, ola, ole,* are long; as, *viólla, gallinhóla, bóla, engóle, miólo, bólo, rebólo, tólo, cebóla;* except *pérola, frívolo, benévolo, malévolo.*

Words ending in *omo, oma, ome,* have the penultima long; as *mordômo, redôma, fóme;* except *Thomé.*

Words ending in *onho, onha, ono, ona,* have the penultima long; as, *bisônho, risonha, dôno, atafôna, dôna;* except *altísono* and *unísono.*

Words ending in *opla, opo, opa, ope, opro, opra, opre, oque,* have the penultima long; as *manópla, tópo, tópa, galópe, assôpro* (when a verb); *assópra, assópre, assopro* (when a noun), *botóque.*

Words ending in *oro, ora, ore,* are long in the penultima; as, *penhóro, penhóra, penhóre, chôro* (when a noun), *choró* (when a verb); except *bácoro, rémora, pólvora, árovre.*

Words ending in *orro, orra,* are long; as, *soccôrro, môrro, cachôrra;* and some others ending in *oso, ose, osa, ozo, oza;* as, *primorósa, primorôsa, industriôso, industriôsa, ciôzo, cióza, descóse.*

Words ending in *oto, ota, ote,* have their penultima long; as, *gôto, gôta, bóta, devóto, fróta, capóte, garróte.*

Words ending in *ovo, ova, ove,* are long in the penultima; as, *ôvo, corcóva, apróve.*

Words ending in *oxo, oxa,* are long in the penultima; as, *rôxo, róxa, pintarrôxo.*

RULES FOR SUCH WORDS AS MAKE THEIR PENULTIMA IN *u*.

Words ending in *ubo, uba, ubro, ubra, ucho, ucha, uco, uca, uço, uça,* make the penultima long; as, *adúbo, adúba;* except *súccubo, íncubo,* and some others; *incúbro, incúbra, machúcho, embúcha, cadúco, cadúca, rebúço, embúça.*

Words ending in *udo, uda, ude, ufo, ufa, ufe, ugo, uga, ujo, uja,* have the penultima long; as, *felpúdo, felpúda, almúde, pantúfo, adufa, adúfe, sanguesúga, caramujo, azambúja.*

Words ending in *ulho, ulha, ulhe, ulo, ula, ule, umo, uma, ume, unho, unha, unhe;* as, *bayúlho, borbúlha, entúlhe, engúlo, engúla, bulebúle;* except *vocábulo, vestíbulo, ángulo, régulo, opúsculo, trémulo, patíbulo, thuribulo,* and some others; *consúmo, consúma, cardúme, testemúnho, testemúnha, empúnhe.*

Words ending in *uno, una, une, upo, upa, upe, uque, uro, ura, ure,* are long in the penultima; as, *desúno,* fortúna, desúne, apúpo, apúpa, apúpe, estúque, madúro, madúra, apúre.

Words ending in *uso, usa, use, uzo, uza, uze, uto, uta, ute, uxo, uxa, uxe*, have the penultima long; as, *parafúso, parafúsa, parafúse, redúzo, redúza, vedúze, condúto, labúta, enxúta, labúte;* except *cômputo* (when a noun), *repúxo, empúxa, empúxe*, and some others ending in *úvo, úva, úve;* as, *viúvo, viúva, enviúve*.

Note. When the penultima is immediately followed by another vowel, observe that,

A before *e* must be accented with the acute accent, and pronounced accordingly; as, *sáe, cáe;* but before *i* it has no accent.

A before *o* must be pronounced and accented thus, *bacalháo;* but when the relative *o* is added to the third person singular of the present indicative, then *a* has no accent; as, *âma-o*.

E before *a* is accented thus, *balêa;* and sometimes with the acute, as *assembléa, idéa*, and some others; and sometimes has no accent at all, as in *gávea, fémea*, and some others.

E before *o* is exceedingly sonorous and long, as in *chapéo, coruchéo;* except *páteo, férreo, plúmbeo, áureo, argênteo*.

I before *a, e, o*, is long; as *dizía, fazía, almotolía;* except such as are borrowed from the Latin; as, *néscia, comédia, féria, sciência, prudência*, and *sábia*, when an adjective, &c. *I* before *o* and *e* is long; as, *desvíe, desvío;* except *vício*, and some others.

O before *a* is accented thus, *corôa, tôa, môa, esmôa*.

O before *e* is long in the words *dóe, móe, róe*, and in the verb *sóe*, when it signifies *to be wont;* but when it signifies *to sound*, it is to be accented thus, *sôe*.

U before *a* is long; as, *rúa, charrúa;* except *mellíflua, insua.*

U before *e* and *o* is long; as, *conclúo, recúo, conclúe, recúe;* except *mellifluo,* and some others derived from the Latin.

CHAPTER IX.

ETYMOLOGY OF THE PORTUGUESE TONGUE FROM THE LATIN.

THE Portuguese has so great an affinity to the Latin, that several words of the latter are preserved in the former, by only allowing a small alteration; as may easily be seen in the following observations:—

1. The *o* of the Latin words is preserved in some of the Portuguese: some Latin words are entirely preserved in the Portuguese; as, *hospede, corda, porta,* &c.

2. The *u* is changed into *o;* as, *forca, goloso, estopa, mosca, anamos,* &c., from *furca, gulosus, stupa, musca, anamus,* &c.

3. The diphthong *au* is frequently changed into *ou;* as, *louvavel, ouro, couve, mouro,* &c., from *laudabilis, aurum, caulis, maurus,* &c.

4. The *e* is preserved in several Portuguese words; as, *certo, servo, erva, terra, ferro,* &c., from *certus, servus, herba, terra, ferrum,* &c.

5. The *e* takes the place of *i;* as, *enfermo, seco,* &c., from *infirmus, siccus,* &c.; and the *i* is sometimes preserved; as in *indigno, benigno,* &c., from *indignus, benignus,* &c.

6. The *b* is also changed into *v;* as, *arvore, duvidar, dever, estava, amava,* &c., from *arbor, dubitare, debere, stabat, amabat,* &c.

7. The *c* is very often changed into *g;* as, *digo, agudo, amigo, migalhi,* &c., from *dico, acutus, amicus, mica,* &c.

8. *Cl* is changed into *ch;* as, *chamar, chave,* from *clamare, clavis,* &c.

9. When the *c* in Latin is followed by *t*, this letter is changed into ç; as, *acção, dicção,* &c., from *actio, dictio,* &c.: and sometimes the *c* before *t* is changed into *i;* as, *feito, leito, noite, leite, peito,* &c., from *factus, lectum, nocte, lacte, pectus,* &c. Finally, both the *c* and *t* are preserved in a great number of words; as, *acto, afflicto, distincto,* &c., from *actus, afflictus, distinctus,* &c.

10. The *d* is often omitted; as, *roer, excluir, raio,* &c., from *rodere, excludere, radius,* &c.

11. The *f* is frequently preserved; as in *filho, fazer, fervor, formoso,* &c., from *filius, facere, fervor, formôsus,* &c.

12. The *g* is changed into *i;* as, *reino,* from *regnum.* Sometimes it is omitted; as in *dedo, frio, setta, sinal, bainha,* &c., from *digitus, frigus, sagitta, signum, vagina,* &c.

13. The *h* is used instead of the *l;* as, *alho,* from *allium.* Sometimes it is added; as, *artelho, alheo, folha, conselho,* &c., from *articulus, alienus, folium, consilium,* &c.

14. The *n* is sometimes added, and sometimes taken off; as, *mancha, ilha, salitre, esposo,* from *macula, insula, sal nitrum, sponsus,* &c.

15. The *mn* is preserved by many Portuguese writers in the words *alumno, calumnia, columna, damno, solemne, somno,* from *alumnus, calumnia, columna, damnum,* &c.

16. The double *n* of the Latin is preserved in several words; as in *anno, innocencia, innocuo, innavegavel, innovar,*

connexo, &c., from *annus, innocentia, innocuus, innavigabilis, innovare, connexus*, &c.

17. The *gn* and *gm* are preserved in several Portuguese words; as in *augmento, fragmento, enigma, benigno, digno, indigno, ignominia*, &c., from *augmentum, fragmentum, enigma, benignus, dignus*, &c.

18. The *e* and the *i* after *n* are sometimes changed into *h;* as in *aranha, vinha, Hispanha, castanha*, &c., from *aranea, vinea, Hispania, castanea*, &c.

19. The *p* is changed into *b;* as in *cabra, cabello, cabeça*, &c., from *capra, capillus, caput*, &c. Sometimes *pl* is changed into *ch;* as, *chaga, choro, chuva*, &c., from *plaga, ploro, pluvia*, &c.

20. The *q* is changed into *g;* as, *igual, alguem, antigo, agoa, aguia*, &c., from *æquus, aliquis, antiquus, aqua, aquila*, &c.

21. The *t* is likewise changed into *d;* as, *cadea, fado, lado, nadar, piedade*, &c., from *catena, fatum, latus, natare, pietas*, &c. The *ti* of the Latin is sometimes changed into *ça*, and sometimes into *ci;* as in *graça, clemencia, paciencia*, &c., from *gratia, clementia, patientia*, &c.

Note. All these alterations are not general in all the words, but are used in several; and on some occasions the Latin word is preserved without any change or variation. And as it would be endless to pretend to show all the affinity between the Portuguese and the Latin, I shall only observe that they sometimes add, and sometimes take off, letters from the Latin roots; as in *facil, debil, final, material, estrepito, estomago, expectador, especular*, &c. from *facilis, debilis, finalis, strepitus, spectator*, &c.

PART III.

THE DIFFERENT IDIOMS OF *ANDAR*, TO GO.

Andar a pé	To go on foot
Andar a cavallo	To ride on horseback
Andar pela rua	To walk in the street
Andar em coche	To ride in a coach
Andar embarcado	To sail
Andar de bolina	To sail with a side wind
Andar para diante	To go forward
Andar para traz	To go backward
Andar atraz de algum	To go behind *or* after one, *also* to follow, to press, to solicit a person
Andar de vagar	To go wandering
Andar com o tempo	To go with the times
Andar perdido	To go astray
Andar de pé	To be poorly, *but not bedridden*
Andar com honra	To act honestly
Anda	Go
Anda para diante	Go on
Andar de pandega	To carouse
Andar de mal a peior	To grow worse and worse
Andar de reixa com alguem	To bear one a grudge
Com o andar do tempo	In the course of time
Andar de galope	To gallop
Andar em corpo	To be uncloaked
Anda o mundo ás avessas	The world has come about

Andar trabalhando n'alguma obra	To be about some piece of work
Andar contente	To go pleased
Andar dizendo	To publish or report

THE DIFFERENT IDIOMS OF *DAR* AND *DAR-SE*.

Dar	To give, to strike
Dar a entender	To give to understand
Dar fé	To credit, to believe
Dar or vender fiado	To sell upon credit
Dar á luz	To publish, to be confined
Dar-se a partido	To side with one
Dar palavra	To promise
Dar uma salva	To fire a volley
Dar fiador	To bail
Dar principio or fim	To begin or to end
Dar conta	To give an account
Dar-se ao estudo	To apply oneself to study
Dar em que fallar	To give room for talking
Dar entrada	To give access to
Dar causa	To give cause
Dar que entender	To vex one sadly, to trouble one
Dar de beber	To give drink
Dar vozes	To cry out
Dar um coscorrão	To give a box on the ear
Dar palmadas	To clap hands
Dar caução	To give security
Dar o faro de alguma coisa a alguem	To give a hint about something
Dar uma éstocada	To give a thrust
Dar os bons dias	To bid one good morning
Dar a guardar	To give to keep

Dar emprestado	To lend
Dar com alguem	To meet with one by chance, to light upon a person
Dar em alguem	To strike one
Dar cartas	To deal *or* give the cards
Dar sobre o inimigo	To fall upon the enemy
Dar os parabens	To congratulate
Dar os parabens a alguem da sua chegada	To bid one welcome
Dar a mão ajudando	To give a helping hand
Dar a escolher	To let one take his choice
Dar enfado a alguem	To molest one
Dar no alvo	To hit the mark
Dar as costas	To run away, to betake oneself to flight
Dar pelo amor de Deos	To give for God's sake
Dar uma volta em redondo	To turn round
Dar uma vista de olhos	To cast a glance
Dar alcance ao que se deseja	To compass one's wish
Dar suspiros	To sigh
Dar ouvidos	To give hearing
Dar em rosto	To upbraid, to cast in the teeth
Dá cá	Give hither
Deu-me uma dôr	I was taken with a pain
Dar que fazer a alguem, or *occupar alguem*	To employ one, to set him at work, to set him upon some business
Dar horas	To strike (hours)
O relogio dá hóras	The clock strikes
Dar a alma a Deus	To die
Dar comsigo em alguma parte	To cast oneself into a place, *or* to go to a place
Dar de jantar	To give some dinner

O sol dá nos olhos	The sun shines in one's eyes
Dar razões	To debate *or* contend
Dar comsigo no chão	To fall upon the ground
Dar fruto	To bear fruit
Dar as mãos	To shake hands
Dar com a porta na cara de alguem	To shut the door upon one
Dar pressa	To press *or* hasten
Esta travessa vai dar á rua larga	This lane strikes, *or* goes into, the broad street
Dei no pensamento de, &c.	It came into my head to, &c.
Não sabe aonde ha de dar comsigo	He does not know where to go
Isto vos ha de dar muito que fazer	This will give you a great deal of trouble
Dar com o corpo em terra	To fall down
Dar em todos, or *dizer mal de todos*	To speak ill of everybody
Dar conta de si	To give account of oneself
Dar á conta	To pay on account
Eu darei conta d'isso	I will accomplish that
Elle deu em ir áquelle lugar	He began to use that place
Dar uma broma a alguem	To jest with some one
Dar-se por culpado	To acknowledge oneself guilty
De nenhuma sorte vos deis por entendido	Take no notice of anything
Dar-se por aggravado	To make a show of anger
Dar-se por satisfeito	To rest satisfied
Dar-se por vencido	To submit, to surrender oneself a prisoner, *or* to yield a point
Dar-se por desentendido	To fain oneself ignorant, to to take no notice of anything

Quando se der a occasião	When occasion shall require it
Dar-se pressa	To be in haste, to make haste
Elle deu-se a toda a sorte de vicios	He gave himself up to all manner of vices
Que se vos dá a vós d'isso?	What is that to you?
Pouco se me dá	I care but little
Não se me dá nada	I care nothing at all
Elles dão-se muito bem	They agree very well together
Esta carne não se dá bem para isso	This meat is not good for that

OF THE DIFFERENT IDIOMS OF THE VERB *ESTAR*.

We use the verb *estar* to make an action of repose, by putting the verb that follows in the gerund; as, *elle está escrevendo*, he is writing.

Estar has several other significations; as,

Estar em pé	To stand upright
Estar bem or *mal*	To be well *or* ill
Estar assentado	To be sitting
Estar para sahir	To be just going out
Estar com o sentido em outra parte	To have one's wits a-wool-gathering
Está muito bem	It is well, it is very well
Está para chover	It is going to rain
Estar para cahir	To be ready to fall
Estar para morrer	To be on the point of death
Estar em duvida	To be in doubt
Estaremos a ver	We will expect the issue
Estar mão sobre mão	To stand idle

Estar em casa	To be at home
Aquillo não me está bem	That does not become me well
Estar dormido	To be asleep
Estar fazendo	To be doing
Estar de nojo	To be in mourning
Estar álerta	To be upon one's guard
Estar de sentinella	To stand sentry
Estar alegre	To be merry
Elle está como quer	He lives in clover
Estar em perigo	To be in danger
Estar encostado	To lean upon
Estar esperando	To expect
Estar muito tempo	To stay a good while
Estar calado	To be silent
Estar or viver com outros	To dwell with others
Estar por cima	To lie over
Estar debaixo	To lie under
Estar bem aviado	To be in a bad plight
Estar á espera	To lie in wait
Estar enamorado	To be in love
Estar de cama	To be bedridden
Estar no campo	To be in the country
Estar com saude, or de saude	To be in health
Estar quieto	To stand still, *or* to be quiet
Estar neutral	To stand neuter
Estarei por tudo o que vos parecer mais conveniente	I shall stand to whatever you shall think proper
A difficuldade está em, &c.	The difficulty consists in, &c.
Estar por alguem	To stand for one, to be of his side
Estar por or em lugar de, &c.	To stand for *or* signify, &c.
Elle estava na altura do Cabo de Boa Esperança	He stood off the Cape of Good Hope

Eu não quero estar a razões comvosco	I will not quarrel *or* dispute with you
Está quanto quizeres	Stay as long as it may please
Aonde estais?	Where are you? [thee
Estarei pelo que disser a pessoa que for de vosso agrado	I will refer it to whom you please
Não podemos estar por isso	We cannot stand to that
Não quero estar pelas vossas razões	I will not take your judgment
Como está vm^{ce}?	How do you do, sir?

Estar, joined with the infinitive of a verb and the particle *para*, signifies to be ready, or about doing a thing, which has always reference to the signification of the verb; as,

Estou para ir	I am going, I am ready to go
Estou para comprar um cavallo	I am about buying a horse
Estou para cazar-me	I am going to be married
Esta casa está para cahir	This house is ready to fall
Estou para dizer	I dare say
Estar com a boca aberta (metaphor)	To stare, to look, to hearken attentively
Estar de dieta	To keep to a diet
Estar fiado em alguem	To trust to, to rely, *or* depend upon one
Estar no fundo	To lie at the bottom
Estar de fronte	To lie over against
Estar em competencia	To stand in competition
Estar ao lume	To stand by the fire
Estar de longe	To stand at a distance
Estar alto	To stand high *or* in a high place
Estar á mão direita de alguem	To be at one's right hand, to have the first place

Elle esteve em perigo de afogar-se	He was like to be drowned
Não estar no caso de, &c.	Not to be able, *or* in case of, &c.
Estar á ordem de alguem	To be at one's disposal
Isso não está nos termos	That is not right, it will not do
Não estou no caso	I am not in a position of
Estar á razões	To contend, to strive, *or* quarrel
Estar bem com alguem	To be in favour with one
Estar bem	To be well, to be at ease
Bem aviado estaria eu, se &c.	It would be very bad for me, indeed, if, &c.
Estar em conceito de homem honrado	To be looked upon as an honest man
Estar na fé de	To believe, to think, *or* suppose
Estar de posse	To possess, to have the possession of a thing
Deixai estar isso	Let that alone
Estar em si	To be in one's right wits
Estar fóra de si	To be out of one's wits
Deixa estar (a sort of threatening)	I will be revenged on you, you shall pay for it

We have already observed the difference between *ser* and *estar*.

OF THE DIFFERENT IDIOMS OF *FAZER* AND *FAZER-SE*.

Fazer signifies *to do, to make, to create*; also *to form of materials*; also *to feign, to seem, to pretend as if*.

Elle fez que não o via	He pretended as if he did not see it

Fazer uma visita	To pay a visit
Elle o fez maltratar	He caused him to be used ill
Fazer pé atraz (metaphor)	To fall *or* draw back, to give ground
Que tendes vós que fazer com isto?	What have you to do with it? *or* what is that to you?
Fazer alarde de alguma cousa	To make a pride of a thing, to glory in it
Fazer fim ao desejo	To satisfy one's desire *or* longing
Fazer por alguma coisa	To take pains, to endeavour, to labour for a certain purpose, to work for a certain end
Faço por isso	I try after it
Fazer ao negocio or *ao caso*	To come to the purpose
Fazer esmolas	To give alms
Fazer gasto	To spend
Fazer gosto	To like, to be pleased with
Fazer o gosto or *a vontade a alguem*	To please one, to comply with one's desires
Fazer parallelo	To parallel, to compare
Fazer fumo	To smoke
Fazer ausencias a alguem	To speak of any one absent
Faz frio	It is cold
Fazer em pedaços	To pull to pieces
Fazer zombaria de alguem	To mock *or* to laugh at a person
Não façais caso d'isso	Do not mind that
Fazer agoada	To take in fresh water
Isto me faz vir a agoa á boca	This makes my mouth water

Fazer alto	To halt
Fazer casa (in playing at backgammon)	To put two men on the some point
Fazer a cêa	To get supper ready
Fazer caras	To make faces
Fazer enredos	To form a secret design against another
Fazer caso	To take notice
Fazer de valente	to act the brave
Fazer muito caso de alguma coisa	To make much of a thing
Não faço caso d'elle	I do not take any notice of him
Fazer festa	To caress, to fondle
Fazer uma festa	To give an entertainment, to feast
Fazer as vezes de alguem	To act as a substitute
Fazer das suas	To do mischief
Fazer lugar	To make room
Fazer mercê	To grant a favour
Fazer ouvidos de mercador	To appear as if one were deaf
Ter que fazer	To be busy
Fazer exercicio	To take exercise
Fazer exercicio (a military word)	To drill
Os soldados estão fazendo exercicio	The soldiers are drilling
Que fazeis aqui?	What are you doing here?
Fazer um vestido	To make a suit of clothes
Fazer uma lei, um discurso	To make a law, a speech
Fazer guerra	To make war
Fazer saber alguma cousa a alguem	To make one acquainted with a thing

PHRASEOLOGY. 261

Fazer enraivecer alguem	To make one mad
Fazer uma conta	To cast up an account
Fazer conta	To intend, *or* to propose
Elle fazia uma conta, e sahio-lhe outra	He was much disappointed
Fazer contas com alguem	To settle accounts with one
Isso não me faz conta	That is not convenient to me
Fazer pausa	To make a stand
Fazer bem	To do good
Fazer dinheiro de alguma cousa	To make money of a thing, to sell it
Tornar a fazer	To make again
Fazer damno	To do harm
Ter que fazer com alguem	To deal with one, *or* to have to do with one
Fazer amizade	To become friends
Fazer honra	To honour
Fazer fé	To make known, to testify, to witness
Fazer-se forte	To fortify oneself
Fazer menção	To mention
Fazer mal	To hurt
Fazer de alguem o que se quizer	To dispose of one
Fazer uma aposta	To lay a wager
Faz vento	The wind blows
Faz hoje oito dias	A week ago
Fazer vida com alguem	To dwell together
Fazer a sua vontade	To do as one pleases
Fazer o possivel	To do one's best
Não fareis nada com isso	You will do no good in it
Não façais mais assim	Do so no more

Se tornardes a fazer assim	If ever you do so again
Desejo que faça a sua fortuna	I wish he may make his fortune
Custou-me muito a fazel-o vir	I had much to do to make him come
Fazer a outrem o que quizeramos que outrem nos fizesse a nós	To do to others as we would have to be done to us
Não tenho que fazer com isso	I have nothing to do with it
Fazer o que alguem manda	To do as one is bid
Fazei de mim o que vos parecer	Do with me as you think fit
Fazer um grande estrondo	To make a great noise
Elle foi o que fez tudo n'aquelle negocio	He was the factotum in that business
Que fareis hoje?	What will you do to-day?
Fazer o seu trabalho	To do one's work
Fazer uma boa casa	To raise, to set up a good house (business)
Fazer a barba	To shave
Fazer a cama	To make the bed
Não sei que lhe fazer	I cannot help it
Fazer grande negocio	To drive a great trade
Fazer o seu officio	To exercise *or* discharge (profession)
Fazer profissão	To profess
Todos o fazião morto	Everybody gave out that he was dead
Fazer vir	To call *or* send for
Fazer entrar, or sahir alguem	To call in *or* out, to bid one come in *or* out
Isto não faz nada	It is no matter
Não sei que fazer d'isso	I have no need of it

Já não tenho que fazer com elle	I have done with him
Fazer um livro	To write a book
Fazer amizade com alguem	To make friendship, to get into friendship with one
Fazer exemplo em alguem, or *castigal-o para dar exemplo*	To make one a public example
Fazer uma coisa muito encubertamente	To do a thing very covertly
Fazer das suas	To play tricks
Elle sempre está fazendo das suas	He is always playing his tricks
Fazer jurar alguem	To put one to his oaths
Fazer saltar, or *voar pelos ares*	To blow up
Fazer boa vizinhança	To keep on good terms with one's neighbours
Fazer lenha	To fell wood
Fazer a ronda	To walk the rounds
Fazer dividas	To run in debt
Faz lua	The moon shines
Fazer violencia	To offer violence
Fazer-se ao trabalho	To inure oneself to hardships
Fazer-se velho	To grow old
Fazer-se feio	To grow ugly
Fazer-se soberbo	To grow proud
Faz-se tarde	It grows late

Fazer-se signifies also *to feign, to pretend, to seem, to make as if.*

Faz-se de surdo	He pretends to be deaf

THE DIFFERENT IDIOMS OF *TER* AND *TER-SE*.

Ter que fazer	To be busy
Ter odio	To hate
Ter por costume	To be wont
Ter alguem por ignorante	To believe one ignorant
Ter cuidado de	To be careful of
Ter cuidados	To be full of care
Ter fastio	To loathe, to see food with dislike
Ter animo	To have courage
Ter boa fama	To be well spoken of
Ter boa cara	To have a pleasant face
Ter necessidade	To be in want
Ter pressa	To be in haste
Ter muita fumaça	To be very proud
Ter grande presumpção	To presume much on oneself
Ter razão	To be in the right
Não ter razão	To be in the wrong
Ter uma coisa na ponta da lingua	To have a thing at one's finger's ends
Ter feições feiticeiras	To be fascinating
Ter má fama	To be ill spoken of
Ter ciumes	To be jealous of
Ter meios com que viver	To be well off
Ter no pensamento	To bear in mind
Ter obrigação	To be obliged
Ter medo	To be afraid
Ter razão, e mais que razão	To be right enough
Que tendes vós com isso?	What is that to you?
Ter carruagem e criados	To keep a carriage and servants
Ter a alguem suspenso	To hold one in suspense

Homem que tem boa feição	A man of good address
Ter mesa franca	To keep open house, to keep a table where a man may come without bidding
Ter frio	To be cold
Ter por bem	To approve of
Tenho-o por douto	I consider him as a learned man
Ter com que	To have wherewith
Não tendes de que vos queixar	You have no reason of complaint
Não tendes que, &c.	It is useless, *or* it will be to no purpose for you to, &c.
Isto não tem nada que fazer com o que eu digo	That is nothing to the purpose
Ter entre mãos	To have in hand
Tenho isso por certo	I hold that for a certainty
Ter d'ir com alguem	To have to go with some one
Ter alguem por si	To be supported *or* protected by one
Temos por nós a authoridade dos mais prudentes	The wisest men are of our opinion
Ter para si	To be of opinion
Ter em muito	To set much by
Ter em pouco	To value but little
Ter em boa conta	To hold in great esteem
Ter mão	To hold, *or* to restrain
Ter mão n'alguma coisa	To bear up, to support, to prop, to keep up, to hold up
Tenha não, or *tem mão*	Hold, stop
Ter-se em pé	To stand, to stand up

Ter-se bem a cavallo	To sit firmly *or* well on horseback
Não me posso ter de riso	I cannot forbear laughing
Não se pode ter, que não falle	He cannot forbear speaking

THE DIFFERENT IDIOMS OF *QUERER*.

Querer signifies *to wish, to be willing,* and *to believe;* as,

Querem alguns	Some believe
Querer bem	To love
Querer mal	To hate
Antes querer	To have rather
Queira Deus	God grant it
Mas quero que assim seja	I grant it, suppose it were so
Que quer dizer aquelle homem?	What does that man mean?
Que quer dizer isto?	What means this?
Isto quer dizer que, &c.	This means that, &c.
Eu quero absolutamente que, &c.	I positively resolve that, &c.
Eu assim o quero	I will have it so
Elle quer que vós obedeçais	He will have you obey
Não quero	I will not
Elle o fará quando quizer	He will do it when he pleases
Elle quer partir ámanhã	He wants to set out to-morrow
O mal que eu lhe quero me venha a mim	I wish him no more harm than I do to myself

HAVER, TO HAVE.

Tu has-de ir	You must go
Elle ha-de vir hoje	He is to come to-day
Se eu houver de ir	If I shall be obliged to go

Aindaque isso me houvesse de custar a vida	Though I were to lose my life for it
Haveis vós de estar em casa?	Shall you be at home?
Eu hei-de achar-me lá	I must be there
Elle ha-de ser bom	He must be good
Eu hei-de receber dinheiro	I am to receive money
Vós é que haveis de jogar	It is your turn to play
Aquillo é que vós havieis de fazer	You should do that
Haver por bem	To take in good part
Haver por mal	To take in ill part
Que ha-de ser	That is to be hereafter
Aquillo nunca ha-de ser	That will never happen
Para haver de fallar, ouvir, &c.	In order to speak, hear, &c.
Que ha-de ser de mim?	What is to become of me?
Livros do deve, e ha-de haver	Books of debtor and creditor
Haver mister	To want
Ha mister apressar-se	It is necessary to make haste

Haver, when impersonal, is rendered into English by the verb *to be*, preceded by *there;* as,

Ha	There is *or* there are
Ha homens tão malvados	There are men so wicked
Havia uma mulher	There was a woman
Ha alguns bons, e outros máos	There are some good and some bad
Ha muitas casas	There are several houses
Ha alguma coisa de novo?	Is there any news?
Ha mais de uma hora	It is more than an hour since
Ha muito tempo	Long since
Ha perto de uma hora que elle sahio	It is almost an hour since he went out
Ha um anno	A year ago
Ha oito dias	Eight days ago

Ha perto de 20 legoas da qui lá	It is nearly 20 leagues thither
Não ha	There is not
Haver-se, v. r.	To behave oneself
Elle sabe como se ha de haver, or *elle sabe como ha de haver-se*	He knows how to behave himself
Elle houve-se de maneira que, &c.	He behaved himself in such a manner that, &c.

Note.—When this verb is used impersonally, it requires the particle *de*, as follows:

Ha-se mister de dinheiro	Money is wanted
Ha-de-se fazer, or *dizer, isto*	This must be done *or* said
Ha-de-se fazer o que elle quizer	People must do what he pleases

Ir, a neuter and irregular verb, *to go, to walk, to march;* also *to grow, to reach any estate gradually, to be going.*

Ir por mar e por terra	To travel by sea and land
Como vão os vossos negocios?	How go your concerns?
Tudo vai bem	All is well, all goes on well
As suas cousas vão muito mal	Things go very ill (or very hard) with him
Ir á mão	To hinder, to obstruct
Ir andando	To go on *or* forward, to keep *or* hold on his way; *also* to proceed, to continue on, to prosecute
Ir passando	To shift, to pass life not quite well, to live, though with difficulty
Onde vai?	Where are you going?
Onde vai isto a dar comsigo?	What of all this?

Ir para baixo	To go down
Ir para cima	To go up
Quanto mais vamos para a primavera, mais compridos são os dias	The nearer the spring the longer the days
Ir de mal para peor	To grow worse and worse
Ir diante	To go before
Ir por diante	To go on or forward
Ir ao encontro	To go to meet
Ir ao fundo	To sink or fall to the bottom
Ir e vir	To go to and fro
Não faço mais do que ir e voltar	I will not stay, I shall be back presently
Isso já la vai	It is a thing past and done
Ei-lo lá vai	There he goes
Que vos parece d'aquella mulher? ei-lo vai, ella não é feia	How do you like that woman? there she goes, she is not ugly
Como as cousas agora vão	As things go now, as the world goes
Por que parte ides?	Which way do you go?
Deus vá comvosco	God go with you
Ir á roda do mundo	To go round the world
Ir com alguem	To go along with one
Esta travessa vai até á rua larga	This lane leads into the broad street
Eu o irei ver de caminho	I will call upon him as I go
Ir continuando o seu caminho	To go along [along
Ir fora do seu caminho	To go out of one's way
Ir um de uma banda, e outro da outra	To go separately
Ir para traz	To go backward
Ir detraz	To go behind
Ir atraz de alguem	To pursue, to go after one

Ir ao alcance de alguem	To go after one, in order to overtake him
Ir buscar	To go for or fetch
Ir para dentro	To go in
Ir para fóra	To go out
Ir peregrinando	To go on a pilgrimage
Ir ver, cantar, &c.	To go to see, to sing, &c.
Ir fazer um negocio	To go upon a business
Ir com a maré	To go with the tide
Ir par a par com alguem	To go side by side with one
Vai para quatro meses que eu aqui cheguei	It is now going on four months since I came hither
Ide em paz	Depart in peace
O tempo vai abrandando	The weather grows mild
Ir (at cards)	To go, to lay, to stake, to set
Ir-se, v. r.	To go, to go away, to go one's way, to depart, *also* to run *or* leak
Ir-se o enfermo	The sick man to die
A quaresma vai-se acabando	Lent draws to an end
Ir-se	To slip *or* pass away (as time)
Nada se vai mais depressa que o tempo	Nothing goes faster than time
Aquellas nuvens vão-se escurecendo	Those clouds are growing dark
Ir-se embora	To go away, *also* to be over
Esperai até que a calma se vá embora	Stay till the heat is over
Vai-te embora; que não sabes enganar a gente	Away *or* go, you know not how to wheedle people
Vai-se fazendo tarde	It grows late
Vai-se chegando a noite	The night draws on

Vai-se chegando o tempo da séga	It grows near harvest
Vai-se acabando minha paciencia	My patience is nearly exhausted
Ir-se escapulindo	To sneak away
Ir-se á mão	To refrain, to forbear, to abstain

Ir-se, to go away, impersonal; as, *vãi-se*, he goes away; *foi-se*, he went away; *ir-se-ha*, he shall go away.

TO PRAY.

Senhor, como amigo, faça-me o favor	Dear sir, do me the favour
Eu vos peço, or *peço vos*	I pray you
Peço-lhe em cortesia	I beseech you
Peço-lhe encarecidamente	I entreat *or* conjure you to do it
Peço-lhe por favor que, &c.	I beg of you that, &c.
Faça-me a fineza	Do me the kindness
Peço-lhe perdão	I beg your pardon

EXPRESSIONS OF KINDNESS.

Minha vida	My life
Minha alma	My soul
Meu amor	My love
Meu querido, minha querida	My dear
Meu coração	My dear love, my love
Filho do meu coração	My dear boy
Filha da minha alma	My dear girl

TO SHOW CIVILITY.

Agradeço a vm^{ce}	I thank you
Dou a vm^{ce} os agradecimentos	I give you thanks

Beijo as mãos de vm^{ce}	I kiss your hand
Fal-o-hei com todo o gosto	I will do it cheerfully
Com todo o meu coração	With all my heart
De muito boa vontade	Heartily, willingly
Veja. vm^{ce} se o posso servir n'alguma cousa	See if it is in my power to serve you
Disponha vm^{ce} como lhe parecer d'este seu criado	Do what you please with your servant
Estou esperando pelas ordens de vm^{ce}	I wait for your commands
Já que vm^{ce} assim o ordena	Since you will have it so
Ás ordens de vm^{ce}	At your service
Fico muito obrigado a vm^{ce}	I am very much obliged to you
Quer vm^{ce} que eu faça alguma coisa?	Have you anything to command me?
Sem ceremonia	Without ceremony
Não tem vm^{ce} mais que fallar	You need but speak
Faça-me a honra de me pôr aos pés da senhora	Present my respects, *or* duty, to my lady
Não sei como agradecer a vm^{ce} tantos favores	I know not how to make a proper return for so many favours
Não sou de cumprimentos	I am not for ceremonies
Deixemos estes cumprimentos	Away with these ceremonies or compliments
Isso é o melhor	That is the best way

TO GIVE TOKENS OF AFFIRMATION, CONSENT, BELIEF, AND REFUSAL.

É verdade	It is true
É isso verdade?	Is it true?
É muito verdade	It is but too true

Para dizer-vos a verdade	To tell you the truth
Com effeito é assim	Really it is so
Quem duvida d'isso?	Who doubts it?
Não ha duvida n'isso	There is no doubt of it
Parece-me que sim, que não	I think so, I do not think so
Apósto que sim	I lay it is
Apósto que não	I lay it is not
Creia-me vm^{ce}	Do believe me
Está vm^{ce} zombando?	Are you jesting?
Falla vm^{ce} de veras?	Are you in earnest?
Fallo de veras	I am in earnest
Pois está feito	Well, let it be so
Pouco a pouco	Little by little
Isso não é verdade	That is not true
Não ha tal coisa	There is no such thing
É mentira	It is false
Estava zombando	I did but jest
Seja muito embora	Let it be so
Não quero	I will not

TO CONSULT.

Que se ha de fazer?	What is to be done?
Que faremos?	What shall we do?
Que lhe parece a vm^{ce} que eu faça?	What do you advise me to do?
Que remedio tem isso?	What remedy is there for it?
Façamos assim	Let us do so
Façamos uma coisa	Let us do one thing
Será melhor que	It will be better that
Seria melhor que	It would be better that
Esperai um pouco	Stay a little

T

Deixai-me com isso	Let me alone
Antes quizera	I had rather
Se isso fosse commigo	Were that with me
Tudo é o mesmo	It is all one

OF EATING AND DRINKING.

Tenho fóme	I am hungry
Morro de fóme	I am dead hungry
Coma vm^{ce} alguma coisa	Eat something
Que quer vm^{ce} comer?	What will you eat?
Quer vm^{ce} comer mais?	Will you eat any more?
Tenho sêde	I am thirsty
Já matei a fome	I am no longer hungry
Tenho muita sede	I am very thirsty
Morro de sede	I am almost dead with thirst
Dê-me de beber	Give me something to drink
Eu beberia um copo de vinho	I could drink a glass of wine
Pois beba vm^{ce}	Drink, then
Tenho bebido bastante	I have drunk enough
Não posso beber mais	I can drink no more
Já matei a sêde	I am no longer thirsty, *or* my thirst is quenched

OF GOING, COMING, STIRRING, ETC.

Donde vem vm^{ce}?	Whence do you come?
Para onde vai vm^{ce}?	Where are you going?
Venho de—vou para	I come from, I am going to
Quer vm^{ce} subir or descer?	Will you come up *or* come down?
Entre vm^{ce}, saia vm^{ce}	Come in, go out
Não se mexa d'aqui	Do not stir from hence

Chegue-se para mim	Come near to me
Vá-se vm^{ce}	Go your way, be gone
Vem cá	Come hither
Espere por mim	Wait for me
Não vá tão depressa	Do not go so fast
Tire-se de diante de mim	Get out of my way
Não me toque	Do not touch me
Deixe estar isso	Let that alone
Estou bem aqui	I am well here
Abra vm^{ce} a porta	Open the door
Feche a porta	Shut the door
Abra or feche a janella	Open the window, *or* shut the window
Venha vm^{ce} por aqui	Come this way
Passe por alli	Pass that way
Que procura vm^{ce}?	What do you look for?
Que perdeo vm^{ce}?	What have you lost?

TO WISH WELL TO A PERSON.

O Céo vos guarde	Heaven preserve you
Deos vos dê boa fortuna	God send you good luck
Desejo vos todo o bem	I wish you everything that is good
Deus vos ajude	God assist you
Deus vos perdoe	God forgive you
Ide com Deus	God be with you
Até ver-nos	Till I see you again
Bom proveito faça a vm^{ce}	Much good may it do you
Bemdito sejas	God bless you

TO ADMIRE.

Óh Deus!	O God!
É possivel!	Is it possible!

Quem teria imaginado, crido, dito!	Who would have thought, believed, said
Que delicia!	How delightful!
Que maravilha! or *que milagre!*	Oh, strange! wonder!
Não me maravilho	I do not wonder
Como pode ser isto? or *Como é possivel?*	How can that be?
Eis aqui como são as coisas d'este mundo	So goes the world

TO SHOW JOY OR DISPLEASURE.

Que gosto!	What pleasure!
Que gloria!	What bliss!
Que alegria!	What joy!
Que contentamento é o meu!	How pleased I am!
Que felicidade!	What happiness!
Sinto isso	I am sorry for it
Sinto isso n' alma	That touches my very soul
Sinto isso no coração	It pierces me to the heart
Oh que desgraça é a minha!	Oh, how unhappy am I!
Affrontar-me d'esta sorte!	To affront me thus!
Assim é que me trata?	Do you use me thus?
Que bella cortesia!	Oh, what fine manners!
Não deveria tratar commigo d'esta sorte	You ought not to treat me thus
Parece-te bem?	Do you think that well?
Olhe como elle me trata	See how he is using me
Olhai o que elle diz	Hear what he says
Peço-lhe que me deixe	Pray leave me alone
Ora deixa-me	Away, away
Deixa-me, vai com Deus	Go, go, God be with you
Vai-te d'aqui, or *vai-te embora*	Go away

Vai tratar da tua vida	Go, mind your own business
Não me quebres a cabeça	Do not torment me any more
Já me tens dito isso um cento de vezes	You have told it to me a hundred times already

TO CALL.

Ouve!	Hark!
Onde estás?	Where art thou?
Uma palavra	A word
Duas palavras somente	Only two words

TO ASK.

Que novas ha?	What news?
Que é isto? que ha?	What is this? what is the matter?
Onde ides?	Where are you going?
Donde vindes?	Whence come you?
Que quereis dizer?	What do you mean?
De que serve?	To what purpose?
Que vos parece?	What do you think?
Quem teve tal atrevemento?	Who has been so bold?
Que dizem? que se diz?	What do they say?
Como diz vm^{ce}?	How do you say?
Por que não me responde?	Why do you not answer me?

TO FORBID.

Deixai estar isso	Let that alone
Não toqueis	Do not touch
Não digais nada	Say not a word
Guardai-vos	Have a care

OF SPEAKING, SAYING, DOING, ETC.

Falle vm.^{ce} alto	Speak loud
Falle vm.^{ce} baixo	Speak low
Com quem falla vm.^{ce}?	To whom do you speak?
Falla vm.^{ce} commigo?	Do you speak to me?
Falle lhe	Speak to him *or* to her
Falla vm.^{ce} Portuguez?	Do you speak Portuguese?
Que diz vm.^{ce}?	What do you say?
Não digo nada	I say nothing
Elle não quer calar-se	She will not hold her tongue
Ouvi dizer que	I was told that . . . .
Assim m-o disserão	I was told so
Assim dizem	They say so
Assim dizem todos	Every one says so
Quem lhó disse a vm.^{ce}?	Who told it you?
Disse-mó o Sr. A.	Mr. A. told it me
Pois elle é que lhó disse?	Did he tell you so?
Pois ella é que o disse?	Did she tell it?
Quando o ouvio vm.^{ce} dizer?	When did you hear it?
Disserão-m-o hoje	I heard it to-day
Não posso crel-o	I cannot believe it
Que diz elle?	What does he say?
Que vos disse-elle?	What did he say to you?
Elle não me disse nada	He said nothing to me
Não lhó diga vm.^{ce}	Do not tell him that
Eu lhó direi	I will tell him *or* her of it
Não diga nada	Say not a word
Disse vm.^{ce} aquillo?	Did you say that?
Não o disse	I did not say it
Não disse vm.^{ce} assim?	Did you not say so?
Que está vm.^{ce} fazendo?	What are you doing?
Que tem vm.^{ce} feito?	What have you done?
Não faço nada	I do nothing

Não tenho feito nada	I have done nothing
Tem vm^{ce} acabado?	Have you done?
Que está elle fazendo?	What is he doing
Que faz ella?	What does she do?
Que quer, or *que ordena vm^{ce}?*	What is your pleasure?
Que lhe falta?	What do you want?

OF UNDERSTANDING, OR APPREHENDING.

Entende-o, or *percebe-o vm^{ce} bem?*	Do you understand him (or it) well?
Percebe vm^{ce} o que elle disse?	Do you understand what he said?
Percebe vm^{ce} o que elle diz?	Do you understand what he says?
Entende-me, or *percebe-me vm^{ce}?*	Do you understand me?
Entendo a vm^{ce} muito bem	I understand you very well
Sabe vm^{ce} a lingua Portugueza?	Do you understand Portuguese?
Não a sei	I do not understand it
Tem-me vm^{ce} percebido?	Did you understand me?
Agora o percebo	Now I understand you
Não se percebe o que elle diz	One cannot understand what he says
Parece tartamudo	He speaks like a stammerer

OF KNOWING, OR HAVING KNOWLEDGE OF.

Sabe vm^{ce} isso?	Do you know that?
Não o sei	I do not know it
Não sei nada d'isso	I know nothing of it
Ella bem o sabia	She knew it well
Porventura não sabia elle isso?	Did he not know of it?

Demos que eu o soubesse	Suppose I knew it
Elle não saberá nada d'isso	He shall know nothing of it
Elle nunca soube nada d'isto	He never knew anything about this
Eu soube-o primeiro, or antes que vm^{ce} o soubesse	I knew it before you
É isto assim ou não?	Is it so or not?
Não que eu saiba	Not that I know of

OF KNOWING, OR BEING ACQUAINTED WITH, FORGETTING AND REMEMBERING.

Conhece-o um^{ce}?	Do you know him?
Conhece-a vm^{ce}?	Do you know her?
Conhece-os vm^{ce}?	Do you know them?
Conheço-o muito bem	I know him very well
Não os conheço	I do not know them
Nós não nos conhecemos	We do not know one another
Conheço-o de vista	I know him by sight
Conheço-a de nome	I know her by name
Elle conheceo-me muito bem	He knew me very well
Conhece-me vm^{ce}?	Do you know me?
Estou esquecido do seu nome	I have forgotten your name
Esqueceu-se vm^{ce} de mim?	Did you forget me?
Conhece-vos ella?	Does she know you?
Conhece o Sr. a vm^{ce}?	Does the gentleman know you?
Parece que não me conhece	It appears he does not know me
O Sr. bem me conhece	The gentleman knows me well
Elle já me não conhece	He knows me no more
Tenho a honra de ser seu conhecido	I have the honour to be known to him
Lembra-se vm^{ce} d'isso?	Do you remember that?

Não me lembro d'isso	I do not remember it
Lembro-me muito bem d'isso	I do remember it very well

OF AGE, LIFE, DEATH, ETC.

Que idade tem vm^{ce}?	How old are you?
Que idade tem seu irmão?	How old is your brother?
Tenho vinte e cinco annos	I am five-and-twenty
Tem vinte e dois annos	He is twenty-two years old
Vm^{ce} tem mais annos do que eu	You are older than I
Que idade terá vm^{ce}?	How old may you be?
É vm^{ce} casado?	Are you married?
Quantas vezes tem vm^{ce} sido casado?	How often have you been married?
Quantas mulheres tém vm^{ce} tido?	How many wives have you had?
Tem vm^{ce} ainda pae e mãi?	Are your father and mother still alive?
Meu pai morreo	My father is dead
Minha mãi morreo	My mother is dead
Ha dois annos que meu pai morreo	My father has been dead these two years
Minha mãi casou outra vez	My mother is married again
Quantos filhos tem vm^{cc}?	How many children have you?
Tenho quatro	I have four
Filhos ou filhas?	Sons or daughters?
Tenho um filho e tres filhas	I have one son and three daughters
Quantos irmãos tem vm^{ce}?	How many brothers have you?
Não tenho nenhum vivo	I have none alive
Todos morreram	They are all dead
Todos havemos de morrer	We must all die

OF THE WORD *HORA*, AS A NOUN.

Hôra	An hour, *also* a particular time
Eu estarei lá dentro de uma hora	I will be there within an hour
Que horas são?	What is it o'clock? what is the time?
São sete horas	It is seven o'clock
A que horas estareis vós lá?	At what hour *or* time will you be there?
As horas que for preciso	In due *or* good time, at the time appointed
Horas desoccupadas	Leisure hours
A ultima hora, or *a hora da morte*	The last *or* the dying hour
Cada hora	Every hour
De hora em hora	Hourly, every hour
Meia hora	Half an hour
Um quarto de hora	A quarter of an hour
Uma hora e meia	An hour and a half
Perto das nove horas	About nine o'clock
Ha uma hora	An hour ago, *or* an hour since
Fóra de horas	Beyond the hour, or very late
A tempo	In time
Recolher-se a boas horas	To keep good hours
Recolher-se fóra de horas	To keep late hours
Horas de jantar, or *de cear*	Dinner *or* supper-time
Perto das horas de jantar	About dinner-time
Ainda estais na cama a estas horas?	Are you in bed at this time of the day?
O relogio dá horas	The clock strikes

Já derão onze horas	It struck eleven o'clock
Muito a boas horas	Early, betimes
A boas horas	In good time, in time, at the time appointed
Em má hora	In an ill hour, unluckily, unfortunately
Toda a hora que	Whensoever, at what time soever
A toda hora que quizerdes	At what time you will
Hora	Time
Horas de fazer oração	Prayer-time
Horas de ir á igreja	Church-time
Horas de ir para a cama	Bedtime
Horas de comer	Meal-times
Já não são horas	The time is past, it is too late
Quando lhe chegar a sua hora	When his dying hour shall arrive
Estar esperando pela sua hora	To wait for God's time
Não ver a hora	To long, to wish with eagerness, continued, with *em* or *de* before the thing desired
São horas de, &c.	It is time to, &c.
Horas canónicas	The set time for the clergy to say their office
Horas	Any little prayer-book, but particularly that in which is the office of the Blessed Virgin
As quarenta horas	So they call the space of three days, in which the consecrated Host is exposed and laid to public view, in certain festivals

Conta das horas	Horography, account of hours
Arte de dividir o tempo em horas	Horometry

ORA, AS AN ADVERB AND INTERJECTION.*

Ora, deixa-o-ir	Pray let him go
Ora, deixa-te d'estas parvoices	Away with these fopperies
Ora, deixemo-nos d'estes cumprimentos	Away with these compliments
Ora, vamos, despacha-te	Come, come, make haste
Ora, vamos, não ha perigo	Away, there is no danger
Ora, vamos, tira, d'aqui isto	Away with this
Ora, vamos, tem vergonha	Away, for shame
Ora, eu não posso soffrer aquillo	I cannot bear that
Ora um, ora outro	Sometimes one, sometimes another
Elles ora estão sobre um pé, ora sobre outre	They stand now on one foot, and then on another
Ora, que quer dizer isso?	How now?
Tudo a que é bom, deve ser amado; ora, Deus é infinitamente bom, logo, &c.	All that is good is to be loved; now God is infinitely good, therefore, &c.
Ora, havia um enfermo	Now, there was a sick man
Por ora	At present, for the present, now, at this time

* When it is an adverb or an interjection, it is now written *ora*, without the *h*.

A VOCABULARY

OF

WORDS MOST USED IN CONVERSATION.

DO CEO E DOS ELEMENTOS.	OF THE HEAVENS AND THE ELEMENTS.
Deus	God
Jesus Christo	Jesus Christ
O Espirito Santo	The Holy Ghost
A Trindade	The Trinity
A Virgem	The Virgin
Os anjos	The angels
Os archanjos	The archangels
Os santos	The saints
Os bem aventurados	The blessed
O céo	Heaven
O paraiso	Paradise
O inferno	Hell
O purgatorio	Purgatory
Os guerubins	The cherubim
O fogo	The fire
O ar	The air
A terra	The earth
O mar	The sea
O sol	The sun
A lua	The moon
As estrellas	The stars
Os raios	The rays

As nuvens	The clouds
O vento	The wind
A chuva	The rain
O trovão	The thunder
O relampago	The lightning
A saraiva	The hail
O raio	The thunderbolt
A neve	The snow
A geada	The frost
O gelo	The ice
O orvalho	The dew
Nevoa	Fog *or* mist
O terremoto	The earthquake
O diluvio	The deluge *or* flood
O calor	The heat
O frio	The cold

DO TEMPO. — OF TIME.

O dia	The day
A noite	The night
Meio dia	Noon
Meia noite	Midnight
A manhã	The morning
Uma hora	An hour
Um quarto de hora	A quarter of an hour
Meia hora	Half an hour
Tres quartos de hora	Three-quarters of an hour
Hoje	To-day
Hontem	Yesterday
Amanhã	To-morrow
Antes d'hontem	The day before yesterday
Depois de ámanhã	After to-morrow
Depois de jantar	After dinner

Depois da cêa	After supper
Uma semana	A week
Um mez	A month
Um anno	A year
Um dia santo	A holiday
Um dia de trabalho	A working day
O nascer do sol	The sun-rising
O pôr do sol	The sunset
O tempo da séga or *da ceifa*	The harvest
O tempo de vindima	The vintage

DAS ESTAÇÕES DO TEMPO.   OF THE SEASONS.

A primavera	The spring
O verão	The summer
O outomno	The autumn
O inverno	The winter

OS DIAS DA SEMANA.   THE DAYS OF THE WEEK.

Domingo	Sunday
Segunda feira	Monday
Terça feira	Tuesday
Quarta feira	Wednesday
Quinta feira	Thursday
Sexta feira	Friday
Sabado	Saturday

DOS MESES.   OF THE MONTHS.

Janeiro	January
Fevereiro	February
Março	March
Abril	April
Maio	May

Junho	June
Julho	July
Agosto	August
Setembro	September
Outobro	October
Novembro	November
Dezembro	December

DIAS SANTOS. — HOLY-DAYS OF THE YEAR.

Dia de Anno-bom	New Year's Day
Dia de Reis, a Epiphania	Twelfth Day
A Candelaria	Candlemas Day
A Purificação	The Purification
O Entrudo	The Carnival, *or* Shrovetide
Quarta feira de Cinzas	Ash Wednesday
A Quaresma	The Lent
Annunciação	Lady Day in March
As Quatro Temporas	The Ember Weeks
A Semana santa	The Holy Week
Domingo de Ramos	Palm Sunday
Quarta feira de Trevas	Wednesday before Easter
Quinta feira de Endoenças	Maunday Thursday, the last Thursday in Lent
Sesta feira da Paixão	Good Friday
Pascoa de Resurreição	Easter Day
Assumpção de N. Sª.	Lady Day in Harvest
As Rogações, or Ladainhas	Rogation Week
Ascensão	The Ascension
Pentecostes	The Pentecost, *or* Whitsuntide
Dia do Corpo de Deus	Corpus Christi Day
Dia de S. João	Midsummer Day
Dia de S. Pedro	Lammas Day

Dia de todos os Santos	All Saints' Day
Dia dos Finados	All Souls
Dia de S. Martinho	Martinmas
Dia de Natal	Christmas Day
Vigilia, or *vespera*	The eve

DA IGREJA E DIGNIDADES ECCLESIASTICAS.	OF THE CHURCH AND ECCLESIASTICAL DIGNITIES.
A nave	The aisle of the church
O zimborio	The dome
O pináculo	The pinnacle
O côro	The choir
A capella	The chapel
Um estante	A reading desk *or* chorister's desk
A sacristia	The vestry
O campanario, or *torres dos sinos*	The belfry *or* steeple
O sino	The bell
O badalo	The clapper of the bell
A pia	The font
Um hysope	A sprinkler
Um confessionario	A confession seat
Uma tribuna	A tribune *or* gallery
Um cemiterio	A churchyard *or* burying-place
Um carneiro	A charnel
Um altar	An altar
Um frontal	Antipendium
Um pallio	A canopy
Uma toalha do altar	The altar-cloth
Um missal	A missal, a prayer-book
Uma sotana	A cassock

Um sobrepelliz	A surplice
Um roquete	A short surplice, a bishop's surplice
O papa	The pope
Um cardeal	A cardinal
Um patriarcha	A patriarch
Um arcebispo	An archbishop
Um bispo	A bishop
Um legado	A legate
Vice-legado	A vice-legate
Um nuncio	A nuncio
Um prelado	A prelate
Um commendador	A commander
Um abbade	An abbot
Uma abbadessa	An abbess
Um prior	A prior
Um reitor	A rector
Um beneficiado	A beneficed clergyman or incumbent
Um frade	A friar *or* monk
A corôa	A shaven-crown
Um guardião	A guardian
Um definidor	A definitor
Um provincial	A provincial
Um geral	A general
Um vigario	A vicar
Um vigario-geral	A vicar-general
Um deão	A dean
Um arcediago	An archdeacon
Um diacono	A deacon
Um subdiacono	A subdeacon
Um conego	A canon
Um arcipreste	Arch-priest
Um clerigo	A clergyman

Um capellão	A chaplain
Um esmoler	An almoner
Um cura	A curate
Benificio simples	Sinecure
Uma freira	A nun
Um prégador	A preacher
Um sacristão	A sexton, a vestry-keeper
Um menino do côro	A choir-boy

O MUNDO VISIVEL. — THE PHYSICAL WORLD.

A natureza	Nature
A materia	Matter
Um átomo	An atom
Uma molécula	A particle
Um corpo	A body
Um sólido	A solid
A solidez	Solidity
Um fluido	A fluid
A fluidez	Fluidity
O gaz	The gas
A luz	The light
Um ser humano	A human being
O espaço, a immensidade	The space *or* immensity

DO SERVIÇO DE HUMA MESA. — OF THE COVERING OF THE TABLE.

A mesa	The table
O aparador	The sideboard
A toalha da mesa	The table-cloth
Uma toalha de mãos	A towel
Um guardanapo	A napkin
Uma faca	A knife

Um garfo	A fork
Uma colher	A spoon
Um prato	A plate
Um saleiro	A saltcellar
Uma galheta	A cruet
Um talher {A place at table} i.e.,	A plate with a knife, spoon, or fork
O assucareiro	The sugar-basin
Baixella, or serviço de prata	A set of silver-plate
Uma cuberta	A course
Um copo	A glass
Uma garrafa	A bottle
Uma taça	A cup
Um cesto para pôr o pão	A bread-basket
Um faqueiro	A case for knives
Louça de barro	Earthenware
Louça de estanho	A pewter service
Baixella, or serviço de porcelana	A china service
Colher da sopa	A table-spoon
Uma colher-de-chá	A tea-spoon
Um trinchante	A carving-knife and fork
Um prato côvo	A soup-dish
Uma travessa	A dish
Um pimenteiro	A pepper-box
Uma mostardeira	A mustard-pot
Uma saladeira	A salad-dish
Uma cafeteira	A coffee-pot
Uma chocolateira	A chocolate-pot
Um bule	A tea-pot
Uma bandeja	A tray
Uma leiteira	A milk-pot
Uma taça	A cup
Um pires	A saucer

Uma poncheira	A punch-bowl
Um saccarolhas	A corkscrew
Um cascanozes	A nut-cracker

AS COMIDAS.	THE MEALS.
O almôço	Breakfast
Almoçar	To breakfast
O jantar	Dinner
Jantar	To dine
A merenda	A luncheon
A cêa	Supper
Cêar	To sup
Consoada	A light supper, as upon a fast-day

DA COMIDA.	OF EATING.
Pão	Bread
Carne	Meat
Peixe	Fish
Carne cozida	Boiled meat
Carne assada	Roast meat
Um pastel	A tart
Sôpa	Soup
Caldo	Broth
Môlho	Sauce
Fructa	Fruit
Queijo	Cheese
Vaca	Beef
Carneiro	Mutton
Vitella	Veal
Cordeiro	Lamb
Gallinha	Fowl
Gallo	Cock
Perú	A turkey

Almondegas	Force-meat balls
Pão fresco, or *pão molle*	New bread
Pão quente	A hot loaf
Pão de toda farinha	Common bread
Pão branco, or *pão alvo*	White bread
Arrôz	Rice
Pão de rala	Brown bread
Pão de cevada	Barley bread
Pão de centeio	Rye bread
Pão de avea	Oaten bread
Pão de milho miudo	Millet bread
Pão de milho grande, ou *de maiz*	Indian corn bread
Um biscoito	A biscuit
Uma migalha de pão	A crumb of bread
Uma fatia de pão	A slice of bread
Uma côdea de pão	A crust of bread
Massa	Dough
Uma torta	A tart
Rosca	Roll
Estofado	Stewed meat
Fiambre	Ham
Carne assada sobre grelhas	Broiled meat from the grill
Carne frita	Fried meat
Picado, or *carne picada*	Mince meat
Um javali, or *porco montez*	A wild boar
Presunto	Ham
Porco	Pork
Cabrito	Kid
Toucinho	Bacon
Um lombo	A loin
Mãos de carneiro	Sheep's trotters
Fressura, or *forçura*	A pluck
Uma cachola de porco	A pig's head

Linguiça, or *lingoiça*	A sausage
Chouriço de sangue de porco	Black-pudding
Fricassé	A fricassee
Fígado	Liver
Leite	Milk
Nata	Cream
Sôro	Whey
Requeijão	Cream cheese
Coalhada	Curdled milk
Um ôvo	An egg
A gemma do ôvo	The yolk of an egg
A clara do ôvo	The white of an egg
Um ôvo fresco	A new-laid egg
Um ôvo molle	A soft egg
Um ôvo duro	A hard egg
Ovos escalfados	Poached eggs
Ovos fritos	Fried eggs
Uma omelette	An omelette
Uma fritura	A fritter
Ovas dé peixe	The roes of fish
Dôces	Sweetmeats
Marmelada	Marmalade

O QUE SE ASSA. — THAT WHICH IS ROASTED.

Um capão	A capon
Uma franga	A pullet
Um frango	A chicken
Pombos	Pigeons
Pombo trocaz	A wood-culver *or* wood-pigeon
Uma gallinhola	A woodcock
Uma narseja	A snipe
Uma perdiz	A partridge

Um tordo	A thrush
Um faisão	A pheasant
Um faisãosinho	A pheasant-poult
Um leitão	A sucking-pig
Um veado	A stag
Um coelho	A rabbit
Uma lebre	A hare
Um adem	A duck
Um ganso	A drake
Uma pata	A goose
Um pato	A gander
Uma calhandra	A skylark
Uma cordorniz	A quail

DE OUTROS PASSAROS. — OF OTHER BIRDS.

Uma águia	An eagle
Uma águia nova	An eaglet
Um abutre	A vulture
Um abestrús	An ostrich
Um esmerilhão	A merlin
Um gavião	A sparrowhawk
Um môcho	The horned owl
Um falcão	A falcon
Um falcão que ainda não vôa	A jess-hawk
Um gerifalte	A gerfalcon
Um sacre	A saker, a saker-hawk
Uma garça	A heron
Um melharuco	Tomtit
Uma garçota	A little heron
Um milhano, or *milhafre*	A kite
Um corvo	A crow *or* raven
Uma gralha	A rook
Um gralho	A jackdaw

Uma alveloa, or *rabeta*	A wagtail
Um canario	A canary-bird
Um pintacilgo	A goldfinch
Um melro	A blackbird
Um tentilhão	A chaffinch
Um rouxinol	A nightingale
Um verdelhão	A green-bird
Um papagayo	A parrot
Uma pêga	A magpie
Um estorninho, or *zorzal*	A starling
Um francelho	A hobby, a musket
Um môcho	Owl
Uma coruja	A screech-owl
Um morcêgo	A bat
Uma ave nocturna, como melro, que mama as cabras	A goat-milker
Um francolim	A goodwit, a moor-cock
Um bufo	A night-crow *or* raven
Uma cerceta	A teal
Um corvo marinho	A cormorant
Um gaivota	A moor-hen *or* gull
Um gaivão	A martlet *or* marten, a kind of swallow
Uma andorinha	A swallow
Um mergulhão	A diver
Uma marreca	A wild duck
Um picanço	A wren, a little bird
Um taralhão	A kind of ortolan
Um pavão	A peacock
Uma pavôa	A pea-hen
Uma arára	A macaw
Um pardal	A sparrow
Uma rôla	A turtle-dove
Um alcion	A kingfisher

Uma cegonha	A stork
Uma cuco	A cuckoo
Uma cisne	A swan
Um pintarrôxo	A robin
Uma grou	A crane
Um pavoncino	A lapwing
Um pelicano	A pelican
Uma tarâmbola	A plover
Um pisco	A bullfinch *or* red-tail

PARA OS DIAS DE PEIXE, OU DE JEJUM.	FOR FISH DAYS, OR FAST DAYS.
Sôpa de hervas, &c.	Vegetable soup
Peixe	Fish
Peixe do mar	Sea-fish
Peixe de agoa doce	Fresh-water fish
Um savel	A shad
Uma anchova	An anchovy
Uma enguia	An eel
Um barbo	A barbel
Um lucio	A pike *or* jack
Uma carpa	A carp
Uma siba	A cuttle-fish
Uma lula	A calamary
Uma cabra	The miller's thumb
Um goraz	A roach
Um congro	A conger
Uma dourada	A dorado, St. Peter's fish, *or* the gilt-head
Um linguado	A sole
Uma lagosta	A lobster
Um bordalo	A sturgeon, sometimes called a shad-fish

Um mugem	A mullet
Um rodovalho	A turbot
Uma sarda	A sort of small mackerel
Uma cavalla	A mackerel
Uma sardinha	A pilchard
Um bacalháo	Dried cod
Um arenque	A herring
Um voador	A flying-fish
Um arenque de fumo	A red herring
Um arenque com óvas	A hard-roed herring
Uma pescada	An ake
Um cadoz	A gudgeon
Uma ostra	An oyster
Uma lamprea	A lamprey
Uma lamprea pequena	A lampern
Um porco marinho	A porpoise
Uma perca	Perch
Uma tinca	A tench
Uma truta	A trout
Um atum	A tunny-fish
Um salmão	A salmon
Um camarão	A shrimp or prawn
Um caranguejo	A crab
Uma ameijoa	A cockle

PARA TEMPERAR O COMER.   TO SEASON MEAT WITH.

Sal	Salt
Pimenta	Pepper
Pimentã de Cayenna	Cayenne pepper
Azeite	Oil
Vinagre	Vinegar
Mostarda	Mustard
Cravo da India	Cloves

Canela	Cinnamon
Loureiro	Laurel
Alcaparras	Capers
Cogumelos	Mushrooms
Tubaras	Truffles
Cebolas	Onions
Ouregão	Organy
Funcho	Fennel
Cebolinhas	Young onions
Alho	Garlic
Laranjas	Oranges
Limões	Lemons
Perrexil	Wild parsley
Salsa	Garden parsley
Ortelã	Mint
Aipo	Celery
Alho pôrro	Leek
Coentro	Coriander
Açafrão	Saffron

PARA SALADA. — FOR A SALAD.

Almeirão	Wild succory
Almeirão hortense or *endivia*	Endive
Alface	Lettuce
Chicoria	Succory
Agriões	Water-cresses
Mastruços, or *masturços*	Cresses
Cerefolio	Chervil
Rabão	Radish root

PARA SOBREMESA. — FOR THE DESSERT.

Maçãs	Apples
Peras	Pears

Uma pêra begamota	A bergamot pear
Pêcegos	Peaches
Uma camoeza	A pippin
Damasco	Apricot
Cerejas	Cherries
Cerejas de saco	Hard cherries
Ginjas	Sour cherries
Ginja garrafal	A very large sort of cherry, the fruit of the dwarf cherry-tree
Laranja da China	China orange
Uvas	Grapes
Passas de uva	Raisins
Uva erpim	Gooseberries
Figos	Figs
Figos lampos	The first figs that come in May
Ameixas	Plums
Passas de ameixas	Prunes
Amoras de sarça or *de silva*	Blackberries
Framoesas	Raspberries
Amoras da amoreira	Mulberries
Marmelos	Quinces
Romãs	Pomegranates
Lima	Lime
Azeitonas	Olives
Amendoas	Almonds
Nêsperos	Medlars
Um melão	A melon
Uma melancia	A water-melon
Castanhas	Chestnuts
Nózes	Wulnuts
Avelans	Hazel-nuts
Morangos	Strawberries

Medrônho	A sort of fruit that grows in Portugal, like a strawberry, said to intoxicate
Um tamara	A date
Um pistacho	A pistachio-nut
Uma alfarroba	A carob
Uma belota	An acorn
Sôrva	Service

DA BEBIDA. — OF DRINKING.

Agoa	Water
Vinho	Wine
Vinho do Porto	Port wine
Vinho de Jerez	Sherry wine
Cerveja	Beer
Cerveja branca	Ale
Café	Coffee
Café com leite	Coffee and milk
Chocolate	Chocolate
Chocolate com leite	Chocolate and milk
Cidra	Cider
Agua-ardente	Brandy
Limonada	Lemonade
Licores	Liquors
Ponche	Punch
Rom	Rum
Chá	Tea
Vinho branco	White wine
Vinho tinto	Red wine

DAS ARVORES E ARBUSTOS. — OF TREES AND SHRUBS.

Um damasqueiro	An apricot tree
Uma amendoeira	An almond tree

Uma cerejeira	A cherry tree
Um castanheiro	A chestnut tree
Uma cidreira	A citron tree
Uma sorveira	A service tree
Uma palmeira	A palm tree
Uma figueira	A fig tree
Um marmeleiro	A quince tree
Uma macieira	An apple tree
Uma macieira da náfega	A jubub tree
Uma romeira	A pomegranate tree
Um limoeiro	A lemon tree
Uma amoreira	A mulberry tree
Uma oliveira	An olive tree
Uma nespereira	A medlar tree
Uma laranjeira	An orange tree
Murta	Myrtle
Uma nogueira	A walnut tree
Um zambujeiro	A wild olive tree
Era	Ivy
Um percegueiro	A peach tree
Uma roseira	A rose-bush
Uma ameixieira	A plum tree
Uma pereira	A pear tree
Romaninho	Rosemary
Um pinheira	A pine tree
Giesta	Broom

DOS REPTIS E ANIMAES AMPHIBIOS.
OF REPTILES AND AMPHIBIOUS CREATURES.

Uma minhóca	An earth-worm
Uma serpente	A serpent
Uma serpente com azas	A flying serpent
Um aspide	An asp

Uma cobra	A snake
Uma cobra de cascavel	A rattlesnake
Uma vibora	A viper
Um lagarto	A lizard
Uma osga	An evet, eft, *or* newt
Um oscorpião	A scorpion
Um crocodilo	A crocodile
Um jacaré, or *crocodilo da America*	An alligator
Um castôr	A beaver
Um cágado	A land tortoise
Uma lontra	An otter

DOS INSECTOS. — OF INSECTS.

Uma aranha	A spider
Uma formiga	An ant
Um caracol	A snail
Uma rã	A frog
Um sapo	A toad
Um oução	A hand-worm
Uma barata	A beetle
Um caruncho	A woodworm
Uma lagarta	A caterpillar
Uma cigarra	A grasshopper
Uma borbolêta	A butterfly
Um grillo	A cricket
Uma lêndea	A nit
Uma pulga	A flea
Uma môsca	A fly
Um carrapato	A tick
Um gafanhôto	A locust
Polilha, or *traça*	Moth
Uma vêspa	A wasp

Uma abêlha	A bee
Um zango, or *zangão*	A drone
Um tavão	An ox-fly
Um boi de Deus	A ladybird
Um mosquito	A gnat

GRÁOS DE PARENTESCO.	DEGREES OF KINDRED.
Pai, or *pae*	Father
Mãi	Mother
Avô	Grandfather
Avó	Grandmother
Bisavô	Great-grandfather
Bisavó	Great-grandmother
Filho	Son
Filha	Daughter
Um irmão	A brother
Uma irmã	A sister
O primogenito	The eldest son
O filho mais moço	The youngest son
Um tio	An uncle
Uma tia	An aunt
Um sobrinho	A nephew
Uma sobrinha	A niece
Um primo	A cousin
Uma prima	A female cousin
Um primo-co-irmão	A male first cousin
Uma prima-co-irmã	A female first cousin
Um cunhado	A brother-in-law
Uma cunhada	A sister-in-law
Irmão de pai	A brother by his father
Um sôgro	A father-in-law
Uma sogra	A mother-in-law
Um padastro	A step-father

x

Uma madrasta	A step-mother
Um enteado	A step-son
Uma enteada	A step-daughter
Um genro	A son-in-law
Uma nóra	A daughter-in-law
Uma néta	A grand-daughter
Um néto	A grandson
Um bisnéto	A great-grandson
Uma bisnéta	A great-grand-daughter
Consorte, masc. and fem.	A consort
Um marido	A husband
Uma mulher	A wife
Um irmão gémeo	A twin brother
Um collaço, or *irmão de leite*	A foster brother
Um filho bastardo	A bastard
Um compadre	A male gossip
Uma comadre	A female gossip
Um afilhado	A godson
Uma afilhada	A god-daughter
Um padrinho	A godfather
Uma madrinha	A godmother
Um parente	A male relation
Uma parente	A female relation
Parente por affinidade, or *consanguinidade*	A kin, a relation either of affinity or consanguinity

DOS DIFFERENTES GENEROS DE ESTADO DO HOMEM E DA MULHER, E DAS SUAS QUALIDADES.

OF THE CONDITIONS OF MEN AND WOMEN, AS WELL AS OF THEIR QUALITIES.

Um homem	A man
Uma mulher	A woman
Um homem de idade	An aged man

Uma mulher de idade	An aged woman
Um velho	An old man
Uma velha	An old woman
Um moço, or *mancebo*	A young man
Uma rapariga	A girl
Um amante	A lover
Uma amiga	A lady friend *or* mistress
Uma criança, or *menino*	A child, a little child
Um rapaz	A boy
Um rapazinho	A little boy
Uma menina	A little girl
Uma donzella	A maiden
Uma virgem	A virgin
Um amo	A master
Uma ama	A mistress
Um criado	A male servant
Criada	A female servant
Um cidadão	A citizen
Um rustico	A countryman
Uma rustica	A peasant woman
Um estrangeiro	A stranger *or* foreigner
Um viuvo	A widower
Uma viuva	A widow
Um herdeiro	An heir
Uma herdeira	An heiress
Um solteiro	A bachelor
Uma solteira	A single woman
Estado de solteiro	Bachelorship
Um homem casado	A married man
Uma mulher casada	A married woman
Destro	Dexterous
Agudo	Sharp
Recatado	Cautious
Astuto	Cunning, sly

Esperto	Sprightly
Doido	Mad
Malicioso	Malicious
Timido	Timid
Valeroso	Brave
Estupido	Stupid
Enganoso	Deceitful
Docil	Docile
Bem criado	Well-bred
Cortêz	Courteous
Justo	Just
Desatento	Uncourteous
Impertinente	Impertinent
Importuno	Troublesome
Descuidado	Careless
Temerario	Rash
Constante	Constant
Devoto	Devout
Deligente	Diligent
Compassivo	Merciful
Paciente	Patient
Ambicioso	Ambitious
Cobiçoso	Covetous
Soberbo	Proud
Cobarde	Coward
Lisonjeiro	Flatterer
Goloso	Dainty
Desleal	Treacherous
Desagradecido	Ungrateful
Inhumano	Inhuman
Insolente	Insolent
Obstinado	Obstinate
Teimoso	Stubborn
Preguiçoso	Slothful

Pródigo	Prodigal
Atrevido	Bold
Alegre	Merry
Zeloso	Zealous
Modesto	Modest
Obediente	Obedient
Um murmurador	A censurer
Officioso	Officious
Um feiticeiro	A sorcerer
Um traidor	A traitor
Malvado	Wicked
Um rebelde	A rebel
Perfido	Perfidious
Um bobo	A buffoon
Um mentiroso	A liar
Altivo	Haughty
Côxo	Lame of the legs
Manco	Lame of the hands
Cégo	Blind
Surdo	Deaf
Pacifico	Pacific
Mudo	Dumb

DOS MORADORES DE UMA CIDADE.
OF THE INHABITANTS OF A CITY.

Um fidalgo	A gentleman
Um nobre	A nobleman
Um mecanico	A mechanic
Um tendeiro	A grocer
Um negociante or *homem de negocio*	A merchant *or* tradesman
O vulgo or *a plébe*	The mob
A canalha	The rabble

Um jornaleiro	A labourer
Um ourives da prata	A silversmith
Um ourives do ouro	A goldsmith
Um livreiro	A bookseller
Um impressor	A printer
Um barbeiro	A barber
Um mercador de seda	A silk-merchant
Um mercador de panno	A woollen-draper
Um mercador de panno de linho, or *fanqueiro*	A linen-draper
Um alfayate	A tailor
Um alfayate remendão	A botcher
Uma costureira	A sempstress
Um chapeleiro or *sombreiréiro*	A hatter
Um sapateiro	A shoemaker
Um remendão (sapateiro)	A cobbler
Um ferreiro	A blacksmith
Um alveitar	A farrier
Um cerralheiro	A locksmith
Um parteira	A midwife
Um medico	A physician
Um charlatão	A quack
Um cirurgião	A surgeon
Um dentista	A dentist
Um selleiro	A saddler
Um carpinteiro	A carpenter
Um pádeiro	A baker
Um carniceiro	A butcher
Um fruteiro	A fruiterer
Uma verduleira	A herb-woman
Um pasteleiro	A pastrycook
Um taverneiro	A vintner
Um cervejeiro	A brewer
Um estalajadeiro	An innkeeper

Um bufarinheiro	A pedler
Um relojoeiro	A watchmaker
Um pregoeiro	A crier
Um joialheiro	A jeweller
Um boticario	A chemist
Um vidraceiro	A glazier
Um carvoeiro	A coalman
Um jardineiro	A gardener
Um letrado	A lawyer
Um procurador	An attorney
Um advogado	A solicitor, *or* a pleader
Um juiz	A judge
Um carcereiro	A jailer
O carrasco	The hangman
Um porteiro	A porter

OS CINCO SENTIDOS. — THE FIVE SENSES.

A vista	The sight
O ouvido	The hearing
O olfacto	The smell
O gôsto	The taste
O tacto	The feeling

AS PARTES DO CORPO HUMANO. — THE PARTS OF THE HUMAN BODY.

A cabeça	The head
Os miólos	The brains
O toutiço	The hinder part of the head
A testa	The forehead
A molleira	The mould of the head
As fontes	The temples
A orêlha	The ear
O cartilagem	The gristle *or* cartilage

O *timpano*	The drum of the ear
A *sobrancelha*	The eyebrow
As *palpebras* or *capellas dos ólhos*	The eyelid
As *pestanas*	The eyelashes
O *lagrimal*	The corner of the eye
O *alvo do ôlho*	The white of the eye
As *meninas dos ólhos*	The eyeballs
O *nariz*	The nose
As *ventas*	The nostrils
O *septo* or *diaphragma do nariz*	The gristle of the nose
A *ponta do nariz*	The tip of the nose
A *bôca*	The mouth
Os *dentes*	The teeth
A *gengiva*	The gum
A *lingoa*	The tongue
Paladar or *céo da boca*	The roof or palate of the mouth
A *queixada*	The jaw
A *barba*	The chin
As *barbas*	The beard
Os *bigodes*	The mustachios
O *pescoço*	The neck
A *nuca*	The nape of the neck
A *garganta*	The throat
O *seio*	The bosom
O *peito*	The breast
O *estômago*	The stomach
As *costélas*	The ribs
A *verilha*	The groin
O *braço*	The arm
O *cotovêlo*	The elbow
O *sobáco*	The arm-pit

A mão	The hand
O pulso	The wrist
A palma da mão	The palm of the hand
Os dedos	The fingers
O dedo polegar	The thumb
O dedo mostrador	The forefinger
O dedo do meio	The middle finger
O dedo annular	The ring finger
O dedo meninho or *minimo*	The little finger
As pontas dos dedos	The tips or tops of the fingers
As juntas e nós dos dedos	The joints and knuckles of the fingers
Um dedo do pé	A toe
A unha	The nail
As costas	The back
Os hombros	The shoulders
As ilhargas	The sides
A côxa	The thigh
O joelho	The knee
A barriga da perna	The calf of the leg
O espinhaço	The spine
O tornozelo	The ankle
O pé	The foot
A planta do pé	The sole of the foot
O coração	The heart
Os bofes or *pulmões*	The lungs
O figado	The liver
O baço	The spleen
Os rins	The kidneys
O fel	The gall
O sangue	The blood
A suór	Perspiration
Uma lagrima	A tear

VESTIDOS DO HOMEM.	A MAN'S CLOTHES.
Um fato	A suit of clothes
Uma casaca	A coat
Uma gravata	A cravat *or* necktie
Uma chapéo	A hat
Uma camisa	A shirt
Um colête	A waistcoat
Um colarinho	A collar
Os punhos	The wristbands
As ceroulas	The drawers
Um chambre	A morning gown
As calças	The trousers
O lenço do pescoço	The necktie
O lenço d'assuar	The handkerchief
Uma casaca	A coat
Um trage de caça	A hunting dress
Os botões	The buttons
Um sobretudo	An overcoat
Uma capa or *capote*	A cloak
Um barrete or *gôrra*	A cap
O chapéo	The hat
O chapéo de chuva	The umbrella
As botas	The boots
Os sapatos	The shoes
As meias	The stockings
As piugas	The socks
Peitinhos	Shirt fronts
As solas dos sapatos	The soles of the shoes
O tacão das botas	The heels of the boots
Os suspensorios	The braces
Um descalçador	A boot-jack
A bengala	The walking-stick
Uma navalha de barba	A razor

As ligas	The garters
As chinellas	The slippers

VESTIDOS DA MULHER.	WOMEN'S CLOTHES.
Uma anágoa	A petticoat
Uma saia	An under-petticoat
O atacador	The lace
Um vestido	A gown
Um lencinho de pescoço	A neckerchief
Um mantelete	A mantelet
Um cinto	A sash
Um chapéo	A bonnet
Um collar	A necklace
Um aderêço de brilhantes	A set of diamonds
Um challe	A shawl
Um manto	A mantle
Um avental	An apron
Os braceletes	The bracelets
Um annel	A ring
Os brincos	The earrings
Um leque	A fan
Um penteador	A combing-cloth
Um toucador	A toilet *or* dressing-table
As sinães	Patches to wear on the face
Um espêlho	A looking-glass
Um regálo or *manguito*	A muff
O espartilho	The stays
Um pente	A comb
Alfinetes	Pins
Uma tesoura	A pair of scissors
Um dedal	A thimble
Uma agulha	A needle
A linha	The thread

Um fio de perolas	A row of pearls
Polvilhos	Powder
Joias	Jewels
Côr	Colour
Um palito	A toothpick
O fuso	The spindle
Uma almofadinho para alfinetes	A small pin-cushion
Uma agulheta	A bodkin
Fitas	Ribbons
O véo	The veil
Renda	Lace
Bilros	Bobbins
Agoa de cheiro	Scented water

OS DOZE SIGNOS CELESTES. — THE TWELVE CELESTIAL SIGNS.

Aries	Aries *or* the ram
Touro	The bull
Gemini or *geminis*	The twins
Cancer	The crab
Leão	The lion
Virgem	The virgin
Libra	The balance
Escorpião	The scorpion
Sagitario	The archer
Capricornio	The goat
Aquario	The water-bearer
Peixes	The fishes

DE UMA CASA E DO QUE LHE PERTENCE. — OF A HOUSE AND ALL THAT BELONGS TO IT.

Uma casa	A house
O alicerse	The foundation

Uma parede	A wall
Um tabique	A light brick wall
Um páteo	A court or yard
Um andar	A floor
A fachada	The front
Uma janella	A window
Uma abobada	A vault
As escadas	The stairs
Os degráos	The steps
Um telhado	A tiled roof
As têlhas	The tiles
Os ladrilhos or *tijolos*	The bricks
Uma sala	A sitting or drawing-room
Uma antecamara or *salêta*	An antechamber
Um salão	A hall
Um tecto	A roof
Uma alcôva	A small room
Uma baranda	A balcony
Um gabinete	A closet
Um quarto	A room
Um guarda-roupa	A wardrobe
Uma adêga	A wine-cellar
Uma cozinha	A kitchen
Uma dispensa	A pantry
Uma chaminé	A chimney
A cavallariça	The stable
Um gallinheiro or *casa das gallinhas*	A hen-house
Um poleiro	A hen-roost
Um jardim	A garden
Uma casa de jantar	A dining-room
Um quarto de cama	A bed-room
A porta	The door
Um postigo	A wicket

O liminar or *lúminar*	The threshold
Uma clara boia	A skylight
O algeróz	The gutter-tile
As beiras or *abas do telhado*	The eaves
A couceira da porta	The hinges
Uma fechadura	A lock
Um cadeado	A padlock
O ferrôlho	The bolt
A tranca da porta	The bar of the door
O cano da chave	The pipe of a key
Uma chave mestra	A master-key
As guardas da fechadura	The wards of a lock
O palhetão da chave	The key bit
A vidraça	The glass of a window
Uma escada feita a caracol	A winding staircase
Escada secreta	Private staircase
Uma viga	A beam
A parede mestra	The main wall
As paredes meianciras	The party walls

MOVEIS D'UM QUARTO DE CAMA.	A BED-ROOM FURNITURE.
A cama or *leito*	The bed
O sobrecéo da cama	The bed tester
As cortinas da cama	The bed curtains
Os lençóes	The sheets
A cabeceira da cama	The head of the bed
O pé da cama	The foot of the bed
Uma cólcha	A counterpane, a quilt
Um colchão	A mattress
Um cobertôr	A blanket
Um cobertôr de felpa	A rug
Uma cama de armação	A bedstead with tester
Um travesseiro	A bolster

VOCABULARY. 319

Um tapete	A carpet
Tapeçaria	Tapestry
Um bahn	A trunk
Um relogio	A clock *or* watch
Uma estufa	A hothouse
Uma chave	A key
Um espreguiçador	A couch
Um enxergão	A paillasse
Uma esteira	A mat
Os folles	The bellows
As tenazes	The tongs
Uma pá	A shovel
Um armario	A cupboard
A vassoura	The broom
Um banco	A bench
Uma bacia or *alguidar*	A basin
Uma quentador	A warming-pan
Uma caixa	A box
Uma palmatoria	A flat candlestick
Um bufete	A sideboard
Uma gaiola	A cage
Um canapé or *sofá*	A sofa
Uma cadeira	A chair
Um castiçal	A tall candlestick
Um braseirinho	A small fire-pan
A chaminé	The chimney
Os ferros da chaminé	The fire-irons
Uma commoda	A chest of drawers
Um espêlho	A looking-glass
Um jarro	An ewer
Uma bacia de mãos	A hand-basin
Um parafogo	A fire-screen
Um apagador	An extinguisher
Caixa do chapeo	Hat-box

Cadeira de braços	Arm-chair
Um candieiro	A lamp
Um colchão	A mattress
Um lavatorio	A wash-hand stand
Uma almofada	A pillow
Uma fronha de almofada	A pillow-case
Um balde	A pail
Uma papeleira	A writing-desk
Um quadro	A picture
Uma mêsa	A table
Uma gaveta	A drawer
Um toucador	A toilet table
Uma lamparina	A night lamp
Uma maleta	A portmanteau

UTENSILIOS DE COZINHA. — KITCHEN UTENSILS.

Uma panella	A saucepan
O testo	The lid of a saucepan
Um ferro para atiçar o lume	A poker
Uma escumadeira	A skimmer
Uma colhér grande	A ladle
Uma caldeira	A kettle
Uma sertã or frigideira	A frying-pan
Um coador	A cullender or strainer
As grêlhas	The gridiron
Um ralo	A grater
Um espêto	A spit
Um almofariz	A mortar wherein things are pounded
Uma mão do almofariz	A pestle
Uma redôma	A glass shade
Um balde	A bucket or pail
O sabão	The soap

O fôrno	The oven
A pá do forno	The peal of the oven
Um vasculho para alimpar o forno	A coal-rake to make clear an oven

CORES.   COLOURS.

Branco	White
Azul	Blue
Azul celeste	Sky-colour
Azul ferrete	Dark blue
Azul claro	Light blue
Côr de camurça	Light yellow
Amarello	Yellow
Côr de rosa	Rose colour
Côr de palha	Straw *or* cream colour
Verde	Green
Côr de verde mar *or* verde claro	Sea-green
Côr vermêlha *or* incarnada	Red colour
Côr vermêlha muito viva *or* carmim	Carmine, a bright red colour
Côr de carne	Flesh colour
Côr carmesim	Crimson red
Côr negra *or* preta	Black colour
Côr de mel	A dark yellow
Furta-côres	A deep changeable colour
Côr viva	A lively and gay colour
Côr triste	A dull colour
Côr escura	A dark colour
Côr carregada	A deep colour
Côr de fogo	Fire colour
Pardo	Grey
Côr de cinza	Ash colour

Y

Escarlate	Scarlet
Leonado	Tawny
Côr de laranja	Orange colour
Côr de azeitona	Olive colour
Rôxo	Purple, violet
Rôxo or *côr de aurora*	Aurora colour

CRIADOS DOMESTICOS. — SERVANTS.

Um capellão	A chaplain
Um secretario	A secretary
Um tutor	A tutor
Uma governante	A governess
Um preceptor	A preceptor
Um mordomo	A steward
Um dispenseiro	A butler
Uma criada	A maid-servant
Um cocheiro	A coachman
Um lacaio	A footman
Um palafreneiro	A groom
Um criado	A man-servant
Um cozinheiro	A man cook
Uma cozinheira	A woman cook
Um porteiro	A door-keeper
Um jardineiro	A flower gardener
Um hortelão	A kitchen gardener
Um creado de quarto	A valet de chambre
Um pagem	A page
Uma ama	A nurse

DAS POVOÇÕES. — OF TOWNS, BUILDINGS, ETC.

Uma capital	A capital
Uma cidade	A city

Uma metrópole	A metropolis
Uma villa	A village
Um lugar	A place
Um casal	A farmhouse
Uma parroquia	A parish
Um bairro	A quarter of the town
Um palacio	A palace
Um castello	A castle
Uma casa	A house
Uma quinta	A country house
Uma casinha	A little house
Uma choça or *cabana*	A hut
Um cemiterio	A churchyard or cemetery
Os arrabaldes	The suburbs
Um chafariz	A public fountain
Uma calçada	A pavement
Uma praça	A square
Uma ponte	A bridge
Um parapeito	A parapet
Um arco	An arch
Um passeio	A promenade
Uma rua	A street
Um jardim	A garden

A TERRA. — THE EARTH.

O globo terraqueo	The terrestrial globe
O hemispherio	The hemisphere
O equador	The equator
Os tropicos	The tropics
O pólo	The pole
Polar	Polar
O norte	The north
Septentrional	Northern

O éste or *oriente*	The east
Oriental	Eastern
O sul or *meiodia*	The south
Meridional	Southern
O oeste or *occidente*	The west
Occidental	Western
Um meridiano	A meridian
A latitude	The latitude
A longitude	The longitude
Um gráo	A degree
Um continente	A continent
Continental	Continental
Uma planicie	A plain or flat country
Um valle	A valley
Uma veiga	A plain pasture ground by a river side
Uma charneca, or *ermo*	A barren sandy land
Um cêrro	A hillock
Um oiteiro	A hill
Uma montanha	A mountain
O cume	The summit
O declive	The declivity
A falda de uma montanha	The skirt of a mountain
Uma cordilheira	A range of mountains
Uma planicie	A plain
Um desfiladeiro	A mountain pass
Um volcão	A volcano
A cratéra	A crater
Um abysmo, precipicio	An abyss
Um cabo or *promontorio*	A cape
Um isthmo	An isthmus
Uma peninsula	A peninsula
Um ilha	An island
A costa	The coast

A praia	The beach
Uma rocha	A rock
Um rochedo	A cluster of rocks
Um escólho or *recife*	A rock under water
Um banco d'areia	A sand-bank
Um deserto	A desert

SUBSTANCIAS MINERAES.	MINERAL SUBSTANCES.
Um mineral	A mineral
Pedras preciosas	Precious stones
Uma mina	A mine
Uma camada	A stratum
O aço	Steel
O iman	The loadstone
A ágata	The agate
Magnético	Magnetic
O bronze	Bronze
O alabastro	Alabaster
Uma amathista	The amethyst
O antimonio	Antimony
A piçarra	Slate
A prata	Silver
A argilla or *greda*	Clay
O arsenico	Arsenic
O betume	Bitumen
O carvão de pedra	Mineral coals
A cal	Lime
Terra calcarea	Calcareous earth
O azinhabre	Verdigris
O cabalto	Cobalt
O coral	Coral
Uma cornelina	The cornelian stone
A caparrosa	Copperas

O cobre	Copper
Um diamante	A diamond
A esmeralda	The emerald
O estanho	Pewter
O ferro	Iron
O granito	Granite
O jaspe	Jasper
O latão	Brass
A maganésia	Magnesia
O marmore	Marble
O mercurio or azougue	Mercury or quicksilver
O chumbo	Lead
O nitro	Nitre
A opála	Opal
O ouro	Gold
O rubim	Ruby
O enxofre	Brimstone
O topazio	A topaz
O zinco	Zinc

COLHEITAS DOS CAMPOS.	PRODUCTION OF THE FIELDS.
Cereaes	Cereals
Aveia	Oats
Beterraba	Beet-root
Trigo	Wheat
Milho	Millet
Canhamo	Hemp
Favas	Broad beans
Feno	Hay
Herva	Herbs or grass
Lentilhas	Lentils
Linho	Hemp
Nabos	Turnips

Ervilhas	Peas
Batatas	Potatoes
Arroz	Rice
Piperigallo	Sainfoin
Centeio	Rye
Cha	Tea
Trevo	Trefoil
Tabaco	Tobacco
Oliveira	Olive tree
Vide	Vine branch

DA AGRICULTURA. OF AGRICULTURE.

Um agricultor	A husbandman
Um quinteiro	A farmer
Um boieiro	A herdsman
Um vaqueiro	A cowkeeper
Um porqueiro	A swineherd
Um pastor	A shepherd
Um cavador	A digger
Um vinhateiro	A vine dresser
Um lavrador	A farmer
Um semeador	A sower
Um roçador	A weeder
Um segador	A reaper
Hortaliça	All sorts of herbage
Pastos	Pasture ground
Um arado	A plough
O ferro do arado	The ploughshare
A rabiça do arado	The plough handle
Uma aguilhada	A goad
Um ensinho	A rake
Uma fouce	A scythe *or* sickle
Uma fouce roçadoura	A weeding hook

Um podão	A pruning knife
Um mangoal	A flail
Um forcado	A pitchfork
Um rego	A furrow
Um bosque	A wood
Uma espiga	An ear of corn
A cabeça da espiga	The grain at the top of the ear of corn
Uma carreta	A waggon
Um carro	A cart
Uma roda	A wheel
O eixo	The axletree of a wheel
O raio da roda	The spoke of a wheel
Um curral de bois	An ox stall
Um curral de ovelhas	A sheepfold
Um chiqueiro de porcos	A hog's sty
Um tarro	A milk-pail
Uma francéla	A cheese-vat
Uma enxada	A hoe *or* spade
Um enxadão	A mattock
Uma canga	A yoke for oxen
Uma sébe	A hedge *or* fence
Uma ramada	A bower
Um rebeirinho	A rivulet
O tempo de tosquia	The time of shearing sheep
Cantiga dos segadores	Harvest home

ANIMAES DOMESTICOS.	DOMESTIC ANIMALS.
Um burro or *jumento*	A donkey
Um carneiro	A sheep
Uma ovelha	An ewe
Um cordeiro	A lamb
Um bode	A buck-goat

Uma cabra	A goat
Um cabrito	A kid
Um gato	A cat
Um gatinho	A kitten
Um cão	A dog
Um cãozinho	A puppy
Um fraldiqueiro	A lapdog
Um lebrel	A greyhound
Um cavallo	A horse
Uma egua	A mare
Um poldro	A colt
Um cavallo inteiro	A stallion
de montar	A riding horse
de carroça	A van-horse
d'aluguer	A hackney horse
de posta	A post-horse
de sella	A saddle-horse
alazão	A sorrel horse
baio	A bay horse

COUSAS PERTENCENTES A GUERRA. THINGS RELATING TO WAR.

Serviço or *vida militar*	Warfare
Militar or *servir na guerra*	To serve in the army
Artilheria	Artillery
Um canhão or *peça de artilheria*	A cannon
Um canhão de ferro	Iron cannon
Um canhão de bronze	Brass cannon
A alma do canhão	The mouth of the cannon
O fogão do canhão	The touch-hole of the cannon
A culatra do canhão	The breach of the cannon

O botão or extremidade da culatra	The pommel
Balas encadeadas	Chain shots
Uma bala de canhão	A cannon-ball or cannon-shot
A carrêta de canhão	The carriage of a cannon
Polvora	Gunpowder
Um canhão de vinte e quatro	A twenty-four pounder
Calibre	Calibre
Carregar	To load
Escorvar	To prime
Fazer pontaria	To level
Petrechos or munições de guerra	Military stores or ammunition
Encravar uma peça	To nail up a gun
Descavalgar uma peça	To dismount a gun
Disparar	To fire
Um tiro de peça	A cannon-shot
O trem de artilheria	The train of artillery
Uma colubrina	A culverin
Um falconete	A falconet
Um petardo	A petard
Um pedreiro	A swivel-gun
Uma bomba	A bomb
Uma bombarda	A great gun
Um morteiro	A mortar-piece
Uma granada	A grenade
Uma espingarda	A firelock
Uma pistola	A pistol
Uma carabina	A carbine
Um mosquete	A musket
Uma machadinha	A battle-axe
Uma lança	A lance
Uma alabarda	A halberd

Uma partasana	A partizan
Um pique	A pike
Calar os piques para resistir á cavallaria	To present the pikes against the cavalry
Um alfonge	A scimitar
Uma espada	A sword
Desembainhar a espada	To unsheathe the sword
O punho da espada	The handle of a sword
A maçã da espada	The pommel of a sword
A guarnição da espada	The hilt of a sword
A folha da espada	The blade of a sword
Meter mão á espada	To clap one's hand on one's sword
Matar	To kill
Ferir	To wound
Desbaratar	To rout
Saquear	To sack
Um punhal	A dagger
Uma bayoneta	A bayonet
Armar a bayoneta	To fix the bayonets
Um capacete	A helmet
Um morrião	A morion
Uma viseira	The vizor of a helmet
O gorjal or *gola*	The gorget
Um peito de armas	A breastplate
Uma couraça	A cuirass
O espaldar	The backplate
Um cossolete	A corslet
Um broquel	A buckler
Um escudo	A shield
Uma adaga	Dagger, a short sword
Uma saia de malha	A coat of mail
O rei de armas	The king-at-arms *or* king of heralds

Um arauto	A herald
Um general	A general
Um tenente general	A lieutenant-general
Um major general	A major-general
Um major	A major
Um sargento	A serjeant
Um marechal	Marshal
Um coronel	A colonel
Um coronel de infanteria	A colonel of infantry
Um official	An officer
Um brigadeiro	A brigadier
Um tenente coronel	A lieutenant-colonel
Um ajudante	An adjutant
Um ajudante de ordens	An aide-de-camp
Um capitão	A captain
Um posto de capitão	A captaincy or captainship
Um tenente	A lieutenant
Um corneta	A cornet
Um alferes	An ensign
As bandeiras	The colours
O estandarte	The standard
O porta estandarte	The standard-bearer
O pagador	The paymaster
Um commissario	A commissary
Um commissario geral	A commissary-general
Um engenheiro	An engineer
Um quartel mestre	A quarter-master
Um cabo de esquadra	A corporal
Um tambor or *caixa*	A drum
Um tambor, or *o que toca tambor*	A drummer
As baquetas	The drum-sticks
Os cordeis do tambor	The drum-strings
Os toques do tambor	The beats of a drum

Tocar a tambor	To beat a drum
A alvorada or *general*	The general, one of the beats of the drum
Passar mostra	To muster, to review forces
Um trombeteiro or *trombeta*	A trumpeter
Um pifano	A fifer or fife
Soldo	Wages, *or* pay for soldiers
Um soldado	A soldier
Soldado que está de sentinella	Soldier on duty
Entrar de guarda	To mount guard
Sentinella	Sentinel, sentry
Render a guarda, sentinellas, &c.	To relieve the guard, &c.
Bloquear	To block up
Um soldado de infanteria	A soldier of infantry
Um granadeiro	A grenadier
Um dragão	A dragoon
Um soldado de cavallo	A trooper *or* cavalry soldier
Montar a cavallo	To get on horseback
Apear-se	To alight
Um guarda da pessôa real	A life-guardsman
Um couraceiro	A cuirassier
Um fuzileiro	A fusilier
Um alabardeiro	A halberdier
Um pioneiro	A pioneer
Um mineiro or *minador*	A miner
Um bombardeiro	A bombardier
O tiro da artilheria, or *o espaço que a bala desparada corre; Alcance*	The range of a gun
Um artilheiro	An artilleryman
A arte da artilheria	Gunnery
General de artilheria	General of artillery
Um voluntario	A volunteer
Recrutas	Recruits

Um explorador, or *corredor de exercito*	A scout
Um espia	A spy
O que leva viveres ao exercito, or *vivandeiro*	Sutler
Um soldado que faz correrias	A marauder, a soldier that goes marauding
Um timbale or *atabale*	A kettledrum
Infanteria	Infantry
Cavallaria	Cavalry
Cavallaria ligeira	Light cavalry
A vanguarda	The vanguard
A retaguarda	The rear
O corpo de reserva	The reserve corps
O corpo de guarda	The body-guard
O piquete	The picquet guard
A ala	The wing of an army
Um batalhão	A battalion
Um destacamento	A detachment
Um regimento	A regiment
Uma companhia	A company
Um esquadrão	A squadron
Uma mochila	A knapsack
O bagagem	The baggage
Batedores do campo	Discoverers
O armazem	The magazines
As muralhas	The walls
Uma amea or *ameya*	A battlement
O parapeito	The parapet
Um castello	A castle
Um forte	A fort
Uma fortaleza	A fortress
Uma fortificação	A fortification
Uma torre	A tower

Uma cidadella	A citadel
Um baluarte	A bulwark
Uma fileira	A file
Uma cortina	A curtain
Meia lua	Half-moon
Uma troneira	A loophole
Um terra pleno	A platform of earth
Um rebelim or *revelim*	A ravelin
Uma contrascarpa	A counterscarp
Uma barreira	A barrier
Uma falsabraga	A fausse-braie
Um fosso	A ditch
Uma guarita	A sentry-box
Uma casamata	A casemate
O corredor or *estrada coberta*	The covered way
Os cestoës	The gabions
Uma estacada or *palissada*	A palisade
Um reducto	A redoubt
Uma atalaya	A watch-tower
Uma manta or *mantelete*	A shield, *or* cover for men from the shot
Faxina	Fascines
Uma mina	A mine
Fazer voar a mina	To spring a mine
Uma trincheira	A trench
Abrir as trincheiras	To open the trenches
Um campo	A camp
Os viveres	The provisions
Uma batalha	A battle
Dar batalha	To give battle
Uma escaramuça	A skirmish
Um sitio or *cêrco*	A siege
Um quartel	A quarter
Uma encamisada	A canteen

Uma sortida	A sally
Bater	To batter
Uma brecha	A breach
Um pontão	A pontoon
Uma escalada	An escalade
Um assalto	An assault
Dar assalto	To storm
Tomar por assalto	To take by storm
A chamada	The chamade
Capitular	To capitulate
Capitulação	Capitulation
Tregoas	Truce
Uma guarnição	A garrison
Um preboste	A provost
Uma leva	A levy
Levantar soldados, or fazer leva de gente	To raise men, to levy or raise soldiers
Levantar o sitio	To raise the siege
Levantar o campo	To decamp
Assentar o campo	To pitch one's camp
Um campo volante	A flying camp
Uma campanha	A campaign
Meter-se em campanha	To begin the campaign, to open the field
Guerrear	To fight
Uma peça de campanha	A field-piece
Uma forragem	A forage
Quarteis de inverno	Winter quarters
Dar quartel	To give quarter
Aquartelar-se	To take quarter
Marchar	To march
Marchar com bandeiras despregadas	To march with flying colours
Tocar a recolher	To beat the tattoo

Entregar uma praça	To surrender a place
Fila da vanguarda	Front rank
Fila do centro	Centre rank
Fila da retaguarda	Rear rank
Direita	Right
Esquerda	Left
Tempos	Motions
Exercicio	Exercise
Fechos	Lock
O cão, or *perro da arma*	Cock
A cronha	The butt
A boca da arma	The muzzle
O cano	The barrel
A vareta	The ramrod
O gatilho	The trigger
Um pellotão	A platoon
Uma divisão	A division
Linha, or *fileira*	Line
Caçadores	Riflemen
Flanco	Flank
Estado Maior	Staff
Frente	Front
Infanteria ligeira	Light infantry
Regulamentos	Regulations

PALAVRAS DE COMANDO. — MILITARY WORDS OF COMMAND.

Sentido	Attention
Armas ao hombro	Shoulder arms
Descançar	Order arms
Metter bayonetas	Fix bayonets
Apresentar armas	Present arms
Calar bayonetas	Charge bayonets

Descançar armas	Support arms
Tirar bayonetas	Unfix bayonets
Cruzar armas	Pile arms
Preparar	Make ready
Carregar	Load
Tirar o cartuxo	Handle cartridge
Escorvar	Prime
Tirar as varetas	Draw ramrods
Atuchar o curtuxo	Ram down cartridge
Apontar	Present
Fogo	Fire
Meter o cartuxo	Cast about
Fogo por pellotões	Firing by platoons
Fogo de filas	File-firing
Alto	Halt
Formar em linha	To form in line
Fogo obliquo	Oblique firing
Formar	Form
Marcha	March
Ordem cerrada	Close order
Desfilar	To file
Columna cerrada	Close column
Meia volta á esquerda	Left flank wheel, backward
Voltar	Wheel
Avançar	Advance
Cerrar as fileiras	Close the ranks

NAVEGAÇÃO. — NAVIGATION.

Um navio	A ship
Uma náo de guerra	A line-of-battle ship
Um navio de carga, or *mercante*	A merchant-ship, a merchantman
Um navio veleiro	A very good sailer, *or* a ship that sails well

Um navio ronceiro	A bad sailer
Uma fragata	A frigate
Uma fusta	A foist
Uma pinaça	A pinnace
Uma barca de passagem	A ferry-boat
Um barco	A boat
Uma barca	A barque
Uma canôa	A canoe
Uma gondola	A gondola
Um esquife	A skiff
Uma chalupa or balandra	A sloop
Uma chalupa pequena	A shallop
Um bergantim	A brigantine
Uma balsa	A raft
O navio almirante	The admiral's ship
Uma armada	A fleet, a navy
Uma frota	A fleet of merchant ships
Uma esquadra	A squadron, part of a fleet
A bordo	On board
A pôpa	The poop, stern, or steerage
A prôa	The prow or head
Peças de prôa para dar caça ao inimigo	Chase guns
Uma tartana	A tartan
Um brulote	A fire-ship
Uma falua	A felucca
Uma caravela	A caravel
Embarcacão pequena para serviço de um navio de guerra	A tender
Um guarda costa	A guard-ship
Um cruzador	A cruiser
Um corsario	A privateer
Um hiate	A yacht

Um navio de transporte	A transport
Uma náo da India oriental	East-Indiaman
Uma náo da India occidental	West-Indiaman
Um navio para levar carvão	A collier
Embarcações pequenas	Small craft
Uma falua	A barge
Embarcação de avizo	Advice-boat
Um paquete	A packet-boat
Um barco de pescar	A fishing-boat
Uma lancha	A lighter
Os remos	The oars
A pá do remo	The blade of the oar
A sentina	The well
O lastro	The ballast
Alastrar o navio	To ballast a ship
Um mastro or *arvore*	A mast
O mastro grande	The main-mast
O mastro de mezena	The mizen
O mastro do traquete	The fore-mast
O gurupés	The bowsprit or boltsprit
A gávea	The round-top, main-top, or scuttle of a mast
A quilha	The keel
A verga or *entena*	The yard
A laiz, or *extremidade das vergas*	The yard-arm
As pranchas que cobrem os costados do navio da parte de fora	The side planks or side of a ship
*Uma véla**	A sail
Uma véla mestra, or *a véla do mastro grande*	The main-sheet
A véla da gávea	The main-top-sail

* By *véla* is often meant the ship itself.

A véla de joanête do mastro grande	The main-top-gallant-sail
Os papafigos	The mizen and fore-sail
A mezêna	The mizen-sail
A gata, or véla de cima da mezêna	The mizen-top-sail
O traquête	The fore-sail
O velacho	The fore-top-sail
O joanete do traquete	The fore-top-gallant-sail
A cevadeira	The sprit-sail
A véla latina	A shoulder-of-mutton-sail
Fazer força de véla	To crowd the sail
Os mastaréos	The top-mast, or top-gallant-masts
Oa mastaréo da mezêna, or mastaréo da gata	The mizen-top-mast
Uma portinhola	A port-hole
As bandeiras	The colours
As flammulas, or galhardetes	The streamers, pendants
A agulha de marear	The mariner's compass
A bitácola	The binnacle
As costuras do navio	The seams of a ship
O léme	The helm or rudder
A cana do léme	The whip or whip-staff
A cuberta	The deck
Cuberta corrida	Flush fore and aft
As escotilhas	The hatches or scuttles
Um escotilhão	A room by the hatches to keep the provisions in
O castello de pôpa	The quarter-deck
O castello de prôa	The forecastle
Garrar a ancora	To drive, or for a ship to drag her anchor
A ancora	The anchor

Meter a ancora dentro	To weigh the anchor
Uma ancora de roboque	A kedger
A ancora de esperança	The sheet anchor
As unhas da ancora	The flukes of the anchor
A argola da ancora	The ring of the anchor
Estar a ancora a pique	The anchor to be a-peak
Uma amarra	A cable
Picar or cortar as amarras	To cut the cables
A sonda or prumo	The sounding-lead
Os cutelos	The studding-sails
A maré	The tide
Uma bozina	A speaking-trumpet
Preparar um navio de velas, cordas, &c.	To rig a ship
Um piloto	A pilot
Um escrivão	A purser
Pilotagem	Pilotage
A carta de marear	The sea-chart
Um capitão	A captain
O capitão tenente	The first lieutenant
Um contramestre	A boatswain
Um marinheiro	A sailor
Um camarote	A cabin
Marinheiro que é camarada ou pertence ao mesmo rancho	A messmate
Uma tormenta	A tempest
Uma borrasca	A storm
Bonança	Fair weather
Calmaria	Calm
Vento em pôpa	The wind full astern, a fore-wind
Navio arrasado em pôpa	A ship that sails before the wind

A derrota	The course *or* way of a ship
Alar a bolina	To tighten the main bowline, to haul up the bowline
Ir pela bolina	To tack upon a wind, sail upon a bowline
Nó da bolina	The bowline knot
Barlavento	Windward
Ganhar o barlavento	To catch the wind
Barlaventear, or *deitar a barlavento*	To ply to windward
Sotavento	Leeward
Escovens	Hawsers
Escôtas	Tacks
Velame, cordas, e o mais que é necessario para preparar um navio	Tackle *or* tackling, the rigging of a ship
Uma corda	A rope
As enxarcias	The shrouds
Arribar	To put into harbour
Bombordo	Larboard
Estibordo	Starboard
Ló	Luff
Meter de ló	To luff *or* keep the ship nearer the wind
Uma bomba	A pump
Dar á bomba	To pump
Balde para deitar agoa na bomba	A pump-can
O pistão da bomba	The sucker of a pump
O braço da bomba	The pump-handle
Um farol	A light, lantern, *or* lighthouse
O vento	The wind

ROSA DA AGULHA, or DOS VENTOS.	THE FLY OF THE MARINER'S COMPASS.
Norte	North
Norte 4ª a nordeste	N. by E.
Nor-nordeste	N. N. E.
Nordeste 4ª a norte	N. E. by N.
Nordeste	N. E.
Nordeste 4ª a leste	N. E. by E.
Les-nordeste	E. N. E.
Leste 4ª a nordeste	E. by N.
Leste	East
Leste 4ª a sueste	E. by S.
Les-sueste	E. S. E.
Sueste 4ª a leste	S. E. by E.
Sueste	S. E.
Sueste 4ª a sul	S. E. by S.
Su-sueste	S. S. E.
Sul 4ª a sueste	S. by E.
Sul	South
Sul 4ª a sudoeste	S. by W.
Su-sudoeste	S. S. W.
Sudoeste 4ª sul	S. W. by S.
Sudoeste	S. W.
Sudoeste 4ª a oeste	S. W. by W.
Oes-sudoeste	W. S. W.
Oeste 4ª a sudoeste	W. by S.
Oeste	West
Oeste 4ª a noroeste	W. by N.
Oes-noroeste	W. N. W.
Noroeste 4ª a oeste	N. W. by W.
Noroeste	N. W.
Noroeste 4ª a norte	N. W. by N.
Nor-noroeste	N. N. W.

Norte 4ª *a noroeste*	N. by W.
Vento travessão or *travessia*	Contrary wind
Dar a embarcação a travéz	To hull
Pairar	To ply backwards and forwards on one station
Esporão	Beak
Colher um cabo	To coil a cable
Largar mais cabo	To pay out more cable
Abrir agoa	To leak or spring a leak
Fazer agoada	To take in fresh water
Arpar um navio	To grapple a ship
Fatexa	Grapple
Pedaço de lôna breada que se põe ao redor do mastro e das bombas para que a agoa não penetre	Tarpaulin
Passador	A fidd or pin of iron to open the strands of ropes
Corda com que se prende o bote, or *lancha á pôpa do navio*	A boat-rope
Um apito	A boatswain's call
As abadernas	The nippers
Uma abita	The bits
Emproar	To steer right forward, to turn the prow straight forward
Guinar o navio	To tack
Parte superior or *mais alta da pôpa de um navio*	Taffrail
As apagafanoes	The leech-lines
As arreigadas	The puttocks
Os brioes	The bunt-lines
As varredouras	The bow-studding-sails

O bartidouro	The boat's-skit
Os bastardos	The parrels
Uma bigota	A dead-eye
Os botalos	The studding-sail-booms
Bracear	To brace
Os braços	The braces
O bragueiro or *vergueiro*	The rudder's rope
Os brandaes	The backstays
As buçardas	The breast-hooks
As cacholas	The cheeks
O cadaste	The stand-post
Um cadernal	A large block with more than one shrive
As cavernas	The floor-timbers
Os colhedores	The lines of the shrouds
Compassar um navio	To trim a ship
Os cossouros	The trucks
A craca	The foulness of the ship's bottom
O cabrestante	The capstan
Dar caça	To chase
As curvas	The knees
Os enbornaes	The scupper-holes
O porão	The hold of a ship
Uma maca	A hammock
O convéz	The deck
O camarote do cirurgião	The cockpit
O frete	The freight
A carga	The cargo
Ordem que o capitão recebe para dar á vela	Sailing orders
Desembarque	Landing
Embargo	Embargo
Ancoragem	Anchorage

Batalha naval	Naval battle
Uma caravela mexeriqueira or *de espia*	A look-out ship
Arriar or *arrear*	To veer
Arrear as velas	The furl a sail
Arrear bandeira	To strike the flag
Levantar ferro, levar ancoras, levar ferro, levar-se or *levar*	To weigh anchor
Leva	The action of weighing or taking up the anchor
Bolear a peça	To move a gun towards starboard *or* larboard
A peça de leva	The signal gun
Rebocar or *levar de reboque*	To tow
Fazer costuras	To splice
A passagem	The passage
Um passageiro	A passenger
Uma viagem	A voyage
Navio cujo capitão tem cartas de corso	Letters of marque
Querenar um navio	To careen a ship
Brear as costuras do navio	To pitch the seams of a ship
Dar á costa	To run a-ground *or* on shore
Soluçar a náo	A ship to roll, *or* to float in rough water
Naufragar	To suffer a wreck, to be wrecked
Naufragio	Shipwreck
Um patrão, or *mestre de embarcação*	The shipmaster
Um carpenteiro de navios	The shipwright

Estaleiro	Ship-yard
Embarcar	To ship
Embarcar-se	To go aboard, to take shipping
Um grumete	A boy (of the crew)
Moço da camara	A cabin boy
Um calafate	A caulker
Calafetar um navio	To caulk a ship
O calafeto	The oakum
Um arsenal or *ribeira das náos*	An arsenal *or* dockyard
Emmastear um navio	To fit a ship, *or* vessel, with masts
Remar	To row
Um remador	A rower
O despenseiro	The steward
Os marinheiros, e toda a outra gente que pertence ao navio, Tripulação	The crew of a ship
A guarnição da náo	The crew and marines who serve on board a man-of-war
A balestilha	The cross-staff
O quadrante	The quadrant
Outante	Hadley's quadrant
De ré	Aft
Paravante	Fore
A situação de uma costa, ilha, &c., a respeito de qualquer outro lugar	The bearing
Quarentena	Quarantine
Baliza	Sea-mark
Larga	Large
Amarar	To bear off

Caçar a vela	To turn the sail to the windward
Cacear um navio	It is said of a ship that is hurried away from her course by strong winds, tides, &c.
Lançar um navio ao mar	To launch a ship
Entrar com vento fresco e bom no porto	To bear in the harbour
Bordo	Tack
Bordo or *banda*	Broadside
Uma caça	A chase
Uma presa or *tomadia*	A prize or capture
Estar de vergadalto	To stand for the offing
Ventos de monção or *geraes*	Trade winds
Andar de conserva	To keep company together, to sail under a convoy
Dar or *fazer um bordo*	To tack the ship, *or* tack about, *or* to bring her head about
Estar á capa, or *pôr-se á capa*	To lie by at sea, to back the sails

DO COMMERCIO, E DO QUE LHE PERTENCE.
OF TRADE, AND OF THINGS RELATING TO IT.

Conta	Account
Conta de venda	Account of sales
Fazer uma conta	To cast up an account
Pedir contas	To call to an account
Dar á conta	To pay on account
Conta corrente	Account current
Dinheiro de contado	Ready money
Fundos publicos	Stocks

O que negocêa em comprar e vender acções	A jobber
O ballanço	The balance
Um fardo	A bale
Um banco	A bank
Um banqueiro	A banker
Quebra	Bankruptcy
Falido or quebrado	Bankrupt
Ajuste or concerto	Bargain
Troca	Barter
Portador	Bearer
Lançador	Bidder
Letra de cambio	Bill of exchange
Negociar uma letra de cambio	To negotiate a bill of exchange
Partida	Parcel
Conhecimento	Bill of lading
Escriptura de obrigação	Bond, engagement
Guarda-livros, or o que em uma casa de negocio tem a seu cargo os livros	Book-keeper
Occupação or negocio	Business
Comprador	Buyer
Dinheiro	Cash
Porte or carreto	Carriage
O caixa or o que guarda a caixa	The cashier or cash-keeper
Cento	Cent
Certidão	Certificate
Cambio	Change, exchange
Freguez	Customer
Gastos	Charges
Barato	Cheap
Caro	Dear
Despacho da alfandega	Clearance

Commissão	Commission
Mercancias	Merchandise
Compromisso	Compromise
Consignação	Consignment
Consumo	Consumption
Conteudo	Contents
Contracto	Contract
Um correspondente	A correspondent
Preço	Price, rate
A alfandega	The custom-house
Os guardas d'alfandega	The custom-house officers
Guardas que estão vigiando até que os navios estejão descarregados	Tide-waiters
Uma feitoria	A factory, settlement
Um escriptorio	A counting-house or office
Credito	Credit
Um credor	A creditor
Corrente	Current
Costume	Custom
Um contractador	A contractor
Trafego or negocio	Traffic or business
Divida	Debt
Um devedor	A debtor
Dinheiro desembolçado	Disbursement
Desconto	Discount
Deposito	Deposit
Direitos que a alfandega torna a dar aos exportadores de certas fazendas, que já os tinhão pago na supposição de serem para consumo interior : servindo isto para animar o commercio	Drawback

Copia	Duplicate
Corretor	Broker
Corretor de letras de cambio	Stockbroker
Assegurador or *segurador*	Insurer *or* underwriter
Endosse	Endorsement
Endossador	Endorser
Levantamento de preço	Enhancement
Entrada	Entry
Equivalente	Equivalent
Exigencia	Exigency
Despeza	Expense
Exportação	Export *or* exportation
Extorsão	Extortion
Feitor or *commissario*	Factor
Feira	Fair
Fio or *arame no qual se enfião os papeis n'um escriptorio*	File for papers
Quatro, cinco, &c., por cento	Four, five, &c., per cent
Frete	Freight
Fretar um navio	To charter a ship
Fundos	Funds
Ganho	Gain *or* profit
O que ganha	Gainer
Fazendas or *effeitos*	Goods, effects
Estrêa	Handsel
Escriptura	Deed
Direitos d' entrada	A duty on imported commodities
Importador	Importer
Renda	Income
Interesse	Interest
Correspondencia	Correspondence
Inventario	Inventory

Insolvencia	Insolvency
Factura	Invoice
Escriptura de arrendamento	Lease
Arrendador	Lessee
Livro de razão	Ledger
Emprestimo	Loan
Dinheiro emprestado	Money lent
Carta	Letter
Sobrescripto da carta	The direction of a letter
Fechar uma carta com sinete	To fold and seal a letter
Mala em que o correio traz as cartas	Mail
Hypotheca	Mortgage
Credor hypothecario	Mortgagee
Fiador	Bail
Pagamento	Payment
Falta de pagamento	Non-payment
Nota promissoria	Note *or* promissory note
Dono	Owner
Pacote	Pack, a truss
Serapilheira	Packcloth, wrapper
Barbante	Pack-thread
Maço de cartas	Packet of letters
Companheiro de alguem no negocio, or *socio*	Partner
Sociedade, or *companhia no negocio*	Partnership
Penhor	Pawn *or* pledge
Aposite de segura	Policy of insurance
Seguro	Insurance
Protestar uma letra	To protest a bill
Aceitar uma letra	To accept a bill
Protesto	Protest
Sacar uma letra	To draw a bill

A A

Correio	Post-office
Correio que leva cartas	Postman *or* letter-carrier
Porte de cartas	Postage
Primagem	Primage
Capital	Capital
Perdas e damnos	Losses and damages
Importancia	Proceeds
Importancia liquida	Net proceeds
Promessa	Promise
Bens	Property
Pontualidade	Punctuality
Compra	Purchase
Recibo	Receipt
Recambio	Re-exchange
Arbitro or *louvado*	Referee *or* arbitrator
Louvamento or *arbitrio*	Reference
Quitação	Release
Remessa	Remittance
Venda das coisas por miudo, como fazem os mercadores de retalho	Retail
Mercador de retalho	Retailler
Riquezas	Riches, wealth
Venda	Sale
Padrão	A pattern
Amostra	Sample
Sinete	Seal
Lacre	Sealing-wax
Ajuste de contas	Settlement of accounts
Logista	Shop-keeper
Contrabandista	Smuggler
Fazenda de contrabando	Contraband, goods smuggled
Fazer contrabando	To smuggle

Modêlo, or *fiel dos pezos e medidas publicas*	Standard measure
Armazem	Warehouse
Subscripção	Subscription
Tara	Tare
Fazenda ruim	Trashy goods
Risco	Risk
Juros	Interest
Usurario	Usurer
Usura	Usury
Mercancias	Merchandise
Valôr	Worth *or* value
Avaria	Average
Direitos	Duties *or* custom
Tributo or *contribuição*	Cess, tribute
Sisa	Excise
Siseiro	Exciseman
Cáes	Wharf
Direito que se paga por desembarcar fazendas no cáes	Wharfage
Collector do mesmo direito or *tributo*	Wharfinger
Dizimos	Tithes
Dizimador or *dizimeiro*	Tithe-gatherer
Louça vidrada, sem ser da China	Dutch-ware
Mercador de atacador	Wholesale dealer
Venda que se faz por atacado	Wholesale

DA MOEDA or DINHEIRO PORTUGUEZ.	OF THE PORTUGUESE COIN.
*Real	A ree, equal to $\frac{27}{400}d$.
Des reis	10 rees, $\frac{27}{40}d$.
Vintem	A vintin, $1\frac{7}{20}d$.
Tostão, or 5 vintens	A testoon, $6\frac{3}{4}d$.
2 tostões	Two testoons, 1s. $1\frac{1}{2}d$.
4 tostões, or um crusado	A crusade, 2s. 3d.
Crusado novo, or 24 vintens	A new crusade, 2s. $8\frac{2}{3}d$.
5 tostões	Five testoons, 2s. $9\frac{3}{4}d$.
10 tostões, or 1000 reis	10 testoons, 5s. $7\frac{1}{2}d$.
Um quartinho de oiro, or 1200 reis	12 testoons, 6s. 9d.
16 tostões	16 testoons, 9s.
Meia moeda de oiro	Half moidore, 13s. 6d.
3200, or 32 tostões	32 testoons, 18s.
Moeda de oiro de 4800	A moidore, 1l. 7s.
Peça de 8000	Joanese, 2l. 5s.
Dobrão, or 12,800	128 testoons, 3l. 12s.

This mark is prefixed to the imaginary money.

A COLLECTION

OF

PORTUGUESE PROVERBS.

A agoa o dá, a ogoa o leva	Lightly come, lightly go
Na agoa revolta pesca o pescador	To fish in troubled waters (to make a benefit of public troubles)
Está como o peixe n' agoa	He lives in clover
Trazer a agoa para o seu moinho	To bring grist to the mill
Levar agoa ao mar	To carry coals to Newcastle
As agoas estão baixas	He or she is at a low ebb
O que não pode ser, deve-se soffrer	What cannot be cured must be endured
Come como um alarve	He eats like a thresher
Alazão tostado antes morto que cançado	A dark sorrel horse will die before he will stop
Uma desgraça alcança a outra	Misfortune never comes alone
Estar na aldêa, e não ver as casas	We say, you cannot see wood for trees; *or* to be like the butcher that looked for his knife when he had it in his mouth
Quem trabalha tem alfaia	He that works has furniture

Fallo-lhe em alhos, responde-me em bugalhos	I talk of chalk, and you of cheese
Em tempo nevado o alho vale um cavallo	Garlic in foggy weather is as good as a horse; it means that garlic is a good defence for travellers against the dampness and cold weather
T'ezo como um alho	As stiff as garlic; that is, a healthy, strong, robust person
Sua alma, na sua palma	As you brew, even so bake
Quem ama a beltrão, ama a seu cão	Love me, love my dog
Cada qual ama seu semelhante	Like will to like, or like loves like
Tambem os ameaçados comem pão	Threatened folks eat bread; we say, threatened folks live long
Contas de perto, e amigos de longe	Short reckonings make long friends
Tão bom é Pedro como seu amo	Like master, like man
Furtar o carneiro, e dar os pés pelo amor de Deos	We say, to steal the goose, and give the giblets in alms
Nem um dedo faz mão, nem uma andorinha verão	One swallow does not make a summer. *Una hirundo non facit ver*, says Horace
Levar palhas e aralhas	To sweep stakes
Na arca aberta o justo pecca	That is, it is opportunity that makes the thief
De um argueiro, fazer um cavaleiro	We say, to make mountains of mole-hills.

Com arte e com engano se vive meio anno ; com engano e com arte se vive a outra parte	That is, all a man's life is a deceit
Quem a boa arvore se chega, boa sombra o cobre	That is, he that relies on good worthy people reaps a benefit
Asno que tem fome, cardos come	We say, hungry dogs will eat dirty pudding
Sôpa de mel não se fez para a boca do asno	Good things are not fit for fools
Mais quero asno que me leve, que cavallo que me derrube	Better be an old man's darling than a young man's slave
Mais valemá avença que boa sentença	It is better to agree at any cost than go to law
Não deites azeite no fogo	Do not throw oil into the fire
Da mão á boca se perde a sopa	Many a slip between the cup and the lip
Em boca cerrada não entra mosca	A close mouth catches no flies
Quem tem boca vai a Roma	That is, a man may go anywhere if he has a tongue to speak and ask his way
Pela bôca morre o peixe	Much taking brings much woe
Cada bufarinheiro louva seus alfinetes	Every man thinks his own geese swans
Quem tem quatro, e gasta cinco, não ha mister bolsa nem bolsinho	He that hath four and spends five hath no need of a purse
Cabra vai pela vinha, por onde vai a mãi vai a filha	Like father, like son

Matar dois coelhos de uma cajadada	We say, to kill two birds with one stone
Quem canta, seus males espanta	The person who sings makes easy his misfortunes
Deitar a capa ao toiro	To throw one's cloak at the bull; that is, to venture all a man has to save his life
Viva el-rei, e dá cá a capa	Let the king live, and give me the cloak; that is, spoken of persons who, under a pretence of authority, rob and plunder other people, and at the same time pretend they are doing justice to the power reposed in their hands
Andar de capa cahida	To be behindhand in the world
O cão com raiva de seu dono trava	A mad dog bites its own master; there is no trusting to madmen *or* people in a rage
Quem com cães se lança, com pulgas se levanta	We say, sleep with beggars and you will get fleas
A carne de lobo dente de cão	That is, to return railing for railing; *or*, as our modern proverb says, give him a Roland for his Oliver; the Latins say, *par pari referre*
A cavallo dado não olhes o dente	Never look in the mouth of a gift horse

Quem faz casa na praça, uns dizem que é alta, outros que é baixa	That is, a man in public business cannot please everybody; *or,* as Solon says, it is rare that statesmen can please all men
Quem quer cavallo sem tacha, sem elle se acha	It is a good horse that never stumbles
Cobra boa fama, e deita-te a dormir	When your name is up, you may lie in bed till noon
Fazer as contas sem a hospeda	To reckon without the hostess; *or,* as we say, the host
Em casa do ladrão não falles em corda	You should not mention a halter to any whose relations or friends have suffered by it; that is, no man should be reminded of the subject of his disgrace
Do coiro lhe sahem as correias	The thongs come out of his skin; that is, he pays for it
Cortar o vestido conforme o panno	To cut one's coat according to the cloth
Cria o corvo, tirarvos-ha o olho	It is said of a person that, being received in distress, shows ingratitude to those who relieved him
Tanta culpa tem o ladrão como o consentidor	The receiver is as bad as the thief
Dádivas quebrantão penhas	Gifts break rocks: that is, kindness overcomes the hardest hearts

Melhor é fazer debalde que estar debalde	It is better to work for nothing than to be lazy and do nothing at all
Deitar azeite no fogo	To make bad worse. Horace says, *Oleum addere camino*
Não é o demo tão feio como o pintão	We say, the lion is not so fierce as his picture
Primeiro estão os dentes, que parentes	We say, near is my coat, but nearer is my skin, &c. Terence says, *Heus proximus sum egomet mihi*
Lá vai a lingoa, onde o dente grita	To scratch where it itches
Quando cuidas meter o dente em seguro, toparás o duro	Harm watch, harm catch, Horace says: —*et fragili quærens illidere dentem Offendet solido*
Dar com a lingoa nos dentes	To denounce oneself, to belie
Ventura te dê Deus, filho; que saber pouco te basta	God give you good luck, child, for a little learning will serve your turn; because it is fortune that raises men more than merit
Cada qual por si, e Deus por todos	Every one for himself, and God for all
Em bons dias, boas obras	The better days the better deeds
Para dia de são cerejo	We say, when two Sundays come together, that is— never

Tudo pode o dinheiro	Money governs the world
O homem propõe, e Deus dispõe	Man proposes, and God disposes
Dorme como um arganaz	He sleeps like a dormouse
A bom entendedor poucas palavras bastão	A word to the wise is enough
Gato escaldado de agoa fria ha medo	We say, a burnt child dreads the fire
No escudellar verás quem te quer bem, ou mal	That is, people's affections are discovered by their liberality
Esmolou são Matheus, esmolou para os seus	Charity begins at home
Não ha melhor espelho que o amigo velho	There is no better looking-glass than an old friend; that is, such a one will not flatter a man, but tell him the truth
Nem estopa com tições, nem mulher com varões	That is, conversation of women is dangerous; it is not safe to play with edged tools
Fallar sem cuidar, é atirar sem apontar	To let one's tongue run without reflecting on what one says is like shooting at random
Falla pouco e bem, ter-te-hão por alguem	Talk little and well, and you will be counted somebody; that is, you'll be esteemed
Quem a fama tem perdida, morto anda n'esta vida	He who has lost his reputation is as good as dead whilst living

A quem má fama tem, nem accompanhes, nem digas bem	Do not keep company with, nor be fond of one that has an ill name
Aproveitador de farelos, esperdiçador de farinha	That is, one that saves at the spigot, and lets it run out at the bung; also, penny wise and pound foolish
Não fazem boa farinha	They cannot agree together
Quem má a faz nella jaz	Self doth self harm
Agora dá pão e mel, e depois dará pão e fel	After sweet meat comes sour sauce
Lingoa dôce como mel, e coração amargoso como fel	A honey tongue, a heart of gall
Bater o ferro quando está quente	To beat the iron whilst it is hot, *or* to make hay whilst the sun shines
Quem com fero mata, a ferro morre	He who kills by the sword dies by the sword
Carregador de ferro, carregado de medo	He who is loaded with iron is loaded with fear; that is, he who loads himself with armour and weapons against danger discovers he is much afraid
Quem te faz festa, não soendo-as fazer, ou te quer enganar, ou te ha mister	He that makes more of you than he is wont to do, either designs to cheat you, or stands in need of you
Não fies, nem profies, nem arrendes, viviráa entre as gentes	Do not trust, nor contend, nor hire, and you will live among men; that is, you'll live peaceably

Se não bebe na taberna, folga n'ella	We say, he does not smoke, but smokes
Achou fôrma para o seu sapato	He has found a last to his shoe; that is, he has met with his match
Não sejais forneiro se tendes a cabeça de manteiga	Do not undertake to be a baker if your head is made of butter; that is, do not take upon you any business you are unfit for
Ao homem ousado a fortuna lhe dá a máo	Fortune favours the bold
Roupa de francezes	Things left at random, *or* exposed to be pillaged
Cahir da frigideira nas brasas	To fall out of the frying-pan into the fire
Perto vai o fumo da chama	We say, there is no smoke without some fire
Quem uma vez furta, fiel nunca	He who once steals, is never trusty; *or*, once a thief, always a thief
Mal vai ao fuso quando a barba não anda em cima	Alas for the spindle when the beard is not over it! By the spindle is meant the woman, and by the beard is meant the man
Cada terra com seu uso, cada roca com seu fuso	So many countries, so many customs
Quantas cabeças tantas carapuças	Several men, several minds
Quem lhe doer a cabeça que a aperte	We say, if any one finds the cap fit him, let him put it on

Se queres saber quem é o villão, metelhe a vara na mão	Set a beggar on horseback, and he will ride to the death
Não ha rosa sem espinhos	There is no rose without thorns, there is no sweet without some pain
Quem não deve, não teme	Out of debt, out of danger
Quando pode, não quer; quando quer, não pode	It is good to make hay while the sun shines
Homem honrado não ha mister gabado	We say, a good face needs no recommendation
Homem grande, bêsta de páo	This proverb intimates that things are not to be valued by their bulk, but according to their intrinsic worth and value; and so we say, a lark is better than a kite
Debaixo de má capa jaz bom bebedor	A tattered cloak may cover a good drinker; that is, men are not to be judged by outward appearance
Quem muito abraça, pouco aperta	All grasp, all lose; or covet all, and lose all.
No açougue, quem mal falla, mal ouve	He that speaks knavishly shall hear knavishly. Terence says, *Qui pergit ea quæ vult dicere, ea quæ non vult audiet*
Quem em mais alto nada, mais prestes se afoga	That is, the highest charges are the more liable and nearer to the downfall
Hospeda formosa, damno faz á bolsa	A beautiful hostess, or landlady, is bad for the purse

O hospede e o peixe aos tres dias fede	Fresh fish, and new-come guests, smell when they are three days old
Horta sem agoa, casa sem telhado, mulher sem amor, marido sem cuidado, de graça é caro	That is, a garden without water, a house untiled, a wife without love, and a husband without troubles, are all alike, being all worth nought
Honra ao bom para que te honre, e ao máo para que te não deshonre	Honour a good man, that he may honour you; and a bad man, that he may not dishonour you
Honra é dos amos, a que se faz aos criados	The honour done to servants redounds to their masters
Officio de conselho, honra sem proveito	An office in the council is honour without profit; that is, to be of the council of a town, by which nothing is got in Portugal
Homem apercebido, meio combatido	A man that is prepared has half the battle over

FAMILIAR DIALOGUES.

Muito bons dias senhor	Good day, sir
Como está vm^{ce}? or *como passa?*	How do you do, sir?
Bem, não muito bem, vou passando	Well; not very well; so so
Muito bem para o servir	Very well, at your service
As suas ordens	At your service
Fico-lhe muito obrigado	I am obliged to you
Agradecido	I thank you
Como está or *passa, o senhor seu irmão?*	How does your brother do?
Muito bem, não muito bem	He is very well; not very well
Elle terá gosto de ver a vm^{ce}	He will be glad to see you
Não terei tempo para ir vel-o hoje	I shall have no time to see him to-day
Faça favor de sentar-se	Be pleased to sit down
Dá uma cadeira ao senhor	Give a chair to the gentleman
Não é necessario	There is no occasion
Tenho que ir a fazer uma visita aqui na visinhança	I must go to make a visit in the neighbourhood
Vm^{ce} tem pressa	You are in haste
Eu logo voltarei	I will be back *or* return presently

Adeus meu senhor	Farewell, sir
Fólgo de o ver com boa saude	I am glad to see you in good health
Beijo as mãos de vm^{ce}	I kiss your hand
Sou seu criado	I am your servant

PARA FAZER UMA VISITA DE MANHA.	TO VISIT IN THE MORNING.
Onde está teu amo?	Where is your master?
Ainda dorme?	Is he asleep still?
Não senhor, elle está acordado	No, sir, he is awake
Está elle já levantado?	Is he up?
Não, senhor, elle ainda está na cama	No, sir, he is still in bed
Que vergonha de estar ainda na cama a estas horas!	What a shame it is to be in bed at this hour of the day!
Hontem á noite fui para a cama tão tarde, que não me pude levantar cedo esta manhã	I went to bed so late last night, I could not rise early this morning
Que fizerão vm^{ces} depois de ceiar?	What did you do after supper?
Dançámos, cantámos, rimos, e jogámos	We danced, we sang, we laughed, we played
A que jogo?	At what game?
Aos centos	We played at piquet
Quanto me peza de o não ter sabido!	How grieved I am, I did not know it
Quem ganhou? quem perdeo?	Who won? who lost?
Eu ganhei dez moedas	I won ten moidores
Até que horas jogarão vm^{ces}?	Till what hour did you play?

BB

Até duas horas depois da meia noite	Till two in the morning
A que horas foi vm^{ce} para a cama?	At what o'clock did you go to bed?
As tres, ás tres horas e meia	At three, at half-past three
Que horas são?	What's o'clock?
Que horas lhe parece que sejão?	What do you think it is?
Parece-me que são apenas oito horas	Scarcely eight, I believe
Sim! as oito! já derão as dez	How! eight! it has struck ten
Então é preciso que me levante quanto mais depressa pudér	Then I must get up with all speed

PARA VESTIR-SE. — TO DRESS ONESELF.

Quem está ahi?	Who is there?
Que quer vm^{ce}?	What do you want
Despacha-te, encende o lume, e veste-me	Be quick, make a fire, dress me
Dá-me a minha camisa	Give me my shirt
Eil-a aqui, senhor	Here it is, sir
Não está quente, está muito fria	It is not warm, it is quite cold
Eu a aquentarei, se vm^{ce} quizer	If you please, I will warm it
Não, não; traze-me as minhas meias de seda	No, no; bring me my silk stockings
Uma d'ellas está rota	One of them is torn
Dá-lhe um ponto, concerta-a	Stitch it a little, mend it
Dei-a ao que as concerta	I have given it to be mended
Fizeste bem	You have done right

Onde estão as minhas chinelas?	Where are my slippers?
Onde está o meu chambre?	Where is my dressing-gown
Pentea-me	Comb my hair
Dá-me o meu lenço	Give me my handkerchief
Eis aqui um lavado	Here is a clean one
Dá-me o que está na minha algibeira	Give me that which is in my pocket
Dei-o á lavandeira	I gave it to the washer-woman
Trouxe ella já a minha roupa?	Has she brought my linen?
Sim, senhor, e não falta nada	Yes, sir, there wants nothing
Que fato quer vm^{ce} para hoje?	What clothes will you wear to-day?
O mesmo de hontem	Those I wore yesterday
O alfaiate ha de trazer logo o seu fato	The tailor will bring your clothes presently
Batem á porta, vê lá quem é	Somebody knocks, see who it is
E o alfaiate	It is the tailor
Deixa-o entrar	Let him come in

O SENHOR E O ALFAIATE. THE GENTLEMAN AND THE TAILOR.

Trazeis o meu fato?	Do you bring my suit of clothes?
Sim, senhor, eil-o aqui	Yes, sir, here it is
Ha muito tempo que estou esperando por elle	You make me wait a great while
Não pude vir até agora	I could not come sooner
Não estava acabado	It was not finished
Ainda não estava forrado	The lining was not sewed

Quer vm.^{ce} vestir a casaca para ver se lhe está bem?	Will you please to try the dress-coat on?
Vejamos se está bem feita	Let us see whether it is well made
Tenho para mim que lhe ha de agradar	I believe it will please you
Parece-me muito comprida	It seems to me to be very long
É costume agora trazel-as compridas	They wear them long now
Abotôe-a	Button it
É muito apertada	It is too tight
Assim deve ser para que lhe esteja bem ao corpo	To fit properly it ought to be tight
Não são as mangas demasiadamente largas?	Are not the sleeves too wide?
Não, senhor, estão-lhe admiravelmente	No, sir, they fit very well
O colete parece-me um pouco estreito	The waistcoat seems rather narrow
Esta é a moda de agora	That is the fashion now
Este vestido está-lhe admiravelmente	This suit becomes you very well
É muito curto, muito comprido, muito grande, muito pequeno	It is too short, too long, too large, too small
Tendes feito a vossa conta?	Have you made your bill?
Não, senhor, não tive tempo	No, sir, I had not time
Trazei-a ámanhã, e pagar-vos-hei	Bring it to-morrow, I will pay you

PARA ALMOÇAR. TO BREAKFAST.

Traze-nos alguma cousa para almoçar	Bring us something for breakfast

Sim, senhor, ha linguiças e pastelinhos	Yes, sir, there are some sausages and patties
Gosta vm^{ce} de presunto?	Do you like ham?
Sim, traze-o; comeremos uma talhada d'elle	Yes, bring it, we will eat a slice of it
Estende um guardanapo sobre aquella mesa	Lay a napkin on that table
Dá-nos pratos, facas, e garfos	Give us plates, knives, and forks
Lava os copos	Rinse the glasses
Dá uma cadeira ao senhor	Reach the gentleman a chair
Assente-se vm^{ce}, assente-se ao pé do lume	Sit down, sir; sit by the fire
Não tenho frio, aqui ficarei muito bem	I am not cold, I shall be very well here
Vejamos se o vinho é bom	Let us see whether the wine is good
Dá cá aquella garrafa com aquelle copo	Give me that bottle and a glass
Faça favor de provar aquelle vinho	Taste that wine, pray
Como lhe agrada? que diz vm^{ce} d'elle?	How do you like it? what say you to it?
Não é mao, é muito bom	It is not bad, it is very good
Eis aqui as linguiças, tira aquelle prato	Here are the sausages, take away that plate
Gosta de linguiças?	Do you like sausages, sir?
Já comi algumas, ellas são muito boas	I have eaten some, they are very good
Dá-me de beber	Give me something to drink
A' saude de vm^{ce}	Your health, sir
Dá de beber ao senhor	Give the gentleman something to drink
Eu bebi ainda agora	I drank but just now

Os pastelinhos erão bem bons	The patties were very good
Estavão um pouco mais cozidos que devião estar	They were baked a little too much
Vm^{ce} mão come	You do not eat
Tenho comido tanto, que não poderei jantar	I have eaten so much that I shall not be able to eat any dinner
Vm^{ce} está zombando, vm^{ce} não tem comido nada	You only jest, you have eaten nothing at all
Tenho comido com muito gosto, tanto das liguiças como do presunto	I have eaten very heartily, both of sausages and the ham

PARA FALLAR PORTUGUEZ. TO SPEAK PORTUGUESE.

Como vai vm^{ce} com o seu Portuguez?	How much progress have you made in Portuguese?
Está vm^{ce} já muito adiantado n'elle?	Are you much improved in it already?
Ainda me falta muito; não sei quasi nada	Far from it; I scarcely know anything
Dizem porem que vm^{ce} o falla muito bem	It is said, however, you speak it very well
Prouvéra a Deus que assim fosse!	Would to God it were true!
Os que dizem isso, estão muito enganados	Those that say so are much mistaken
Esteja vm^{ce} na certeza que assim mó disserão	I assure you I was told so
Posso fallar algumas palavras que aprendi de cór	I can say a few words which I have learnt by heart
É unicamente o que é necessario para começar a fallar	Only so much as is necessary to begin to speak

O começar não é bastante, é preciso que vm^ce acabe	The beginning is not all, you must make an end
Vá sempre fallando, ou bem ou mal	Be always speaking, whether well or ill
Tenho medo de commeter erros	I am afraid to commit blunders
Não tenha vm^ce mêdo; a lingoa Portugueza não é difficil	Never fear, the Portuguese language is not difficult
Conheço isso, e tambem que ella é muito engraçada	I know it, and that it has abundance of graces
Que felicidade seria a minha se eu a soubesse bem!	How happy should I be if I were master of it!
A applicação é o unico meio para aprendel-a	Application is the only way to learn it
Quanto tempo ha que vm^ce aprende?	How long have you been learning?
Apenas ha um mez	Scarcely a month yet
Como se chama o seu mestre?	What is your master's name?
Chama-se ———	His name is ———
Ha muito tempo que o conheço	I have known him a long time
Elle tem ensinado a muitos dos meus amigos	He has taught several friends of mine
Não lhe diz elle ser preciso que falle sempre Portuguez?	Does not he tell you that you must constantly talk Portuguese?
Sim, senhor, assim me diz muitas vezes	Yes, sir, he often tells me so
Pois, porque não falla vm^ce?	Why do you not talk then?
Com quem quer vm^ce que eu falle?	With whom would you have me talk?

Com os que fallarem com vm^{ce}	With those who will talk to you
Eu quizera fallar, mais não me atrevo	I would fain talk, but dare not
É preciso que vm^{ce} não tenha medo, nem se peje dos que o ouvirem fallar	You must not be afraid, you must be bold

DO TEMPO. — OF THE WEATHER.

Que tempo faz?	What sort of weather is it?
O tempo está admiravel	It is splendid weather
O tempo está máo	It is bad weather
Faz frio? faz calor?	Is it cold? is it hot?
Não faz frio, não faz calor	It is not cold, it is not hot
Chove? não chove?	Does it rain? does it not rain?
Não o creio	I do not believe it
O vento está mudado	The wind is changed
Teremos chuva	We shall have rain
Hoje não ha de chover	It will not rain to-day
Chove, chove a cantaros	It rains, it pours
Está nevando	It snows
Troveja	It thunders
Cahe pedra	It hails
Relampeja	It lightens
Faz muito calor	It is very hot
Geou a noite passada?	Did it freeze last night?
Não, senhor, mas agora está geando	No, sir, but it freezes now
Parece-me que ha nevoeiro	It appears to me to be foggy
Vm^{ce} não se engana, assim é	You are not mistaken, it is so

Vm^{ce} tem um a grande constipação or *defluxo*	You have caught a violent cold
Ha quinze dias que o tenho	I have had it this fortnight
Que horas são?	What is the time?
É cedo, não é tarde	It is early, it is not late
É tempo de almoçar?	Is it breakfast-time?
Pouco falta para serem horas de jantar	It will be dinner-time immediately
Que faremos depois de jantar?	What shall we do after dinner?
Daremos um passeio, or *iremos passear*	We will take a walk
Vamos dar uma volta	Let us take a turn now
Não vamos fora com este tempo	We must not go abroad this weather

PARA PERGUNTAR QUE NOVAS HA.

TO INQUIRE AFTER NEWS.

O que ha de novo? or *que novas ha?*	What is the news?
Sabe vm^{ce} alguma cousa de novo	Do you know any news
Não tenho ouvido nada de novo	I have heard none
De que se falla pela cidade?	What is the talk of the town?
Não se falla de nada	There is no talk of anything
Não tendes ouvido fallar de guerra?	Have you heard any talk of war?
Não ouço fallar nada d'isso	I have heard nothing of it
Porem falla-se de um cerco	There is a talk, however, of a siege

Fallou-se d'isso, mas não é verdade	It was so reported, but it is not true
Antes pelo contrario falla-se de paz	On the contrary, there is a talk of peace
Assim o creio	I believe so
Que se diz na côrte?	What say they at court?
Falla-se de uma viagem	They talk of a voyage
Quando vos pareçe que el rei partirá?	When do you think the king will set out
Não se sabe. Não se diz quando	It is not known. They do not say when
Onde, or *para onde, se diz que elle irá?*	Where do they say he will go?
Uns dizem que irá para Flandres, e outros para Alemanha	Some say he will go to Flanders, others to Germany
E que diz a Gazeta?	And what says the Gazette?
Eu não a li	I have not read it
É verdade o que se diz do Sr. ——?	Is that true which is reported of Mr. ——?
Pois que se diz d'elle?	What of him?
Dizem que está ferido mortalmente	They say he is mortally wounded
Muito me pesaria d'isso; elle é um homem de bem	I should be sorry for that, he is an honest man
Quem o ferio?	Who wounded him?
Dois marotos que o investirão	Two rogues that were set upon him
Sabe-se o porque?	Is it known upon what account?
A noticia que corre é, que deu n'um d'elles um bofetão	The report is, that he gave one of them a slap on the face

Eu não creio isso. Nem eu tão pouco	I do not believe it. Nor I either
Comtudo, cedo saberemos a verdade	However, we shall soon know the truth

PARA ESCREVER. — TO WRITE.

Dai-me uma falha de papel, uma penna, e uma pouca de tinta	Give me a sheet of paper, a pen, and a little ink
Ide ao meu quarto, e achareis em cima da mesa tudo o que vos for preciso	Step to my room, you will find on the table whatever you want
Não ha pennas	There are no pens
Ha grande quantidade d'ellas na escrivaninha	There are a great many in the standish
Não prestão para nada	They are good for nothing
Lá ha outras	There are some others
Não estão aparadas	They are not made
Onde está o vosso canivete?	Where is your penknife?
Sabeis vós aparar pennas?	Can you make pens?
Eu aparo-as a meu modo	I make them my own way
Esta não está má	This is not bad
Em quanto acabo esta carta, fazei-me o favor de fazer um maço das restantes	While I finish this letter, do me the favour to make a packet of the rest
Que sello quer vm^{ce} que eu lhe ponha?	What seal will you have me put to it?
Sella-o com o meu sinete, or com as minas armas	Seal it with my cypher, or with my crest
Tem vm^{ce} posto a data?	Have you put the date?
Parece-me que sim, mas ainda não a assignei	I believe I have, but I have not signed it

A quantos estàmos hoje do mez?	What day of the month is this?
A oito, a dez, a quinze, a vinte	The eighth, the tenth, fifteenth, twentieth
Ponde o sobrescrito	Put the address
Ahi está ou seu criado; quer vm^{ce} que elle leve as cartas ao correio?	There is your servant; shall he carry the letters to the post-office?
Leva as minhas cartas ao correio, e não te esqueças de pagar o porte	Carry my letters to the post-office, and do not forget to pay postage
Não tenho dinheiro	I have no money
Ahi está uma moeda de oiro	There is a moidore
Vai depressa, e vem logo	Go quickly, and return at once

PARA COMPRAR. — TO BUY.

Que quer vm^{ce}?	What do you want, sir?
Quero um bom panno fino para um fato	I want a good fine cloth to make me a suit of clothes
Tenha vm^{ce} a bondade de entrar, e verá o mais bello panno que ha em Londres	Be pleased to walk in, sir, you will see the finest in London
Deixe-me ver o melhor que vm^{ce} tem	Show me the best you have
Aqui tem vm^{ce} um excellente, que agora se costuma usar	There is a very fine one, which is much worn at present
É um bom panno, mas a côr não me ograda	It is a good cloth, but I do not like the colour
Ahi tem vm^{ce} outra peça que tem a côr mais clara	There is another lighter piece

Agrada-me a côr, mas o panno não é forte, não tem corpo	I like that colour well, but the cloth is not strong, it is too thin
Veja esta peça; vm^{ce} não achará em nenhuma parte outra tão boa como ella	Look at this piece, sir; you will find none like it anywhere else
Quanto pede vm^{ce} por cada vara?	What do you ask for it a yard?
O seu justo preço é ——	It is fairly worth ——
Sr. não é meu costume pôr-me a regatear; faça-me favor de me dizer o ultimo preço	Sir, I am not used to stand bargaining; pray tell me your lowest price
Já disse a vm^{ce} que aquelle é o seu justo preço	I have told you, sir, it is worth that
É muito caro, dar-lhe-hei a vm^{ce} ——	It is too dear, I will give you ——
Não posso abater um vintem	I cannot abate a farthing
Vm^{ce} não deve levar esse preço	You must not charge that price
Vm^{ce} quiz saber o ultimo preço, e eu disse-lhó	You asked me the lowest price, and I have told you
Hora, vamos, córte lá duas varas d'elle	Well, cut off two yards of it
Asseguro-lhe que não ganho nada com vm^{ce}	I assure you I don't get anything by you
Ahi tem cinco moedas de ouro, dê-me a demasia	There are five moidores; give me the change
Tenha a bondade de me dar outra em lugar d'esta, porque não é de pezo	Be pleased, sir, to let me have another for this; it wants weight
Ahi está outra	There's another

PARA UMA JORNADA.	FOR A JOURNEY.
Que especie de caminho, ha d'aqui a ——?	What sort of a road is it from hence to ——?
A estrada é bella, boa	The road is fine, good
É soffrivel	It is tolerable
É quasi impracticavel no inverno	It is almost impassable in winter
Agora está coberta de lama por causa do degêlo	It is all over mud now, because of the thaw
Não é má n'esta estação	It is pretty good in this season
Estava coberta d'agua ainda não ha muito tempo	It was overflowed a little while ago
Está cheia d'atoleiros	It is very boggy
É larga ou estreita a estrada?	Is the road broad or narrow?
É espaçosa	It is wide
É commoda	It is convenient
Os caminhos não são mui bons	The roads are very indifferent
Encontrão-se boas estalagens na estrada?	Are there any good inns upon the road?
Ha boas e más	There are some good and some bad ones
São soffriveis	They are tolerable
Em geral são mui más	They are generally very bad
Há pelo caminho cidades notaveis?	Are there any remarkable towns on the way?
Offerecem ellas alguma cousa curiosa?	Is there anything interesting in them?
Que conducção posso tomar d'aqui a ——?	What conveyance can I have to ——?
Póde tomar um lugar na diligencia	You can take a place in the stage coach

Póde ir pelo caminho de ferro até ——	You can go by the railroad as far as ——
Vá pelo barco de vapor até a ——	Go by the steamboat as far as ——
Pode tomar a posta	You may travel post
Passa-se por muitas cidades?	Do we go through many towns?
Ha perigo na estrada?	Is there any danger upon the road?
A estrada é segura?	Is the road safe?
Sim, senhor; e muito frequentada	Yes, sir; it is a great thoroughfare
Não ha que ter mêdo de ladrões	There is no danger of robbers
Com tudo, sempre será bom não atravessar a mata de noite	However, you had better not travel in the forests by night
São bem servidas as postas?	Are the post-houses well provided?
Póde-se contar com cavallos de muda?	Can we depend upon having fresh horses?
É necessario esperar muito tempo pelos cavallos?	Shall we have to wait long for horses?
Quanto se paga por cavallo?	How much must be paid for each horse?
Um franco e meio por posta	One franc and a half per post
Quanto se dá aos postilhões?	How much must be given to the postilions?

DA CEA E DA POUSADA.

Com que afinal temos chegado á estalagem

Apeêmo-nos, senhores

Pega nos cavallos d'estes senhores, e trata d'elles

Vejamos agora o que vm^{ce} nos vai da para ceiar

Um capão, meia duzia de pombos, uma salada, seis codornizes, e uma duzia de calhandras

Querem mais alguma coisa?

Isto é bastante; dai-nos algum vinho que seja bom, e uma sobremesa

Deixem isso por minha conta, eu lhes prometo que ficarão bem servidos

Alumia aos senhores

Dai-nos de ceiar o mais depressa que for possivel

Antes que vm^{ces} tenhão descalças botas, estará a cêa na mesa

Tende cuidado que tragão para cima as nossas malas e pistolas

Descalçai-me as botas, e depois ireis ver se tem dado algum feno aos cavallos

OF SUPPER AND LODGING.

So, we have arrived at the inn

Let's alight, gentlemen

Take these gentlemen's horses and take care of them

Now let's see what you'll give us for supper

A capon, half-a-dozen of pigeons, a salad, six quails, and a dozen of larks

Will you have nothing else?

That's enough; give us some good wine and a dessert

Let me alone, I will please you, I warrant you

Light the gentlemen

Let us have our supper as soon as possible

Before you have pulled your boots off, supper shall be on the table

Let our portmanteaus and pistols be carried upstairs

Pull off my boots, and then you shall go to see whether they have given the horses any hay

Levai-os ao rio, e tende cuidado que lhes dem alguma avêa	Take them to the river, and see that they give them some oats
Eu terei cuidado de tudo, estejão vm^{ces} descançados	I will take care of everything, do not trouble yourself
Senhores, a cêa está prompta, está na mesa	Gentlemen, supper is ready, it is upon the table
Nós vamos já	We will come presently
Vamos cear, senhores, para nos irmos deitar cedo	Let us go to supper, gentlemen, that we may go to bed in good time
Sentêmo-nos, senhores, sentemo-nos á mesa	Let us sit down, gentlemen, let us sit down at table
Dai-nos de beber	Give us something to drink
Á sua saude, meus senhores	To your health, gentlemen
É bom o vinho?	Is the wine good?
Não é mao	It is not bad
O capão não está bem assado	The capon is not done enough
Dai-nos algumas laranjas, e uma pouca de pimenta	Give us some oranges, and a little pepper
Porque não come vm^{ce} d'estes pombos?	Why do you not eat of these pigeons?
Eu tenho comido um pombo, e tres calhandras	I have eaten one pigeon and three larks
Dize ao estalajadeiro que lhe queremos fallar	Tell the landlord we want to speak to him

DO SALTAR E DO CORRER. — OF LEAPING AND RUNNING.

Hora vamos, quer vm^{ce} saltar?	Come, will you go and leap?

Não e bom saltar logo despois de comer	It is not good to jump immediately after dinner
De que modo de saltar gosta vm^{ce} mais?	What leaping do you like best?
O mais commum e a pés juntos	The most usual is with one foot close to the other
Quer que saltemos só com um pé?	Shall we hop with one leg?
Como quizér	As you please
Este é um salto muito grande	This is a very great leap
Quantos pés saltou vm^{ce}?	How many feet have you leaped?
Mais de quatro	More than four
Aposto que salto por cima d'aquelle barranco	I wager I leap clearly over that ditch
Vm^{ce} salta com um páo comprido	You jump with a long stick
Demos uma carreira	Let us run races
Quer vm^{ce} que corrâmos a pé ou a cavallo?	Shall we run on foot or on horseback?
De uma e outra sorte	Both ways
Começemos a correr d'aqui	This shall be the starting-place
Correremos até chegar a esta arvore	This tree shall be the goal
Tenho corrido trez vezes desde a lugar assignalado até á arvore	I have run three times from the starting-place to the tree
Vm^{ce} não esperou pelo signal para principiar a correr	You did not stay for the signal to start
Aquelle cavallo corrêo muito bem	That horse has run his race very well
Quantas carreiras tem elle dado?	How many heats has he run?
Tres ou quatro	Three or four

CARTAS DE COMMERCIO.	LETTERS ON BUSINESS.
Londres, 30 *de Janeiro de* 1827.	The 30th Jan., 1827.
Senhor F. F.	Mr. F. F., London.
Recebi as suas de 3 *e* 5 *do passado, no dia* 5 *do corrente, vindas pelo navio F. P., capitão B. B.; pelas quaes vejo, que* Vm^{ce} *pretende carregar as fazendas que recommendei ao seu cuidado pela minha ultima, no primeiro navio para esta.*	Yours of the 3rd and 5th of last month came to hand on the 5th current by the ship F. P., Captain B. B.; and therein I take notice that you intend to put on board the next good ship bound hither the goods I recommended to your care in my last.
Inclusas remetto a Vm^{ce} *mais algumas amostras; porem desejo que queira recommendar ao tintureiro que as côres sejão vivas e firmes.*	Herewith I send you more patterns; but I would desire you to be solicitous with your dyer that the colours may be lively and durable.
Pelo ultimo navio que d'aqui partio lhe remetti a conta de venda da sua partida de meias de seda, e das tres caixas de chapéos, pelo navio A.; e achando Vm^{ce} *algumas partidas de qualquer*	By the last ship I remitted you account of sales of the parcel of silk stockings, and the three boxes of hats, by the ship A.; and if you meet with a

d'estes dois generos que lhe agradem, as pode mandar, pois são agora mui procurados; deve comtudo ter muito cuidado em que sejão da ultima moda. Tenho verificado o ajuste das 20 pipas de azeite da proxima safra, para partirem pelos primeiros navios: igualmente tenho carregado no navio N., Capitão F., as suas 20 pipas de vinho tinto; assim como tambem as doze e tres quartos de branco, cuja factura remetto inclusa: os conhecimentos lh'os remetterei pelo correio, Hei-de estimar chegue tudo a salvamento. E quanto por agora se me offerece a dizer-lhe; no entretanto sou,

de Vm^{ce}
m^{to} Venerador e Criado,
N.

parcel of either or both to your mind, please to send them, such articles being now in demand; but great care must be taken of the fashion and make. I have taken care to secure your twenty pipes of oil for the first ships in the season, and put on board the ship N., Captain F., your twenty pipes of red, and twelve pipes and three quarter casks of white wine, of which the invoice goes herewith, and the bills of lading shall be sent by the post, and I hope will come safe to hand; which being all that is necessary at present,

I remain, Sir,
Your humble servant,
N.

Senhor Diogo Jones.

Vou por esta avisar a Vm^{ce} que pelo navio Derby, lhe remetti duas saquinhas de diamantes, importando em pagodas 4396, 25 fan., 10

Mr. James Jones.
Sir,
These will advise you, that by this ship, the Derby, I have made the return of your stock in my hands, viz.: two bulses of

casks, em retorno dos seus fundos em meu poder; os quaes fiz registrar nos livros da companhia, em conformidade com as suas ordens.

Inclusos achará o conhecimento, factura, e a sua conta corrente fechada, que desejo cheguem a salvamento, e me alegrarei de que faça grandes interesses.

Como eu estou para voltar par a Europa, á minha chegada a Londres, terei a honra de o ver, e lhe darei então uma relação exacta do commercio da India.

Tenho o prazer de ser,
Seu humilde Venerador,

Forte de S. Jorge,
12 de Jan., 1826.

diamonds, amounting to pagodas 4396, 25 fan., 10 casks, having registered them according to your order in the company's books. Enclosed is a bill of lading, together with invoice, and your account current closed, which I wish may come safe to you, and turn to a good account. As I am returning to Europe, on my arrival in London I shall have the honour to see you, and give you an exact account of the trade in India.

I am, Sir,
Your humble servant,

Fort St. George,
Jan. 12, 1826.

Lisboa, 4 de Março de 1825.
Sñr. João Ferrier,
Londres.

Acho-me favorecido com a sua de 3 do passado, e vejo, que em execução das minhas ordens, tem Vm^{ce} comprado os quinhentos barris de arenques de fumo a 11l. per last.

Lisbon, March 4, 1825.
Mr. John Ferrier,
London.
Sir,

I am favoured with yours of the 3rd of last month, and find, in compliance with my order, you have bought the five hundred barrels of red herrings at

Estou certo de que esse é o menor preço por que Vm^{ce} os poude obter, e não tenho a menor duvida de que hão de corresponder em sua qualidade.

O meu navio se está a aparelhar para os ir buscar, e visto elle não demandar mais de novo pés d'agua, poderá mesmo carregar no seu cáes (como Vm^{ce} teve a bondade de me dizer), o que poupará quatro pence por barril, de despesas. Julgo que elle poderá carregar sete centos barris, ou mais. O capitão, visto não ter despesas a fazer, não necessitará de dinheiro.

Agradeço-lhe muito a sua informação referente ao cambio entre Londres e esta praça, mas como julgo as Letras sobre o Thesouro um pouco arriscadas, Vm^{ce} se servirá sacar sobre mim ao cambio mais vantajoso possivel, ficando na certeza de que os seus saques serão honrados com a pontualidade do costume.

*Tenho o prazer de ser,
De Vm^{ce}
m^{to} at^{to} Venerador.*

£11 per last. I make no doubt but that was the lowest price you could get them for, and the goodness of them corresponds. My ship is getting ready with all speed to go down to fetch them, and she may be laden at your quay, as she draws no more than nine feet of water (as you are pleased to mention), which will save the charge of fourpence per barrel; I judge she will carry seven hundred barrels or more. The captain will not have occasion for any money, so will want no supply. I thank you for the information you gave me in relation to the exchange between London and this place; but as I look upon the remittance of the money hence as hazardous in Exchequer bills, you will be pleased to draw on me at the most commodious exchange possible, and your bills at the usual course, which shall meet with all due honour from, Sir,

Your humble servant,

Londres, 18 de *Março* de 1826.	London, March 18, 1826.
Sñr. J. Morrice,	Mr. J. Morrice,
Cadiz.	Cadiz.

Sir,

Tenho recebido em seu devido tempo as suas differentes cartas, assim como tambem a minha conta corrente, a qual tenho lançado nos meus livros de conformidade com Vm^{ce}.

A sua ultima é de 29 do passado, e n'ella me manda o recibo das tres letras, importando em seis mil peças de oito, que meu irmão Jozé lhe remetteu por minha conta e ordem : espero fazer triste negocio com ellas depois de um desembolso de tanto tempo, e com um cambio tão desfavoravel. Acho que os limites que elle lhe deu, forão muito abaixo do cambio, e preço da prata : porêm, visto eu ter esperado todo este tempo, e não haver probabilidade de um ou outro baixar, Vm^{ce} se servirá remetter-me o meu dinheiro, ao cambio corrente, para esta praça, ou Amsterdam, como lhe parecer

Your several letters came to hand in due time, as did my account current, which I have noted in conformity with you. Your last to me was of the 29th ult., wherein you give me receipt of the three bills, amounting to six thousand pieces of eight, which my brother Joseph sent to you for my account and by my order. I shall make but a sad bargain of them, after so long a disbursement; besides, they cost me a dear exchange. I find his limits to you were much under the price of plate and exchange; now since I have waited all this time, and there being no probability of their falling, be pleased to send my money, as the exchange comes, either for this place or Amsterdam, which you judge will turn most to account. If the plate or *mais conveniente aos meus interesses.*

Se o preço da cochonilha, ou da prata descesse tanto que Vm^{ce} julgasse ser mais conveniente para mim empregar o meu dinheiro em qualquer d'estes dois generos, do que remetter-me letras, n'esse caso o poderá fazer, deixando eu isso inteiramente á sua disposição, na certeza de que tratará dos meus interesses com o mesmo disvelo como se fossem seus proprios.

Estimarei saber da chegada do comboio, porque poderia ser produzisse alguma mudança favoravel no commercio, e que cada um podesse fazer uso dos seus capitaes; pois ao presente as circumstancias não convidão a nada. É quanto por agora se me offerece a dizer-lhe. No entretanto tenho a satisfação de ser.

*De Vm^{ce},
m^{to} attento ven^{or}, e C^o.*

cochineal should fall to a price which you may conceive will answer better than by remittance at a due exchange, in such case invest my money in either of them: this I shall leave entirely to you, being persuaded you will act in my affairs as if they were your own. I should be glad to hear of the fleet's arrival; for perhaps it might give some favourable turn to business, so that one could make some use of one's money, for at present it does not invite one to anything: which is all from,

Sir,

Your humble servant.

Londres, 3 de Abril de 1826.

Sñr.ˢ Mills & C.ⁱᵃ
Porto.

Esta serve para informar a Vm.ᶜᵉˢ que de sexta feira a oito dias se hão de abrir os livros do Banco de Inglaterra, para pagar os dividendos vencidos até áquelle dia, em que eu não deixarei de receber o que lhes pertence dos juros respectivos até esse tempo, em virtude dos poderes que me conferirão para esse fim, e depois de os ter recebido, lh'os remetterei.

De Vm.ᶜᵉˢ
m.ᵗᵒ at.ᵗᵒ Ven.ᵒʳ., e Criado,

London, 3rd of April, 1826.

Messieurs Mills & Co.
Oporto.

This may serve to inform you that the books will be opened at the Bank of England on Friday se'nnight, to pay the dividends due up to this time to the parties concerned, when I shall be ready to receive whatever belongs to you both, with the respective interests thereon, by virtue of your powers given to me for that purpose, and, on receipt thereof, shall remit the same to you, whom God preserve many years.

Your most humble
servant.

PART IV.

CONTAINING

SEVERAL USEFUL and ENTERTAINING PASSAGES,
COLLECTED FROM THE BEST PORTUGUESE WRITERS.

ENTRE os bons ditos de Souzeni, poeta Persiano, se conta que, bebendo com outro poeta, seu amigo, certo licor, se queixava de que era muito quente; e dizendo-lhe, Amigo, pobre de ti, 'que d'aqui a poucos dias te farão beber no inferno agoas sulfúreas e ardentes, que te abrazarão as entranhas.'—'Não importa,' replicou Souzeni: 'bastará que me lembre algum dos teus versos, que ellas se farão mais frias que a neve.'

Catharina Parthenay, sobrinha da celebre Anna Parthenay, deu esta bella resposta a Henrique IV. 'Saiba V. M. que eu sou muito pobre para ser sua consorte; e que ao mesmo tempo descendo de uma familia muito illustre para ser sua dama.'

Uma Princeza Catholica, e de rara virtude, vendo reduzido o Marechal de Saxonia ás agonias da morte, disse, que era para sentir o não se poder rezar um *De profundis* pela alma de um que tinha feito cantar tantos *Te Deums*.

A Dom Christovão de Moura, Marquez de Castello Rodrigo, e Vice-Rei de Portugal por Dom Philipe Terceiro, indo por uma sala do Paço de Lisboa um soldado honrado, que tinha bem servido na India, lhe dava um memorial e pedia que se lembrasse dos seus papeis, porque havia largo tempo que andava pretendendo, respondeo-lhe o Marquez, que havia muita Gente para despachar, e não se podião despachar todos com brevidade. O soldado, adiantando o passo, se atravessou diante sem descomposição; e, fazendo parar o Vice-Rei, lhe disse com grande confiança: 'Senhor Dom Christovão, despache V. S. os homens, e deixe a Gente.' O Marquez acceitou o memorial e o despachou no mesmo dia.

Mandando um Fidalgo em Lisboa abrir em uma rua os alicerces para se fazerem umas casas, sem licença da camara, e passando por alli o procurador da cidade, pôz pena aos officiaes, que não trabalhassem na obra sem licença dos Vereadores; e os officiaes dizendo-o ao Fidalgo, mandoulhes elle que não deixassem de trabalhar, e que não fizessem caso do que dizia aquelle villão ruim. Tornando o procurador da cidade por alli, e achando os officiaes trabalhando, mandou que déssem com elles no cêpo; e não faltando quem lhe contasse o que o Fidalgo disséra, teve-o em ôlho; e no tempo que elle hia atravessando pelo Rocio para sua casa, sahio-lhe ao caminho a cavallo, e com uma lança que levava, dando na sua sombra, lhe disse: 'Porque o que dissestes foi em minha ausencia, dou em vossa sombra; se m'o tivesseis dito no rosto, déra na vossa pessôa.'

Abou Hanifah, o mais celebre doutor dos Mussulmanes, tendo recebido uma bofetada, disse ao que o tinha insultado: 'Eu poderia vingar-me, pagando-vos na mesma moeda; mas não o quero fazer. Poderia accusar-vos ao califa; mas não quero ser accusador. Poderia nas minhas orações queixar-me a Deus d'esta affronta; mas nem isso quero fazer. Por fim, poderia pedir a Deus, que se quer no dia do juizo vos castigasse; porem o mesmo Senhor me livre de semelhante pensamento; mas antes, se succedesse que n'este instante chegasse aquelle formidavel dia, e se a minha intercessão tivesse alguma efficacia para com Deus, não quizera por companheiro senão a vós para entrar no Paraiso.' Que admiravel exemplo para os Christãos aprenderem a perdoar as injurias!

Da Peregrinação.

Passadas que se dão peregrinando, são degráos para a casa do desengano. Das suas fontes sahem os rios muito pequenos, e crescem correndo, e levão mares ao mar. Homens que da sua terra não sahem são navios que acabão no estaleiro. A sabedoria, como vinda do céo, anda n'este globo terrestre peregrina; não é facil acha-la senão peregrinando; errando por este mundo, se aprende a não cometter erros. Vapôres, que na terra erão lodo, apartados d'ella fazem-se estrellas. Aos homens que querem luzir, deve a patria servir, como aos planetas o horizonte, de berço, para ensaio do seu luzimento; longe do ponto ortivo e remontados a mais alta região apurão as influencias, e duplicão as luzes. Que nome terião hoje no mundo Socrates, Pithagoras, e Platão, e outros sabios da antiguidade, se a modo de cepos, ou troncos, que aonde nascerão fazem raiz e no seu primeiro chão apodrecem, não buscárām fora da Patria as noticias que lhes faltavão. Não se ornára Hercules com os despojos dos Monstros que domou, se os não fôra buscar pelo mundo; á sua dilatada viagem devem os Argonautas a conquista do vello de oiro. Se não corrêra Ulysses remotos climas, fora a Ilha de Ithaca de toda a sua gloria o theatro. Homens perpetuamente caseiros, são gallos que só sabem do seu poleiro. Sabios peregrinos, imitão no seu curso as fontes que passando por vêas de prata, ouro, esmeraldas, e saffiras, tomão, e comsigo levão a flor de suas preciosas qualidades. Zombe embora Plutarco dos que louvão a peregrinação, e diga, que se parecem com os que julgão as estrellas errantes mais nobres, e felices, que as fixas. Não ha escola mais util para a vida, que as muitas vidas ou modos de viver, que na variedade das Nações se observam. Veem-se muitas cousas nunca vistas, aprendem-se muitas que se não sabião, faz-se o homem capaz de toda a casta de negocios, e folga de ver este mundo antes de sahir d'elle. Até para os principes, que das suas cortes fazem na terra o seu paraiso, bom he que peregrinem, para conhecerem o mundo, que elles governão. Os commodos, as delicias, os obsequios dos subditos, podem dar o conhecer a hum homem que nasceu soberano, mas com este conhecimento, não o fazem digno da soberania: se não sahira Alexandre da sua Macedonia, não passára dos limites de regulo, e não chegára a avassallar o mundo.

Do Tempo futuro.

Trate o homem do presente, e não queira penetrar no futuro; quem de tão longe põe a mira, não pode dar no alvo. Muitas vezes bom é ignorar o que ha de succeder;

porque se for bom, a dilação, é tormento; e se for máo, o trabalho é sem proveito. Para futuros não ha segurança. Ao Embaixador, que na guerra movida por Luiz XI., Rey de França, a Carlos Duque de Borgonha, procurava attrahir ao Imperador Frederico, com promessa de se repartirem com elle os despojos, e os estados, respondeo o dito Imperador com este apologo: 'Tres caçadores com a esperança de apanharem um urso, se comprometterão na repartição d'elle. Chegados á boca da caverna, sahio a fera com tão grande impeto, que um dos caçadores botou a fugir, outro subio a uma arvore, e o outro se estendeu no chão fingindo-se morto; chegou-se o urso a elle, poz-lhe o focinho no nariz, e nos ouvidos, e não lhe conhecendo folego, nem signal de vida, o deixou por morto. O que estava na arvore disse ao companheiro, Homem, que te disse o urso, quando te fallou á puridade, com o focinho nos ouvidos?—Disse-me que era mal feito, dispor da pelle e carne do urso, antes de o verem morto.' Com isto o Imperador deu a entender ao Embaixador, que era preciso apanhar primeiro ao Duque de Borgonha, e que depois se trataria da repartição dos seus estados. Dos successos do tempo futuro só Deos tem certeza.

Dos Ricos.

Em lugares estereis, sem hervas nem plantas, produz a natureza o oiro, para mostrar que os amadores das riquezas não têm fé, nem honra. Os ricos facinorosos, que ainda que celebrados nas historias, são o opprobrio da sua posteridade, poderão ter boa fama, se lhes não facilitára este metal a execução de seus damnados intentos. Em todas as idades forão as riquezas antagonistas da virtude; ellas inventaram os mais enormes delictos; ellas ensinaram os filhos a tirar a seus pais a vida ; ensinaram os poderosos a opprimir os innocentes, arruinar as familias, saquear os templos, e despir os altares; ellas induziram os amigos a que faltassem á fé, incitaram os vassallos a negar aos principes a obediencia, aos libidinosos derão meios para violar a pudicicia das donzellas, e estragar a honra dos maridos ; finalmente ellas, ainda que boas para a vida civil, são causa de todos os males ; e posto que os sabios se soubéram aproveitar d'ellas, a cubica, e o máo uso das mesmas, encheram o mundo todo de criminosos. Homens ricos ordinariamente se perdem, por terem muito, e saberem pouco ; desprezão o saber, porque lhes parece, que para todo o genero de vida lhes basta o ter. A Aristippo perguntou Dionysio, porque razão os filosofos frequentavão as casas dos ricos, e não os ricos as dos filosofos. Respondeo Aristippo, que os filosofos conhecem o que lhes falta, e os ricos ignorão o de que necessitão. Senhores ricos, e filosofos pobres, não podem fazer cousas grandes, porque a estes lhes falta dinheiro, e áquelles o espirito. Dizia Diogenes, que muitos ricos são como as plantas, que nascem em desertos e despenhadeiros, porque dos frutos que ellas dão não comem os homens, mas os corvos, milhafres, e feras ; tambem as riquezas de muitos não são para sugeitos benemeritos, mas para chocarreiros, espadachins, rufiões, e meretrizes.

Estado da Lusitania até ao tempo em que foi reduzida a Provincia Romana. Por A. C. do Amaral. Extrahido das Memorias da Academia de Lisboa.

Uma historia sincera envergonha-se da gloria vã, que se busca em antiguidades mentirosas : degosta-se d'esses sonhos agradaveis, pasto de uma esteril recreação; e se saborea só com a verdade pura. Tal é a sorte d'este escripto, dirigido a fazer prezentes aos Portugueses os verdadeiros costumes e Leis de seus Maiores: rejeita tudo quanto a impostura, ou a credulidade moderna lhe conta dos Seculos que a Providencia quiz esconder-lhe: e se contenta com as escassas memorias que pode colher dos raros monumentos antigos que lhe restão. Não tenta entrar pelas espessas trevas dos primeiros 36 Seculos do mundo, em que não acha quem o encaminhe. Pois que os Hebreos unicos guias Seguros, que introduzem em muitos outros paizes, nem um só passo dão para este que habitamos; e apenas dão motivo a conjecturar, que das Colonias sahidas do Oriente para povoar a terra, algumas se estenderam até a esta extremidade; mas nem donde, nem quando viessem o pode colher a historia.

Não acha depois dos Hebreos outros de quem se fie, senão os Romanos: e ainda estes pouco lhe sabem dizer de hum Paiz tão apartado, em quanto a ambição de o senhorear os não avizinha a elle: mal conservão uma obscura tradição de que a estas partes vierão Celtas, Iberos, Persas, Lusos, e Gregos; de uns apenas ficára resto na derivação do nome; de outros na herança de alguns costumes. A navegação com que alguns Povos do fundo do Mediterraneo começão a enriquecer, os traz até estas ultimas Costas, e vai logo espalhar pelo Mundo a fama das ricas minas, e do fertil torrão deste Paiz desconhecido ainda, antes que da qualidade de seus habitantes: não tarda comtudo a mostra-se esta; continua a vir em busca dos thesouros descobertos a ambição estrangeira; e vê erguer d'aqui, quaes feras acossadas nos seus covis, homens bravos para defender os bens que a Providencia lhes destinára. E esta he a primeira scena que se nos representa no Terreno Lusitano; hum

Campo de Batalha, continuada já com os Fenicios, já com os Carthaginezes; que depois de disputarem por largo tempo com estes Barbaros a sorte das armas, os deixão ainda por domar aos Romanos quando lhes cedem a conquista do Mundo. Mas ao justo motivo da defeza propria succedem depois outros, que facilmente põe as armas na mão a uns homens, a quem a falta do commercio e de artes quasi não deixa outro meio de enriquecer, que a pilhagem; nome com que muitas das suas guerras são infamadas pelos Povos mais polidos que elles. E o mesmo habito de pelejar lhes vai alimentando um natural feroz, que já os não deixa accommodar com o socego da paz, e que os faz buscar inimigos dentro em casa, quando lhes faltão os de fóra.

Estes vicios, e virtudes de guerra, he o que de principio n'elles distinguem os Romanos, não os vendo senão armados no campo; e de que não podem deixar de dar testemunho estes mesmos vaidosos desprezadores de tudo o que não he Romano. Mas em fim á medida que se lhes chegão mais perto, e se envolvem com elles, já vão divisando por entre alguns claros que as armas deixão, a forma do seu governo interior.

Vem que este Terreno, que designão pelo nome de Lusitania, é habitado de Povos differentes independentes uns dos outros, e governados cada um por suas Leis, e costumes particulares; leis raras, e costumes singelos, ainda com a marca da Natureza não contrafeita.

Como a segurança propria é quem só forma estes corpos, não largão da liberdade que receberam da natureza, mais que o puramente preciso para conservar essa mesma segurança. A guerra a que são dados é que os obriga a criar um Superior, a que jurão fidelidade; mas conseguida a paz, expira o governo do General, e a obediencia dos Soldados.

Se ha que estabelecer de novo para o bem commum da Sociedade, servem-se do meio usado das puras Democracias, Assembleas geraes, em que cada pessoa tem o arbitrio de approvar, ou rejeitar o que se propõe: e ainda n'esta acção respira o ar militar, em que são criados; um bater da espada no broquel he o signal de approvação; um sussurro inquieto o de desapprovar.

A simplicidade da Legislação segue a das penas; são os reos do crime capital apedrejados, e para que o horror do crime se extenda alem ainda do castigo, todo o que passa depois da execução he obrigado a lançar alguma pedra sobre o cadaver do justiçado.

Não desmente da parte Legislativa, a do Commercio interior ainda pouco sujeito a fraudes; não os move a contratar a sede insaciavel do ouro, que mal conhecem: as mutuas necessidades, a que só procurão soccorrer, os ensina a trocar entre si as cousas precisas á vida. Estas lhes dictão tambem o que devem conceder ao corpo; comeres, e bebidas simples, quaes a Natureza as produzia: vestidos sem mais estudo que o do fim para que os usão; cama sem regalo, nem despeza; enfim a tudo o preciso para o conservação se accode com o menos apparato que pode ser.

A esta sobriedade bem propria de si para dar a saude e vigor do corpo, ajuntão o trabalho aturado; os homens o da guerra quasi continua, e nos intervallos d'ella o de exercicios semelhantes á guerra; as mulheres o da cultura dos campos, o de todo o trato domestico, que com discreta economia lhes é cedido pelos homens occupados com as armas. E se faz memoria dos seus bailes, e contares não são tanto fructo do ocio, como do innocente prazer da vida social.

D'este modo sobrio e trabalhado de vida era consequencia a raridade de doenças: para alguma, que acaso haja, não he venal a cura, nem o remedio, não se tendo alguem por desobrigado de concorrer para um officio de rigorosa humanidade; hé o enfermo exposto em publico; e os que tem sido feridos do mesmo mal ensinão os remedios com que conseguirão a saude.

Nos que habitavão as vizinhanças do Minho, como erão os Gronios, ou Gravios, os Amphilocios, e outros, se vêm assaz retratados os costumes de Gregos, de quem os Antigos querem que elles descendão; Jogos, e certames publicos, cazamentos, arte de augurar tudo he de Gregos. Idolatras como seus Maiores, nada conservão da Religião pura que a Razão lhes mostrára, mais que o reconhecimento de que ha um ente maior que elles, a que devem dar culto; porem estragado este natural sentimento pela corrupção do coração, imaginão Divindades indignas, a que honrão com um culto igualmente indigno. Se querem dar-lhes graças pelo feliz successo de uma batalha, as mãos direitas dos prisioneiros são o triste troféo que lhes levantão. Se antes de qualquer acção procurão saber o seu bom ou mão exito, dentro ás entranhas de um inimigo é que vão buscar este fatal segredo: se querem fazer religioso um juramento, é preciso que as entranhas quentes de um homem, e de um cavallo lhes sirvão de banho, em que depois de mettidas as mãos, as pôe sobre o altar, junto ao qual se deve fazer esta ridicula ceremonia. Emfim, é sempre sangue o que applaca uns Deoses, que estes Idolatras guerreiros formavão á sua semelhança.

Estes são os poucos vestigios, e quasi apagados, que se encontram dos costumes domesticos dos Lusitanos, que de ordinario só se vião no campo de batalha, detendo, ou fazendo retroceder os passos aos Conquistadores do mundo. Mal o poderá crer quem mede a força de um Estado pelo fausto de seus habitadores, pela magnificencia de suas obras, e por todo o esplendor que encanta os sentidos; quem não avalia quanto pode um Povo, em que todos os individuos são aptos para a defesa da Patria, em que a tantos Soldados como homens endurecidos todos no trabalho, e todos animados do amor da liberdade.

Um povo como este foi o que sem arte, e sem disciplina, em tendo na frente um homem que o soubesse mandar, escarneceu por muitas vezes das tropas mais bem reguladas, e deu muitos dias de magoa e de deslustre aos soberbos Romanos. Viriato, Sertorio, e ainda outros de menos nome forão instrumentos da gloria Lusitana, que sobrepujando á emulação ficou eternizada nos escritos de seus mesmos inimigos, e nos marmores que o tempo consumidor não acabou de gastar.

Por mais de Seculo e meio andarão os Romanos na porfiada lida de subjugar este ultimo pedaço da Hespanha que já contão toda por uma porção certa dos seus dominios: todos os annos lhe nomeão Governador; mas por mais que tentem mandar Pretor como para Provincia pacifica, a cada passo se vem obrigados a lhe mandar Consul armado; depois de terem separado o seu Governo do de quasi todo o resto da Hespanha. E se de quando em quando algum d'estes Generaes consegue a gloria de a pacificar, e sujeitar ás Leis Romanas, pouco tempo lhe dura verde o louro; na sua mesma cabeça lhe mercha ou ao mais tarde na de seu successor; até que a longa experiencia os desengana, que he preciso mudar de systema; e que só costumando primeiro os Lusitanos a se sujeitar como amigos, he que os poderão insensivelmente ir passando a obedecer como Vassalos.

Sobre a Poesia Bucolica dos Poetas Portuguezes. Por Joaquim de Foyos. Extrahido das Memorias de Litteratura da Academia de Lisboa.

Assim como entre as duas especies de oração, por que o homem tanto excede aos outros animaes, se cultivou primeiro o Verso, assim de todas as sortes de Poesias parece ter sido primeria a Bucolica. Ainda que o genero humano não nasceo da terra, e dos duros troncos des arvores, como imaginarão muitos Poetas, e parece que chegarão a crer alguns Filosofos; com tudo depois do diluvio, espalhados os homens por toda a face da terra, e perdidos pouco a pouco os conhecimentos que herdaram de seus maiores, e só conservavão na Sociedade, he summamente provavel, que uma grande parte d'elles viesse successivamente a passar por estes tres generos de vida: Selvagem, Pastoral, Agricola. Os muitos Povos, que ainda hoje habitão, e se achão na primeira, e segunda d'estas vidas, confirmão a verdade d'esta conjectura. Mas o homem, vivendo uma vida silvestre nos bosques, separado de toda a Sociedade, e sustentando-se unicamente de caça, e dos fructos espontaneos da terra, nem se acha em circunstancias de adiantar os seus conhecimentos, nem tem tempo para cultival-os, occupado, e attento todo em buscar o necessario fysico, que não pode achar sem muita difficuldade, e trabalho. E ainda que aconteça, que por vezes lhe sobre algum espaço livre d'estas continuas fadigas, satisfeitos todos os seus naturaes desejos e appetites, cançado o corpo, e entorpecidos os membros, lhe entorpecerão juntamente as faculdades da alma, desacostumadas a discorrer e a exercitar-se em outros objectos, e se entregará docemente ao somno. Não succederá assim aos Pastores, que tendo gado que com seu leite lhes subministre o sustento, e com suas

pelles o vestido, passarão uma boa parte da sua vida
quietos e descançados, sem mais outro cuidado que o de
conduzir e defender os seus rebanhos e manadas. Obrigados de necessidades mutuas, e attrahidos do natural
deleite que causa a companhia dos que têm as mesmas
precisões que nós, n'ellas nos podem dar algum auxilio,
e recebel-o, se chegarão, quando o permittir a abun-
dancia, dos pastos, uns para os outros, communicarão
entre si os seus pensamentos, e desejos, praticarão sobre
as cousas que mais amão, celebrarão a sua felicidade.

Uma vez juntos os homens, e em ocio, contentes, e
sem cançaço, impossivel é, que não inventem diversos
jogos, e toda a sorte de desenfado e recreação para evitar
o tedio de uma vida socegada e satisfeita. Entre estes
divertimentos não devia ter ultimo lugar a Poesia. As
faculdades do homem têm uma natural disposição para
ella; ou a Poesia consista na imitação, como querem
Platão e Aristoteles, ainda que clara e distinctamente
nunca nos dissessem o que esta imitação seja; ou em uma
oração levantada sobre as expressões vulgares, invertida com
figuras, e armonios amente modulade, e compassada com
o metro e com o rhythmo. Em qualquer d'estas cousas que
façamos consistir a Poesia, ou em todas ellas, para todas
recebeo o homem da Natureza uma admiravel propensão.

As nossos sensações são não sómente a origem e funda-
mento de todas as nossas idéas, mas transformando-se de
diversos modos, são todos os nossos juizos e raciocinios,
as nossas artes, as nossas Sciencias, e em uma palavra,
tudo quanto sabemos e conhecemos. Mas a imitação é
uma sensação facil, e para que está disposta a con-
formação dos nossos orgãos e das nossas potencias, e por
consequencia uma sensação que nós achamos por extremo
grata e deleitavel. D'este mesmo principio se segue
outro, o qual aqui igualmente pertence, e vem a ser,

que é natural ao homem não so a oração, e a harmonia, mas tambem essa mesma oração variada com differentes tropos e figuras; isto he, com diversos modos de exprimir as cousas, e os pensamentos, já com a mesma harmonia, isto é, com o rhythmo, e já com o metro.

Conhecer-se-ha claramente a dependencia que estes dois principios têm entre si, se considerarmos que a imitação (a qual eu já mostrei ser um exercicio summamente gostoso ao homem, e um modo facillimo assim de elle apprender como de communicar aos outros os seus sentimentos), uma vez feita, e praticada com a oração, traz necessariamente comsigo todas aquellas variedades da mesma oração que apontei acima. D'aqui vem affirmarem agudamente, e com razão justissima, os mais celebres Filosofos que quizerão descer a discussões d'este genero, que a Poesia era tão antiga como o genero humano. Certamente parece ter nascido logo com as primeiras Sociedades, que elles formarão, e quando elles conservavão ainda muito, assim da rusticidade como da singeleza e innocencia natural. Do que parece ou claramente provado, ou deduzido com assaz probabilidade, que a Poesia nasceo e se inventou entre Pastores. Mas em que genero de Poesia se exercitarão estes primeiros homens? Não será difficil conhecel-o, se reflectirmos qual seria a materia que, segundo as circunstancias em que se achavão, se lhes offerecia para os seus cantos. Aristoteles foi de parecer, que dos primeiros inventores os que tinhão genio elevado imitavão acções illustres, e feitas por personagens grandes, e pelo contrario os que tinhão engenho mais rasteiro cantavão as acções dos homens vis, em cujo vituperio compunhão obras ridiculas, assim como os outros se exercitavão em hymnos e encomios.

Porem este erudito e intelligente Filosofo não falla, naquelle lugar, da primeira origem da Poesia rigorosamente, mas sim do modo com que ella, depois de inventada, se foi dividindo em diversas especies; porque suppõe tempos em que he já grande a desigualdade dos homens; o que não tem lugar nas primeiras e simplicissimas sociedades de Pastores.

É pois summamente verosimil, que estes homens quizessem imitar aquellas cousas que com mais frequencia se offerecião aos seus sentidos, que satisfazião as suas necessidades, e que constituião a bem aventurança da sua socegada vida e felice estado, por que nellas empregavão toda a sua attenção e cuidado. Cantarião pois os seus rebanhos, os montes e os valles em que os apascentavão, os rios e fontes, a que os levavão a beber; a alva e serena madrugada que os chamava ao trabalho, a sesta que os convidava ao descanço, e os rafeiros que lhes guardavão o gado. Cantarião, como era natural, as paixões e affectos da sua alma; porém não affectos violentos, e desesperados, que não erão proprios daquelle vida, mas doces e suaves, e que só lhes causavão aquella inquietação e desasocego a que se não pudesse seguir fim algum funesto.

Como estes argumentos são todos proprios da Poesia Bucolica, segue-se legitimamente, que ella foi a primeira que no Mundo inventaram os homens. Sendo pois a Poesia Pastoral a primeira origem de toda a erudição humana, e os primeiros esforços que fizerão as faculdades do homem para se pulirem e cultivarem, justamente me persuadi, que a Academia, instituida toda para utilidade publica, e que álem de outros mais gloriosos e louvaveis empenhos, tomou a si o de dar a conhecer os principios e progressos da nossa Litteratura, havia de levar em gosto que hum Socio seu tratasse dos merecimentos dos nossos Poetas Bucolicos. D'este trabalho, Senhores, posto que maior que minhas forças, me quiz encarregar, por ser dos mais leves e faceis que tão illustre corpo podia commetter a algum de seus membros.

Vós tratareis verdades sublimes, por extremo remotas e escondidas á commum comprehensão dos homens; medireis o espaço immenso dos Céos; poreis Leis aos corpos mais vastos, mais distantes, e até mais rebeldes do Universo; com vossas porfiadas investigações e rara sagacidade obrigareis a Natureza a que vos descubra e patentêe aquilla mesmo que ella punha maior estudo em occultar. Assim para felicidade dos outros homens augmentareis aperfeiçareis os seus conhecimentos; mas sereis muito particularmente felices vós, e feliz a Patria, em cuja utilidade haveis de empregar os vossos talentos e todos estes trabalhos e fadigas: e alla vo-lo saberá agradecer com o premio que só desejão as almas grandes, do louvor e da gloria. Eu, gozando-me e comprazendo-me do vosso alto merecimento, de que vos quizestes me coubesse tambem alguma parte, me contentarei com examinar a propriedade e elegancia de uma palavra; a verdade, novidade, e belleza de um pensamento; a innocencia e sã singeleza de um Pegureiro: e isto *prope aquæ rivum*, ou quando muito, *sub ramis arboris altæ*.

Mas, tornando ao meu assumpto, de que me fizerão desviar os vossos justos louvôres, não são pouco relevantes, nem concorrem medianamente para a instrucção e cultura dos homens, os trabalhos dos Poetas. Negal-o seria não conhecer o modo por que se dilatão e aperfeiçoão as nossas faculdades, e ignorar inteiramente a Historia dos varios progressos do entendimento humano. A restauração das letras, com que se desterrou a ignorancia e barbaridade, a que nos tinhão reduzido as Nações do Norte e as continuas irrupções dos Sarracenos, tem as suas sementes nos Trovadores Provençaes e Lombardos, que fructificando felizmente chegarão a produzir os dois abalisados engenhos de Dante, e Petrarca. Cultivada por estes dous grandes homens, e por alguns mais seus contemporaneos a Lingua Toscana, preparou a Italia, e á sua imitação a toda a Europa, para um conhecimento profundo da Lingua Latina e da Grega. Com taes disposições e auxilios se intruirão as Nações Europeas nas Artes e Sciencias, e em toda a sorte de erudição d'aquelles sabios Povos; e inflammadas cada vez mais no desejo de saber, têm levado muitas das Artes e Sciencias dos antigos a um ponto incrivel de perfeição, &c.

Analyse e Combinações filosoficas sobre a Elocução e Estilo de Sá de Miranda, Ferreira, Bernardes, Caminha, e Camões. Por Francisco Dias.

Quando entrei n'esta composição, julguei que devia tomar um ponto fixo donde viesse deduzindo a sua analyse, e que o Sá de Miranda devia indispensavelmente formar a epoca donde, segundo a ordem do tempo, havia de dimanar todo o seu progresso, como de um escritor que lançou os fundamentos da Poesia Portugueza. Mas antes que entrasse n'esta diligencia, vi que me era de precisa necessidade fazer uma descripção exacta do estado em que se achava a Lingua quando o Poeta Miranda appareceo, e sondar as qualidades principaes da composição e estylo daquelle Padre da Poesia Portugueza, donde passou para Ferreira, para Bernardes, para Caminha, e ultimamente para Camões, o maior Poeta da Nação, e o que mais enriqueceo e apurou o nosso idioma; discorrendo por aquelles pontos que mais me parecerão dignos de comparação no genero Sublime, como mais nobre, e como aquelle que mais esforço pede da fantasia humana;

fazendo juizo de cada um dos Poetas da Analyse, e finalmente indicando as origens donde nascerão as expressões e formulas combinadas; no que julgo ter satisfeito ao Assumpto, que é certamente mais difficultoso do que parece.

Na execução d'este tão trabalhoso argumento me conduzi, segundo as luzes que pude adquirir na lição de Aristoteles, Cicero, Longino, Quintiliano, e muito mais na de Locke, Condillac, Du Marsais, e em especial na do sobre todos sabio Commentario que o grande Voltaire fez ás Obras de Pedro Corneille, onde se vêm as regras do gosto na sua maior elevação.

Todas estas materias são novas em Portugal, e por consequencia não tive a quem seguir; e apezar dos defeitos, posso dizer,

———— *que aqui vereis presente*
Cousas que juntas se achão.
CAMÕES, *Lus.*

Introducção.

É o talento da palavra a mais nobre faculdade do ente racional, como instrumento com que não só expõe as suas idéas, mas até pinta os mais occultos sentimentos do espirito, com rasgos tão vivos e sublimes que os faz passar aos corações mais izentos de interesse. Aquella Filosofia inata ao coração do homem que preside a todas as acções que mais o elevão, foi quem formou os sinaes representativos das suas idéas simplices e compostas, e quem, á força de infinitas combinações, lhe fez conceber o grande pensamento do transumpto mental consignado nas palavras por uma successão de idéas não interrompidas, cujo nexo constitue a pintura eterna não só do fysico, mas, o que é mais prodigioso, do moral humano.

Aquella mesma filosofia, que dirigindo e elevando o espirito humano desde as idéas simplices até as implexas lhe deu as primeiras noções da expressão simples é primitiva, como mais adaptada ás necessidades do homem; á proporção que lhe foi ampliando a esfera dos seus conhecimentos, lhe foi ministrando expressão complexa, isto é, figurada, com a qual pinta aos olhos, e dá corpo e vida ás mais sublimes abstracções que pode conceber o entendimento humano.

D'este immenso aggregado de idéas simplices e compostas, como consequencia natural, procedeo a vivacidade da expressão, e a riqueza das Linguas que se elevaram ao mais distincto grão de perfeição, segundo o numero de acontecimentos e revoluções notaveis: e muito mais segundo o trato frequente com as nações estranhas, e communicação social dos povos entre si; por isso mesmo que das grandes crizes procede a effervescenia das paixões, que pondo em movimento e actividade a massa das idéas, gera nóvos pensamentos, e nova elocução.

D'aqui se infere, que os melhores de todos os idiomas devem forçosamente ser os d'aquelles povos que mais revoluções experimentaram, e que melhor conheceram, as leis da Sociedade. Vê-se pois pelo que nos ensina a historia, que as Nações mais pulidas e sabias, tanto na linguagem como nos costumes, forão quasi sempre as que, situadas junto ao mar, conheceram mais cedo a necessidade de communicação dos povos estranhos por meio do Commercio; ou aquellas cujos acontecimentos lhes derão lugar distincto nos annaes do genero humano.

Por isso vemos, que as Linguas geraes do Malabar, Coromandel, e da China, regiões maritimas, assim como tambem a Arabe, são as mais bellas e antigas de todas as Linguas da Asia. Os Povos da Grecia, que gozando do mais formoso espectaculo da Natureza, experimentarão tantas e tão notaveis revoluções, inventarão o mais significativo e harmonico de todos os Idiomas, onde se achão consignados os mais insignes monumentos do genio, e donde procedeo a magestade da Lingua dos Romanos, não mais famosos pelas suas conquistas que pelos escriptos immortaes com que illustrarão os Seculos. O mesmo se deve considerar dos Italianos, Francezes, Hespanhoes, e Inglezes, cujos Idiomas tendo origem na Lingua Latina, se têm elevado ao mais alto ponto de perfeição possivel, e nos quaes existem monumentos para quem todo o louvor he diminuto.

Mas este concurso de circunstancias parece que ainda não foi a causa sufficiente da perfeição das Linguas: ainda ali se diviza hum vacuo, que preciza ser occupado. Aqui vem a Poesia, com toda a sua pompa e magestade, gerando nóvos pensamentos, pulindo e aperfeiçoando os Idiomas, dando a tudo alma e vida, já elevando-se aos maiores assumptos nos louvores do Ente Supremo, e no Panegyrico dos grandes homens, persuadindo a imitação das acções nobres e dignas dos mais distinctos applausos. Ella lhe abre os seus thesouros, ella os enriquece, ella lhes dá força, elegancia, e harmonia, sem o que serião uns cadaveres seccos e inanimados. Sem a Poesia nada serião talvez os Gregos e os Romanos, que tanto encherão o mundo com a fama das suas victorias, com a grandeza das suas acções, e muito mais com a perfeição, com que cultivarão todas as artes de génio, de que tantos e tão admiraveis testemunhos nos deixarão principalmente nos seus escritos. A Poesia pois, que teve entre os antigos um caracter de harmonia muito diverso da Poesia moderna, veio pella ignorancia dos Seculos a tal decadencia, que pouco faltou par ficar inteiramente ignorada.

Das reliquias da Lingua Latina e Grega se formarão os Idiomas modernos, com diversa Syntaxe; e com elles resuscitarão, ou por melhor dizer, formarão os Provençaes uma Poesia toda nova na disposição das cesuras e combinações harmonicas.

Os Italianos, restauradores de quasi todas as Artes, forão os primeiros que tratarão a Poesia com dignidade, aperfeiçoando os metros e harmonias, que os mesmos Provençaes e Sicilianos tinhão inventado; e tanto se applicarão a ella, que já no decimo quarto Seculo era famoso Poeta o celebre Dante, quem fixou todas as accentuações harmonicas do hendecasyllabo, que ficou sendo o mais necessario metro da Poesia Italiana, Castelhana, e Portugueza.

Entraram os Mouros em Hespanha, e com elles a Poesia: porem o desasocego da guerra não deu lugar aos antigos possuidores d'esta Região, tão infestada de Nações estranhas, a cultivar a Poesia seriamente, nem a pulir os seus Idiomas tão cedo como os Italianos. Da longa dominação que os Romanos tiverão em Hespanha se havia nella introduzido o uzo da Lingua Latina, que veio a ser vulgar: d'ella, e de varios dialectos barbaros, se formarão os dois mais bellos, e sonoros Idiomas de Hespanha, e talves da Europa, o Castelhano, e o Portuguez.

Estas duas Linguas se forão igualmente aperfeiçoando, de sorte que a um mesmo tempo chegaram ao seu auge. Com tudo, sendo a Nação Portugueza mais moderna, e occupando muito menos espaço de torreno que a Castelhana, veio mais cedo a produzir monumentos que assaz distinguiram e acreditaram o seu Idiôma. As historias de João de Barros dadas á luz no meio do Seculo decimo sexto, e traduzidas em todas as Linguas cultas da Europa, fizerão mostrar ao Mundo litterario, que a Lingua Portugueza era a mais filha da Latina. Um numero sufficiente de Escriptores, que logo depois vierão, acabarão de determinar o genio da Lingua, cujo caracter he elegancia a perspicuidade. Sendo pois a Lingua Portugueza desde a sua origem mui doce e sonora, resultado natural da quantidade proporcionada das suas vogaes e consoantes, das quaes as primeiras não são tão frequentes e conjunctas que enfraqueção a harmonia, e a fação languida e pouco notada, como se vê na Lingua Italiana; nem as segundas com nimia frequencia se atropellão, e produzem sons rudes e asperos, como nas Linguas do Norte. Todas estas felices disposições, álem do genio, convidavão a Nação á cultura da Poesia, para que sempre teve natural inclinação. Deixemos a miuda investigação d'estas causas, a qual será mais propria de quem tentar escrever a historia da Lingua. Deixemos tambem as Poesias anteriores ao Seculo de quinhentos, muitas das quaes existem em algumas Bibliothecas antigas, como as d'El Rei D. Diniz, na do Convento da Ordem de Christo em Thomar, e outras andão empregadas no celebre Cancioneiro de Resende, collecção preciosa, donde se podem extrahir as maiores luzes a respeito da Natureza e origem da nossa Poesia: e começando a tratar do auge a que esta elevou a Lingua Portugueza, as graças e numero que lhe communicou, principiaremos a discorrer de uma época mais vizinha a nós, e esta seja determinada pelo famoso Sá de Miranda.

Vejamos pois os assumptos que este Poeta tratou, a qualidade de sua imitação em geral, o uzo que fez do hendecasyllabo, até ao seu tempo pouco ou nada conhecido em Portugal, a em toda a Hespanha; como tratou, como aperfeiçoou o Soneto, do qual se deve reputar inventor entre nós, novas graças que accrescentou á nossa Lingua, e como finalmente preparou aos Poetas que lhe succederam hum novo caminho para se elevarem até á immortal Lusiada.

Mas antes que entremos n'este exame, vejamos primeiro o estado em que o Sá de Miranda achou o Idioma.

A Nação Portugueza, que até ao fim do reinado de D. Fernando jazia na ignorancia, occupada unicamente da cultura das suas terras quanto lhe era preciso para o consumo interior do Reino, e para entreter uma ligeira sombra de commercio exterior, continuamente vexado pella tyrannia Arabica, que, infestando os mares, era eterno obstaculo á navegação; vivendo como desterrada na solidão dos campos, sem communicação, nem policia, fallava uma linguagem informe e grosseira, chea de sons rudes, que as Linguas barbaras lhe tinhão communicado: e a pezar de ter uma origem tão pura, como a Lingua Latina donde procedia, só conservava alguma energia natural nascida das significações primitivas das suas vozes, que, álem, de serem masculadas de infinitas anomalias e dissonancias, erão privadas de translações, que dão força e elevação aos Idiomas. Cheia pois de construcções erroneas, de diphtongos ásperos, e desinencias rudes, pobre de termos, sem idéa do nexo que subsiste nas particulas, sem syntaxe, sem harmonia, o seu periodo incerto e desunido vicillára sem caracter.

A grande revolução de D. João I., fazendo a mais viva commoção no genio dos Portuguezes, com ella lhe vierão novos estimulos de gloria, que eleva o espirito; novas emprezas, novos pensamentos, nova força, nova energia ás suas enunciações; novos objectos do discurso, e novo linguagem. Um Latim barbaro, até alli organo das Leis e instrumentos publicos, cessou de ser a linguagem do Foro.

Da conquista de Ceuta nasceo a idéa, a grande idéa dos descubrimentos, que mostrando a necessidade de cultivar as Mathematicas e a Astronomia, taes quaes existião naquelles tempos obscuros, alargou a esfera da Mechanica, que fazendo novas investigações sobre a acção dos ventos, e resistencia das agoas, extrahindo a somma da combinação dos movimentos, resultantes da acção e reacção d'estes dois Elementos, alcançou mais perfeito conhecimento das leis dos liquidos, e do equilibrio, e aperfeiçoou finalmente a Arte de navegar. Novos Astros, novos mares e costas, novas ilhas, novos mundos enchem de admiração todo o universo.

EXTRACTOS POETICOS.

From the Third Canto of the Lusiad of Camões.

Estavas linda Inez posta em sossego,
   De teus annos colhendo o doce fruto,
   Naquelle engano da alma, ledo e cego,
   Que a fortuna não deixa durar muto:
   Nos saudosos campos do Mondego,
   De teus formosos olhos nunco enxuto
   Aos montes ensinando e ás ervinhas
   O nome que no peito escrito tinhas.

Do teu principe alli te respondião
   As lembranças, que na alma lhe moravão,
   Que sempre ante seus olhos de trazião,
   Quando dos teus formosos se apartavão:
   De noite em doces sonhos, que mentião;
   De dia em pensamentos, que voavão:
   E quanto em fim cuidava, e quanto via,
   Erão tudo memorias de alegria.

D'outras bellas senhoras e princezas,
   Os dezejados talamos engeita,
   Que tudo, em fim, tu puro amor desprezas,
   Quando hum gesto suave te sugeita.
   Vendo estas namoradas estranhezas,
   O velho pay sesudo, que respeita
   O murmurar do povo e a fantasia
   Do filho, que casar-se não queria:

Tirar Inez a mundo determina,
   Por lhe tirar o filho, que tem preso,
   Crendo co'sangue só da morte indina,
   Matar do firme amor o fogo aceso.
   Que furor consentio, que a espada fina,
   Que pode sustentar o grande peso
   Do furor Mauro, fosse levantada
   Contra huma fraca dama delicada?

Trazião-na os horrificos algozes
   Ante o Rey, já movido a piedade,
   Mas o povo com falsas, e ferozes
   Razões, á morte crua o persuade.
   Ella com tristes e piedosas vozes,
   Sahidas só de magoa e saudade
   Do seu Principe e filhos que deixava,
   Que mais que a propria morte a mogoava;

Para o céo cristalino levantando
   Com lagrimas os olhos piedosos,
   Os olhos, porque as mãos lhe estava atando
   Hum dos duros ministros rigorosos:
   E depois nos meninos atentando,
   Que tão queridos tinha, e tão mimosos,
   Cuja orfandade como mãi temia,
   Para o avô cruel assim dizia.

Se já nas brutas feras, cuja mente
   Natura fez cruel de nascimento,
   E nas aves agrestes, que sómente
   Nas rapinas aerias tem o intento,
   Com pequenas crianças vio a gente
   Terem tão piedoso sentimento,
   Como coa mãy de Nino já mostrarão,
   E cos Irmãos que Roma edificarão:

·O' tu que tens de humano o gesto, e o peito,
  Se do humano he matar huma donzella
  Fraca, e sem força, só por ter sugeito
  O coração, a quem soube vencella,
  A estas criancinhas tem respeito
  Pois o não tens á morte escura della :
  Mova-te a piedade sua e minha,
  Pois te não move a culpa que não tinha.

E se vencendo a Maura resistencia
  A morte sabes dar com fogo e ferro,
  Sabe tambem dar vida com clemencia
  A quem para perdella não fez erro.
  Mas se to assi merece esta innocencia,
  Põe-me em perpetuo e misero desterro,
  Na Scythia fria, ou lá na Libia ardente,
  Onde em lagrimas viva eternamente.

Põe-me onde se use toda a feridade,
  Entre leoens e tigres, e verei,
  Se nelles achar posso a piedade,
  Que entre peitos humanos não achei ;
  Alli co' amor intrinseco e vontade,
  Naquelle por quem morro criarei
  Estas reliquias suas, que aqui viste,
  Que refrigerio sejão da mãi triste.

·Queria perdoar-lhe o Rey benino,
  Movido das palavras, que o magôão,
  Mas o pertinaz povo, e seu destino
  (Que desta sorte o quiz), lhe não **perdôão**.
  Arrancão das espadas de aço fino
  Os que por bom tal feito alli pregôão ;
  Contra huma dama, ó peitos carniceiros,
  Ferozes vos mostraes e cavalleiros ?

Qual contra a linda moça Policena,
   Consolação extrema da mãy velha,
   Porque a sombra de Achiles a condena,.
   C' o ferro o duro Pyrro se aparelha;
   Mas ella os olhos, com que o ar serena,
   (Bem como paciente, e mansa ovelha)
   Na misera mãy postos que endoudece,
   Ao duro sacrificio se offerece :

Taes contra Inez os brutos matadores
   No collo de alabastro, que sostinha
   As obras cõ que amor matou de amores
   A' quelle que depois a fez rainha:
   As espadas banhando, e as brancas flores.
   Que ella dos olhos seus regado tinha,
   Se incarniçavão fervidos, e irosos,
   No futuro castigo não cuidosos.

Bem puderas, ó sol, da vista destes,
   Teus rayos apartar aquelle dia,
   Como da seva mesa de Thyestes
   Quando os filhos por mão de Atreu comia::
   Vós ó concavos valles que pudestes
   A voz extrema ouvir da boca fria,
   O nome do seu Pedro, que lhe ouvistes,
   Por muito grande espaço repetistes.

Assi como a bonina, que cortada
   Antes de tempo foi, candida e bella,
   Sendo das mãos lascivas mal tratada,
   Da menina, que a trouxe na capella,
   O cheiro traz perdido, e a cor murchada,.
   Tal está morta a pallida donzella,
   Secas do rosto as rosas, e perdida
   A branca e viva cor, co' a doce vida.

As filhas do Mondego a morte escura,
　Longo tempo chorando memorarão,
　E por memoria eterna em fonte pura
　As lagrimas choradas transformarão;
　O nome lhe puzerso, que inda dura,
　Dos amores de Inez que alli passarão;
　Vede, que fresca fonte rega as flores,
　Que lagrimas são agoa, e o nome amores.

From the fifth Canto of the same.

Porem ja cinco soes erão passados,
　Que dalli nos partiramos, cortando
　Os mares nunca d'ontrem navegados,
　Prosperamente os ventos assoprando;
　Quando huma noite estando descuidados,
　Na cortadora proa vigiando,
　Huma nuvem que os ares escurece,
　Sobra nossas cabeças apparece.

Tão temerosa vinha, e carregada,
　Que poz nos coraçoens hum grande medo,
　Bramindo o negro mar de longe brada
　Como se desse em vão n'algum rochedo;
　O' potestade, disse, sublimada,
　Que ameaço divino, ou que segredo,
　Este clima, e este mar nos apresenta,
　Que mór cousa parece que tormenta?

Não acabava, quando huma figura
  Se nos mostra no ar robusta e valida,
  De disforme e grandissima estatura,
  O rosto carregado, a barba esquallida,
  Os olhos encovados, e a postura
  Medonha, e má, e a cor terrena e pallida,
  A boca negra, os dentes amarellos.

Tão grande era de membros, que bem posso
  Certificarte, que este era o segundo
  De Rhodes estranhissimo Colosso,
  Que hum dos sete milagres foi do mundo:
  Co' hum tom de voz nos falla horrendo e grosso,
  Que pareceo sahir do mar profundo,
  Arrepiãose as carnes, e o cabello
  A mi, e a todos, só de ouvillo e vello.

E disse: O' gente ousada mais que quantas
  No mundo cometterão grandes cousas,
  Tu, que por guerras cruas taes e tantas,
  E por trabalhos vãos nunca repousas,
  Pois os vedados terminos quebrantas,
  E navegar meus longos mares ousas,
  Que eu tanto tempo ha que guardo e tenho,
  Nunca arados de estranho ou proprio lenho;

Pois vens ver os segredos escondidos
  Da natureza, e do humido elemento,
  A nenhum grande humano concedidos,
  De nobre ou de immortal merecimento;
  Ouve os damnos de mi que apercebidos
  Estão a teu sobejo atrevimento,
  Por todo o largo mar, e pela terra,
  Que inda has de subjugar com dura guerra.

Sabe que quantas naos esta viagem,
  Que tu fazes, fizerem de atrevidas,
Inimiga terão esta paragem
  Com ventos, e tormentas desmedidas;
E da primeira armada, que passagem
  Fizer por estas ondas insoffridas,
Eu farei de improviso tal castigo,
Que seja mór o damno que o perigo.

Aqui espero tomar, se não me engano,
  De quem me descubrio summa vingança;
E não se acabará só nisto o damno
  De vossa pertinace confiança:
Antes em vossas naos vereis cada anno
  (Se he verdade o que meu juizo alcança)
Naufragios, perdições de toda sorte,
Que o menor mal de todos seja a morte.

E do primeiro illustre que a ventura
  Com fama alta fizer tocar os Ceos
Serei eterna e nova sepultura,
  Por juizos incognitos de Deos:
Aqui porá da Turca armada dura
  Os soberbos e prosperos tropheos;
Comigo de seus damnos o ameaça
A destruida Quilôa, com Mombaça.

Outro tambem virá de honrada fama,
  Liberal, Cavalleiro e namorado,
E comsigo trará formosa Dama,
  Que Amor por grão mercê lhe terá dado:
Triste ventura e negro fado os chama
  Neste terreno meu, que, duro e irado,
Os deixará de hum crú naufragio vivos,
Para verem trabalhos excessivos.

Verão morrer com fome os filhos caros,
　Em tanto amor gerados e nascidos;
　Verão os Cafres asperos e avaros
　Tirar á linda Dama os seus vestidos:
　Os crystallinos membros e preclaros
　A' calma, ao frio, ao ar verão despidos;
　Despois de ter pizada longamente
　C' os delicados pés a area ardente.

E verão mais olhos que escaparem
　De tanto mal, de tanta desventura,
　Os dous amantes miseros ficarem
　Na fervida e implacavel espessura.
　Alli, depois que as pedras abrandarem
　Com lagrimas de dor, e magoa pura,
　Abraçados as almas soltarão
　Da formosa, e miserrima prisao.

Mais hia por diante o monstro horrendo,
　Dizendo nossos fados, quando alçado
　Lhe disse eu: Quem es tu, que esse estupendo
　Corpo, certo, me tem maravilhado!
　A boca, e os olhos negros retorcendo,
　E dando hum espantoso e grande brado,
　Me respondeo com voz pesada e amara,
　Como quem da pergunta lhe pezára:

Eu sou aquelle occulto e grande Cabo
　A quem chamais vós outros Tormentorio,
　Que nunca a Ptholomeo, Pomponio, Estrabo,
　Plinio, e quantos passarão, fui notorio:
　Aqui toda a Africana costa acabo
　Neste meu nunca visto Promontorio,
　Que para o Polo Antarctico se estende,
　A quem vossa ousadia tanto offende.

Fui dos filhos asperrimos da Terra,
　Qual Encelado, Egeo, e o Centimano,
　Chamei-me Adamastor, e fui na guerra
　Contra o que vibra os raios de Vulcano:
　Não que puzesse serra sobre serra,
　Mas conquistando as ondas do Oceano
　Fui Capitão do mar, por onde andava
　A armada de Neptuno, que eu buscava.

Amores da alta Esposa de Peleo
　Me fizeram tomar tamanha empresa,
　Todas as Deosas desprezei do Ceo
　Só por amar das aguas a Princeza:
　Hum dia a vi co' as filhas de Nereo
　Sahir nua na praia, e logo presa
　A vontade senti de tal maneira,
　Que inda não sinto cousa que mais queira.

Como fosse impossivel alcançalla,
　Pela grandeza fea de meu gesto,
　Determinei por armas de tomalla,
　E a Doris este caso manifesto:
　De medo a Deosa então por mi lhe falla;
　Mas ella co' hum formoso riso honesto
　Respondeo: Qual será o amor bastante
　De Nympha que sustente o d' hum Gigante?

Com tudo, por livrarmos o Oceano
　De tanta guerra, eu buscarei maneira,
　Com que com minha honra escuse o damno
　Tal resposta me torna a mensageira.
　Eu quem cahir não pude neste engano,
　Que he grande dos amantes a cegueira
　Encheu-se me com grandes abundanças
　　peito de dezejos e esperanças.

Já, nescio, já da guerra desistindo,
   Huma noite de Doris promettida,
   Me apparece de longe o gesto lindo,
   Da branca Thetis, unica, despida:
   Como doudo corri de longe abrindo
   Os braços para aquella que era vida
   Deste corpo, e começo os olhos bellos
   A lhe beijar as faces, e os cabellos.

Oh que não sei de nojo como o conte!
   Que crendo ter nos braços quem amavá,
   Abraçado me achei co' hum duro monte
   De aspero mato, e de espessura brava:
   Estando co' hum penedo fronte afronte,
   Que eu pelo rosto angelico apertava,
   Não fiquei homem não, mas mudo, e quedo,
   E junto a hum penedo outro penedo.

O' Nympha a mais formosa do Oceano,
   Já que minha presença não te agrada,
   Que te custava ter-me neste engano,
   Ou fosse monte, nuvem, sonho, ou nada?
   D' aqui me parto irado, e quasi insano
   Da magoa, e da deshonra alli passada,
   A buscar outro mundo, onde não visse
   Quem de meu pranto, e de meu mal se risse.

Erão já neste tempo meus irmãos
   Vencidos, e em miseria extrema postos;
   E, por mais segurar-se os Deoses vãos,
   Alguns a varios montes sotopostos:
   E como contra o Ceo não valem mãos,
   Eu que chorando andava meus desgostos
   Comecei a sentir do fado imigo
   Por meus atrevimentos o castigo.

Converte-se-me a carne em terra dura,
  Em penedos os ossos se fizeram ;
  Estes membros que vês, e esta figura,
  Por estas longas aguas se estenderam :
  Emfim minha grandissima estatura
  Neste remoto cabo converteram
  Os Deoses, e por mais dobradas magoas,
  Me anda Thetis cercando destas agoas.

Assim contava, e co' hum medonho choro
  Subito dante os olhos se apartou ;
  Desfez-se a nuvem negra, e co' hum sonóro
  Bramido muito longe o mar soou.
  Eu, levantando as mãos ao sancto coro
  Dos Anjos, que tão longe nos guiou,
  A Deos pedi, que removesse os duros
  Casos que Adamastor contou futuros.

From the second Canto of the same.

Ouvio-lhe estas palavras piedosas
  A formosa Dione, e commovida
  De entre as Nymphas se vai, que saudosas
  Ficarão desta subita partida.
  Já penetra as estrellas luminósas,
  Já na terceira Esfera recebida
  Avante passa, e lá no sexto Ceo,
  Para onde estava o Padre se moveo.

E como hia affrontada do caminho,
   Tão formosa no gesto se mostrava,
   Que as estrellas, e o Ceo, e o ar vizinho,
   E tudo quanto a via namorava,
   Dos olhos, onde faz seu filho o ninho,
   Huns espiritos vivos inspirava,
   Com que os Polos gelados accendia,
   E tornava de fogo a Esfera fria.

E por mais namorar o Soberano
   Padre, de quem foi sempre amada, e cara,
   Se lhe apresenta assi, como ao Troyano
   Na selva Idea já se apresentára.
   Se a vira o caçador que o vulto humano
   Perdeo vendo a Diana na agua clara
   Nunca os famintos galgos o mataram,
   Que primeiro desejos o acabaram.

Os crespos fios de ouro se esparziam
   Pelo collo que a néve escurecia;
   Andando as lacteas tetas lhe tremiam
   Com quem Amor brincava, e não se via:
   Da alva petrina flamas lhe sahiam,
   Onde o menino as almas accendia;
   Pelas lizas columnas lhe trepavam.
   Desejos, que como hera se enrolavam.

C' hum delgado sendal as partes cobre
   De quem vergonha hé natural reparo:
   Porem nem tudo esconde, nem descobre
   O véo dos roxos lirios pouco ovaro:
   Mas para que o desejo accenda e dobre,
   Lhe põe diante aquelle objecto raro.
   Já se sentem no Ceo por toda a parte
   Ciumes em Vulcano, amor em Marte.

E mostrando no angelico semblante
  C' o riso huma tristeza misturada,
Como dama que foi do incauto amante
  Em brincos amorosos mal tratada,
Que se queixa e se ri n' hum mesmo instante,
  E se mostra entre alegre magoada ;
Desta arte a Deosa, a quem nenhuma iguala,
Mais mimosa que triste ao Padre falla.

From the first Idyll of Boccage.

A' foz do Tejo, em bronca penedia,
  Minada pelas ondas salitrosas,
  Prisioneiro de amor Tritão gemia.

Luzião lhe as espadoas escamosas,
  Sustentava o maritimo instrumento,
  O buzio atroador nas mãos callosas ;

Conchas da cor do liquido Elemento
  Parte do corpo enorme lhe vestião,
  Igual na ligeireza ao proprio vento.

Da barba salsas gotas lhe cahião,
  E nos olhos, que Amor affogueava,
  Em borbotões as lagrimas fervião.

Lilia, que hum Bosque proximo habitava,
  Lilia a Napea desdenhosa e bella,
  Amorosos clamores lhe arrancava :

Hum dia a vio na praia, e só de vella
  Seu coração feroz enfeitiçado,
  Voou, gemendo, para os olhos della.

Das entranhas do Pelago salgado,
 "Louco de Amores, louco de saudades,
 O queixoso Amador tinha saltado.

Do Pai, que abafa as negras tempestades,
 Já seu voraz tormento era sabido,
 E das outras Equoreas Divindades.

De aereas esperanças illudido,
 Grão tempo seu espirito saudoso,
 Rastejando a cruel, vagou perdido;

Grão tempo glorias vãs sonhou teimoso,
 Antes que desse fructuosa entrada
 Ao acre desengano o peito ancioso, &c.

THE END.

www.ingramcontent.com/pod-product-compliance
Lightning Source LLC
Chambersburg PA
CBHW020122020526
44111CB00049B/623